D1038384

THE JOHN HARVARD LIBRARY

OUR COUNTRY

By

JOSIAH STRONG

Edited by Jurgen Herbst

THE BELKNAP PRESS OF
HARVARD UNIVERSITY PRESS
Cambridge, Massachusetts
1 9 6 3

Distributed in Great Britain by Oxford University Press, London

Library of Congress Catalog Number 63-19148

Printed in the United States of America

CONTENTS

OUR COUNTRY

EDITOR'S INTRODUCTION

"The book is out at last."

Thus the March 1886 issue of the periodical *Home Missionary* informed its readers of the publication of Josiah Strong's *Our Country*. "It has been long delayed in the printer's hands," the editors of the magazine went on to say, "but it is well worth waiting for. Its fourteen chapters—230 pages—are filled with matter of deepest interest to every friend of his country and of Home Missions. . . . Mr. Strong has massed an amount of facts not to be found elsewhere in the same compass, and an array of arguments for the prosecution of home missionary work that no patriot or Christian will find it easy to resist or evade." [1]

Strong's book was more than a compilation of facts in support of American home missions. Its success—one hundred and seventy-five thousand copies were sold before 1916, and individual chapters were reprinted in newspapers and magazines, and published separately in pamphlet form [2]—demonstrated the power of its message which, according to the chief librarian of Congress, compared in intensity with that of *Uncle Tom's Cabin*.[3] Strong had gauged correctly the mind and mood of Protestant America and, in the Quaker phrase, spoke "to his readers' condition." The book, consequently, mirrors the thoughts and aspirations of this dominant segment of American society towards the close of the nineteenth century, and it is therefore a historical document of major importance.

[1] Vol. 58, pp. 384–385.

[2] See Preface to the Revised Edition, below, note 1, and *Gospel of the Kingdom: Studies in Social Reform,* 8 (July 1916), 97.

[3] In *Outlook,* May 10, 1916, p. 56.

While the power of *Our Country* propelled the book to fame, its theme can hardly be called new. To faithful readers of the *Home Missionary*, the book's publication came as no surprise. The monthly organ of the American Home Missionary Society had printed articles with the same title for more than forty years. In 1841 an entire issue had been devoted to a tract entitled "Our Country—Its Capabilities, Its Perils, and Its Hope," which had been republished in 1842 with only minor revisions and additions as a separate pamphlet.[4] In 1858 the Society issued *Our Country Number Two: A Plea for Home Missions*, a booklet of 144 pages made up largely of materials that had previously been published in the *Home Missionary*. And now the third version of *Our Country* awaited the reader's perusal. A full-length book it was this time, available in paper and in cloth, brought up to date with the latest facts designed to support the cause of home missions.

"Our Country" had been the perennial theme in the writings of the Presbyterian and Congregational clergymen who led the American Home Missionary Society from the earliest days of its existence. As home missionaries they differed from foreign missionaries not only in the geographical location of their work but also in its emphasis. The original purpose of missionary work, the conversion of the native heathens, had disappeared almost completely from the program of home missions. In 1798 the Missionary Society of Connecticut, one of the forerunners of the American Home Missionary Society, still intended "to Christianize the Heathen of North America, and to support and promote Christian Knowledge in the new settlements within the United States."[5] Yet in 1858 the editors of *Our Country* wrote that the Society's purpose was "to give 'pastors and teachers' to the multiplying communities of this land, to plant a church in the center of every new village or neighbor-

[4] Published by the Executive Committee of the American Home Missionary Society (New York, 1842), 60 pp.

[5] Quoted in Joseph B. Clark, *Leavening the Nation: The Story of American Home Missions* (New York, 1903), p. 28.

hood . . ."[6] The home missionaries were concerned less with pagan natives than with supposedly Christian settlers.

In its origins, *Our Country* had been intended by its authors to be "a plea for the early establishment of gospel institutions in the destitute portions of the United States," the "destitute portions" being the American West, and destitution being the weakness or absence of evangelical Protestantism among the settlers. To Protestant American missionaries in the early 19th century, the conversion of the inhabitants of the western heartland of America to evangelical Christianity was a prerequisite for the work of foreign missions: "To seek the conversion of the heathen without the conversion of our countrymen," the 1842 pamphlet stated, "would be to seek the end without the means."[7] The end, of course, was the acceptance of the Protestant Gospel by all peoples everywhere, and the evangelization of the American West was the necessary first step.

The conversion of the unconverted Americans in the West was viewed not only as Christian duty, but also as patriotic challenge, for the writers of *Our Country* assumed that Protestant America was God's special instrument in His great work, and so to be a Protestant Christian and an American patriot was one and the same.

> What man [wrote the editors] that has the least spark of patriotic feeling, is ready to surrender back his beloved country to the cold embrace of its original paganism? Who can bear to give over his own children's children to the unrestrained influence of a baptized infidelity, or to the darkness and misery of foul-mouthed atheism . . . ?[8]

The work that lay before them in this sacred and patriotic crusade was formidable: there were heathen Indians to be conquered, "infidel" Roman Catholics, Mormons, and Camp-

[6] *Our Country* (New York, 1858), p. 87. On the substitution of missionary activities among white settlers for Indian missions see chapter 2 of Peter G. Mode, *The Frontier Spirit of American Christianity* (New York, 1923).

[7] *Our Country* (New York, 1842), p. 13.

[8] *Our Country* (1842), pp. 58–59.

bellites, as well as "foulmouthed" rationalists. But the struggle was necessary if the victory of Christ was to be secured.

Of the dangers threatening in the West, the editors of the *Home Missionary* singled out the spread of Roman Catholicism for particular emphasis. Taking their cue from Eastern nativist agitators, they cried out against the Roman Catholic "system of ignorance, priestcraft, and superstition," [9] and echoed such standard texts of American nativism as Samuel F. B. Morse's *Foreign Conspiracy Against the Liberties of the United States,* which declared "popery" to be "the *antagonist* to our *free system,*" "a *political* as well as a *religious* system" that espoused despotic rather than democratic government and that was directed from abroad.[10] The pages of the *Home Missionary* reflecting these sentiments exhorted Americans to support greater missionary endeavors in the West, "for there the great battle is to be fought between truth and error, between law and anarchy, between Christianity, with her Sabbaths, her ministry and her schools, on the one hand, and the combined forces of Infidelity and Popery on the other." [11]

But Romanism was only one, if the most important, of the challenges facing the home missionaries in the West. Westerners were a heterogeneous people, widely scattered over an immense territory, always on the move, lacking a stable, religious community life, and exhibiting a deplorable tendency to think only of "making money." The settlers, suffering from a shortage of doctors, teachers, and ministers, wrote the editors of *Our Country,* enjoyed neither physical nor spiritual care and consequently neglected their duties as Christian citizens. When they remained within the Protestant fold, they frequently fell victim to sectarian rivalry. In the 1858 edition the editors added slavery to the list of obstacles to home missions. "This mournful system," they wrote, "is a curse to all concerned in it, and

[9] Quoted from the New York *Observer* of October 20, 1827, in Ray A. Billington, *The Protestant Crusade, 1800–1860* (New York, 1938), p. 119.

[10] Morse, *Foreign Conspiracy,* 4th ed. (New York, 1836), pp. 19, 27.

[11] "The Great and Good Work," *Home Missionary,* 12 (August 1839), 73.

an enemy of God and man."[12] The prospect for America, which had been "predestined, concealed, discovered, and reserved, to be the seat of a Protestant Christian nation,"[13] was dark. Ignorance of the dangers that existed and of the ultimate promise must at least be overcome. The alarm must be sounded. Westerners had to be awakened, and Easterners aroused to come to the aid of their fellow countrymen.

Since ignorance and error lay at the root of the evils rampant in the West, the missionary task was essentially an educational one. To Congregational and Presbyterian ministers deriving their faith from the Puritans of colonial New England, the working association of religion and education, of preaching and teaching, was second nature. Thus at the height of the nativist agitation in 1835 Lyman Beecher held that "the conflict which is to decide the destiny of the West, will be a conflict of institutions for the education of her sons . . . A land supplied with able and faithful ministers, will of course be filled with schools, academies, libraries, colleges, and all the apparatus for the perpetuity of republican institutions."[14] Twelve years later Horace Bushnell warned the home missionaries not to devote all their energies to a destructive "crusade against Romanism . . ." It were better and more constructive to provide "a talented and educated body of Christian teachers, and keep them pouring into the wilderness . . ."[15] The real danger was barbarism: Romanism was but its result, and education was the great weapon of patriotism and Protestantism.

The preoccupation of the American Home Missionary Society with the West, in the pre-Civil War period, brought with it a comparative neglect of the country's other sections. The East was not a field for home missions. The South, especially on its western frontier, presented a special problem. Here was

[12] *Our Country* (1858), p. 82.
[13] Clark, *Leavening the Nation,* p. 11.
[14] Lyman Beecher, *A Plea for the West,* 2nd ed. (Cincinnati, 1835), pp. 12, 24. See also note 1 of Introduction.
[15] Horace Bushnell, *Barbarism the first Danger: A Discourse for Home Missions* (New York, 1847), pp. 30, 28. See also Strong's quotations from Bushnell on pp. 214 and 220–221, below.

a dearth of Congregational and Presbyterian ministers and churches, and obvious needs for the services of the Society. The Society had every intention of fulfilling the Biblical command: Go, and preach the Gospel. Yet its missionaries reported that slave-owning congregations resented the coming of Northern ministers whose sermons implied or expressed a critique of the peculiar institution. The Society found it increasingly difficult to recruit missionaries from the North for service in the South. Its representatives in the slave states diminished from fifty-two in 1835 to thirty-six in 1845, and to a mere three in 1860.[16] Fearful of jeopardizing its effectiveness in the South, the Society hesitated to endorse an abolitionist policy, only to find that thereby it stood to lose the support of its antislavery benefactors in the North. Caught in this predicament, the Society concentrated even greater attention on the Far West and Northwest, allowing, for all practical purposes, the South to go its way unaided.

The image of America, and particularly of the West, created by the home missionaries in this early period was thus a peculiarly unbalanced one. Just as the slavery issue in all its un-Christian immorality was never explored in the pages of the *Home Missionary,* so the fear of Catholicism displayed there was far out of proportion to its actual existence in the West.[17] The American Home Missionary Society, one historian writes, "carefully selected for publication in the *Home Missionary* and in the annual reports" those few letters which dwelt upon "the Catholic danger," and thus sought to capitalize on the appeal of this fear in the East.[18] Above all, the almost exclusive concern with the West served to distort the picture. It was soon realized that if the message of *Our Country* was ever to become more than a limited missionary slogan it would have to be restated within a broader, nationwide perspective.

Events, too, made such restatement necessary. The changes

[16] Colin B. Goodykoontz, *Home Missions on the American Frontier* (Caldwell, Idaho, 1939), p. 292.

[17] See Goodykoontz, *Home Missions,* p. 234, n. 59.

[18] Billington, *Protestant Crusade,* p. 130.

wrought by the Civil War and Reconstruction forced the directors of the American Home Missionary Society to reappraise their work. Not only was America changing, but the Society itself was different from what it had been in pre-Civil War days. The Presbyterians had withdrawn their support in 1861, partly because they felt that their Congregational brothers favored Congregational churches in the Northwest over Presbyterian missions in the Southwest,[19] and so for the period beginning in 1861 we must speak more properly of the Congregational Home Missionary Society—a change in name which was not accepted officially until 1893—and characterize its work as the reaching out of New England Congregationalism. In addition, there were changes in the nature of the Society's concerns as a result of the inescapable pressures of industrial civilization.

Changed conditions required a new presentation, and for this task the Congregational Home Missionary Society commissioned the Reverend Josiah Strong, its representative in Ohio.

There was no expectation that the result of this assignment might be anything but a routine revision and expansion of the old familiar story. The Reverend Mr. Strong was known as a restless, energetic man; but nothing in his past activity suggested the likelihood of an outstanding achievement. Born in 1847 in Napierville, Illinois, of a family that traced its ancestry back to a Congregational church elder resident in the Massachusetts Bay Colony in 1630, the young Josiah grew up in Illinois and Ohio. At the age of twenty-two he graduated from the Western Reserve College of Hudson, Ohio, a town where his family then resided. He enrolled immediately at the Lane Theological Seminary in Cincinnati, where, no doubt, he absorbed much of the evangelical enthusiasm that had been imparted to it by its former president, Lyman Beecher. In the summer of 1871 Strong married, and ten days later, on September 8, he was ordained pastor of the Congregational Church in

[19] See Goodykoontz, *Home Missions*, p. 300.

Cheyenne, Wyoming, a town that lay in the heart of the western missionary field. But then, as always, Strong was restless, and he moved soon again. He returned within two years to his *alma mater* in Hudson, Ohio, to serve as college chaplain and instructor in theology. This post he held for three years, but then went again to a mission church, this one in Sandusky, Ohio. After five years there he took on the duties of the Secretary for the Congregational Home Missionary Society in Ohio, Kentucky, West Virginia, and western Pennsylvania. It was in this position, and while residing once more in Hudson, Ohio, that he began the writing of *Our Country*. But even before he had finished the book he accepted another call, this time to be minister in the Central Congregational Church in Cincinnati, where he remained until in 1886 the book's success brought him a doctorate of divinity from the city's Western Reserve University and an appointment as the General Secretary of the Evangelical Alliance for the United States, with offices in New York.[20]

"We are living in extraordinary times." This is the keynote of Strong's book. History was rushing toward its culmination, he wrote, and America's destiny was to be sealed by man's actions in the present and in the immediate future. The star of empire, steadily traveling westward, now stood over the American West, "there to remain, for there is no further West." Not only was the world's rule to be passed on to western America, but this rule was also to be history's last. In its world-wide extent it had no precedent and could have no parallel. The com-

[20] The university, founded in 1882, was the successor of Strong's *alma mater,* Western Reserve College at Hudson, Ohio, the "Yale of the West." Some writers have attributed Strong's honorary degree to Adalbert College; Adalbert College is Western Reserve University's undergraduate college for men.

For additional biographical information on Strong see the article in the *Dictionary of American Biography,* XVIII (New York, 1936), 150–151; Edward T. Root, "Josiah Strong: A Modern Prophet of the Kingdom of God," *New Church Review,* 29 (June 1922), 47–54; and Dorothea R. Muller, "Josiah Strong and the Challenge of the City," Ph.D. dissertation, New York University, 1955 (University of Michigan, microfilm).

ing of Christ's Kingdom was near, and home missionaries must not be found unprepared, their task of conversion unfinished. They held the power "to hasten or retard the coming of Christ's kingdom in the world by hundreds, and perhaps thousands, of years." The destiny of the world lay in their hands.

Profoundly responsive to this sense of historic mission, Strong could not be content with simply rewriting a missionary pamphlet. He understood his subject to go far beyond the concerns of an organization devoted to assisting churches in the wilderness, for the wilderness was to be "the Gibraltar of the ages." Its surrender or its deliverance would reveal the meaning of history. Strong's goal was to impress upon Christians everywhere, East and West, the conditions required for salvation, to arouse all to an awareness of the crisis, and to the demands it made upon them.

Writing as a Congregational minister, Strong set forth his view of America's historic mission and contemporary crisis within the framework of the so-called New England theology. He tempered a Calvinistic belief in America's predestined task with an exhortation to the human will, and taught that America's salvation "may be certain in the counsels of God; but it is not necessary. I believe it to be conditioned on the Church's rising to a higher spirit of sacrifice." God had promised to use America as an instrument in the world's redemption. Americans must meet the conditions to make possible the fulfillment of God's promise. They must sacrifice money and time to support and join the missionaries in the work of conversion. That Americans would understand and exercise their role in God's plan of redemption was Strong's fondest hope. Behind all the facts of science and history paraded in the pages of *Our Country* lay the faith of a Protestant minister.

The opening chapters do rehearse, though with a new emphasis, the inherited themes of the previous *Our Country*'s. Natural resources are the subject of chapter two; Western supremacy, of chapter three; immigration, of chapter four; "Romanism," of chapter five; education, of chapter six; and Mormonism, of chapter seven. These familiar topics Strong brought up to date with the latest facts and figures, and he presented them in a framework of interpretation which, in its essentials, did not differ from that of 1842 and 1858. And like the editors before him, he found little room for the discussion of slavery; he noted briefly only its abolition as the logical result of the idea of individual liberty.

In chapters eight to eleven, however, Strong moved beyond these traditional topics of the home missionaries. There he turned to what his contemporaries called the "Social Question," and wrote of alcoholism, socialism, private wealth, and the city, adding his voice to others of his time—Protestant ministers like Washington Gladden and Francis G. Peabody, academic social scientists and civil servants like Richard T. Ely and Carroll D. Wright—then giving new direction to the concerns of theology and of social science.[21] Just as the Social Gospel turned Protestant theology towards the "city wilderness" and the new social science departments of the universities and the state labor departments were beginning to concentrate on the scientific study and correction of the cities' ills,[22] so the Congregational Home Missionary Society, thus led by Strong, emerged from its parochial setting and addressed itself to a new world and to millions who otherwise might never have heard of or cared for Protestant missions.

The city, for Strong, was the real testing ground of Ameri-

[21] For references to Strong as a Social Gospel minister see Shailer Mathews, "The Development of Social Christianity in America," *Journal of Religion*, 7 (July 1927), 376–386, also in G. B. Smith, ed., *Religious Thought in the Last Quarter-Century* (Chicago, 1927), pp. 228–239. On the Social Gospel see the standard history of James Dombrowski, *The Early Days of Christian Socialism in America* (New York, 1936); and of Charles H. Hopkins, *The Rise of the Social Gospel in American Protestantism, 1865–1915* (New Haven, 1940); and see Henry F. May, *Protestant Churches and Industrial America* (New York, 1949); Arthur Mann, *Yankee Reformers in the Urban Age* (Cambridge, 1954); Sidney Fine, *Laissez-Faire and the General Welfare State* (Ann Arbor, 1956); and Jurgen Herbst, "Francis Greenwood Peabody," *Harvard Theological Review*, 54 (January 1961), 45–69.

[22] For a contemporary bibliography of the scientific study of social conditions see Francis G. Peabody, ed., *A Guide to Reading in Social Ethics and Allied Subjects* (Cambridge, 1910).

can democracy, and thus by implication of Protestant Christianity. In the city the world would see "whether we are capable of self-government." "It is the cities and towns which will frame state constitutions, make laws, create public opinion, establish social usages, and fix standards of morals in the West." East and West could not be separated: the cities were gateways through which could come to the West socialism, anarchism, the power of monopolies, the spoils system, and intemperance.

Strong's new prospect of a disappearing rural and emerging urban America reminds one of Frederick Jackson Turner's recognition of the disappearing Western frontier.[23] In many, but not in all respects, the convictions of Strong and Turner were the same. Both men agreed that the West as previously known was fast disappearing, and that the frontier lay as much in the East as in the West. Like Turner Strong held that America "shall enter upon a new era, and shall more rapidly approximate European conditions of life." But unlike Turner Strong did not see in this fact of economic and social change, in this shift from country to city, a matter of fundamental importance. The observable change, to Strong, was but a matter of statistics, and he dealt with it in the book's briefest chapter, "The Exhaustion of the Public Lands." Much more important was the relevance of this historical development to his concern for America's abiding mission.

Strong's overriding concern now as before was the permanence of God's plan of redemption. World history remained the progressive revelation of God's will, and the rise of the city was part of the world's progress. Progress, Strong wrote, is the coming of civilization, and "what is the process of civilizing but the creating of more and higher wants. Commerce follows the missionary." Rising wants bring mounting discontents, yet, at the same time, the cities as centers of civilization broke down isolation, that "mother of barbarism" which had been the

[23] See Turner, "The Significance of the Frontier in American History," American Historical Association, *Annual Report for 1893* (Washington, D.C., 1894), pp. 199–227.

curse of the rural West. Progress overcame old and brought new problems, yet it did not touch the truth of the Gospel. It did not bring into question the Christian virtues preached by the missionaries, and in this sense the Social Gospel was not a new gospel but only the Gospel of old applied to new conditions. Strong noted and described America's transformation in order to plead that ethical commands which had proven their worth in a rural society be retained to guide the nation in a new age.[24]

Modern readers can scarcely miss or fail to be struck by Strong's vigorously expressed belief in the superiority of the Anglo-Saxon race. This race, according to Strong, was God's chosen people. Infused with many different strains, it had made its final home in America. The admixture of alien immigrants was dangerous: "Glory is departing from many a New England village, because men alien in blood, in religion, and in civilization, are taking possession. . ." Yet the Anglo-Saxon race was too strong and healthy, too rapidly increasing in numbers, to be overcome by others. Its physical vitality and its most treasured possession—the ideas of civil liberty and of "a pure spiritual Christianity"—had made it "the greatest missionary

[24] After the publication of *Our Country,* Strong devoted all his energies to practical solutions of urban problems. From 1886 to 1898 he served as Secretary of the American Evangelical Alliance—the forerunner of the Federal Council of Churches—and thereafter he founded the League of Social Service and, in 1902, the American Institute for Social Service. How strongly the views expressed in *Our Country* directed his later work may be seen by the program of a Washington conference, sponsored by the Evangelical Alliance in 1887, and devoted to a discussion of "the present perils and opportunities of the Christian church and of the country," and of "a hearty co-operation of all Evangelical Christians" to meet this "momentous crisis." Addresses were given on "The City as Peril," "Immigration," "The Misuse of Wealth," "Estrangement from the Church," "Ultramontanism," "The Saloon," "Perils to the Family," "The Social Vice," "Illiteracy," "Reaction of the Church to the Capital and Labor Question," "The Christian Resources of Our Country," "Necessity of Co-operation in Christian Work," "Co-operation in Cities," and "Individual Responsibility Growing out of Perils and Opportunities." Strong himself spoke on "Methods of Co-operation in Christian Work." See *National Perils and Opportunities: The Discussions of the General Christian Conference* (New York, 1887). Quotations are from pp. v and vii, and from the table of contents.

race." And so, curiously, its "marked superiority" was due, Strong said, "in large measure to its highly mixed origin." Immigrants were thus a blessing in disguise, for their presence spurred on Anglo-Saxons to prove the superiority of their own ways by assimilating inferior races. "The strains of other bloods . . . may be expected to improve the stock, and aid it to a higher destiny." Race, to Strong, was more a matter of faith and morals than of blood and national origin. Anglo-Saxon morality and physical prowess were the guarantees of victory. "Does it not look," asked Strong, "as if God were not only preparing in our Anglo-Saxon civilization the die with which to stamp the peoples of the earth, but as if he were also massing behind that die the mighty power with which to press it?" God's design had worked the superiority of the Anglo-Saxon race. "But for the salt of Christianity" wrote Strong, this race would speedily decline. Kept pure in morals by it, Anglo-Saxons were an instrument in the hands of God.

In exploring these themes and theories, Strong relied heavily on the authority of modern science, an emphasis that had been lacking in the earlier versions of the book. Science, Strong held, was characterized chiefly by its meticulous respect for "facts," and a glance at the sources consulted by Strong reveals the extent to which the book may claim to be based on "facts and figures." Statistics compiled by economists, geographers, demographers, and sociologists supplied the book's "scientific bedrock." Strong based his argument that the progress of civilization meant the increasing centralization of human affairs and a growing interdependence of society's members on statistical data, and geographers' evidence allowed him to say confidently that modern interdependent civilizations were to be found in the belt of intermediate climates, primarily in the habitat of the Anglo-Saxon race. To such sociological, economic, and geographical information Strong added the psychologist's findings concerning the social and climatic causes of mental illness, and concluded that "the American people are rapidly becoming the most nervous, the most highly organized, in the world," nervousness—a term he borrowed from

George M. Beard [25]—being the price of an advanced civilization.

The natural sciences too were drawn upon. Strong found endorsement for his faith in history's onward move in biological science. The theory of evolution and the doctrine of the survival of the fittest provided dramatic proof of America's manifest destiny, for Darwin's theory of natural selection confirmed the emergence of the Anglo-Saxons as the superior race. Darwin, Strong wrote, "even intimates that the world's history thus far has been simply preparatory for our future, and tributary to it." The Anglo-Saxons of America will "move down upon Mexico, down upon Central and South America, out upon the islands of the sea, over upon Africa and beyond. And can any one doubt that the result of this competition of races will be the 'survival of the fittest?' " In the light of this scientific proposition it was irrelevant "whether the extinction of inferior races before the advancing Anglo-Saxon seem to the reader sad or otherwise . . ." Only the facts counted, and they vigorously corroborated the concept of America's mission under divine design.

Yet Strong never lets his readers forget that despite all his excursions into the facts and fancies of science and his survey of American society, he was concerned primarily with an analysis of the spiritual and moral condition of the American people. And he never loses sight of the very practical and concrete purpose of *Our Country:* to raise contributions for the Congregational Home Missionary Society. The work of the spirit depended, he explained, on material gifts from men of wealth. The acquisition, possession, and expenditure of money thus was a theme central to Strong's concerns. Money, he wrote, "is power in the concrete." Unfortunately, this power was exercised all too often without regard for spiritual considerations.

[25] George Miller Beard (1839–1883), American physician, gained international fame with his *The Medical and Surgical Uses of Electricity* (1871). This book presented the results of his research in electrotherapeutics. In 1874–75 Beard founded the *Archives of Electrology and Neurology*. A prolific writer, he was a pioneer in the study of neurology and a crusader in the reform of Amercan psychiatric practice.

"The love of money," Strong reported, "is the besetting sin of commercial people, and runs in the blood of Anglo-Saxons who are the great wealth-creators of the world." It had created in America the extremes of social classes, "the dangerously rich and the dangerously poor; and," added Strong, "the former are much more to be feared than the latter." Capitalists, like socialists, were men subversive to American democracy because as representatives of unrestrained individualism they wielded power irresponsibly and without regard for moral ends. In America's emerging industrial society Strong saw a demonstration of the truth that "great material prosperity is likely to be accompanied by spiritual dearth." Yet money in itself was not an evil. "It represents the school, the college, the church, the printing press, and all evangelizing machinery. . . . It is the modern miracle worker." All depended on its use. If Strong appealed to men of wealth, he did not assume them to be inherently corrupt. He did not urge upon them self-denial and asceticism. "Away with the idea of penance. It belies God, and caricatures the Christian religion." Wealth, Strong wrote, "contains mighty possibilities, both for good and evil . . ." When placed in the hand of the home missionaries, then "the money power has been Christianized." Thus a material force could be made to serve a spiritual cause in concrete ways.

Our Country was to help realize the mighty possibilities of a Christianized money power. In theological language, it was to help transform "the kingdoms of this world" into "the kingdoms of our Lord." The task of *Our Country* was to enlist wealth in the service of God. Strong, the theologian, preached that all of man's possessions belonged to God, that ownership of earthly goods imposed upon man the responsibilities of stewardship. "Our possessions," wrote Strong, "are his property [and] should be used in his service—not a fraction of them, but the whole." If all Christians, the rich and the poor alike, acted upon this assumption there would be no "social question." There would be no greed and envy, no industrial warfare, no liquor power, no monopolies. To have Americans accept the stewardship of wealth idea, to have them give freely to the work of home missions, Strong said, was to hasten the arrival of the Kingdom. "Surely," he wrote in *The New Era*, "to be a Christian and an Anglo-Saxon and an American in this generation is to stand on the mountain-top of privilege." [26] To enjoy such a position of privilege in a time of crisis "demands the acceptance of Christian stewardship . . . The church must consecrate the power which is in money. Oh! that men would accept the testimony of Christ touching the blessedness of giving!"

Strong's book struck deep responses in the American people. Most Americans were aware, however vaguely, that the United States was changing, and in *Our Country* many found a "scientific" explanation of what the changes were. The facts and figures Strong supplied added up to a portrait Americans could recognize. They were witnesses to the changing pattern of European immigration that Strong described and which census figures corroborated: in 1880 64.8 per cent from the continent's Northwest, in 1885 46.5 per cent; in 1880 29.8 per cent from Central Europe, in 1885 44 per cent; in 1880 1.4 per cent from Eastern Europe, in 1885 5 per cent.[27] They were experiencing the increasing strength of Catholicism in the western states of New Mexico, Montana, Arizona, and Nevada, and in the eastern cities of Massachusetts and Rhode Island.[28] And their lives were intimately involved in the increasing importance of the cities that Strong detailed from the census reports.

Similarly, Strong exploited the moral and religious concerns that lurked below the surface of local and national politics.

[26] *The New Era or the Coming Kingdom* (New York, 1893), p. 354.

[27] Based on *Historical Statistics of the United States, 1789–1945* (Washington, D.C., 1949), pp. 33–34. Northwest Europe includes Great Britain, Ireland, Scandinavia, the Netherlands, Belgium, Luxembourg, Switzerland, and France; Central Europe includes Germany, Poland, and Austria-Hungary; Eastern Europe includes Russia, the Baltic States, Rumania, Bulgaria, and European Turkey; Southern Europe includes Italy, Spain, Portugal, Greece, and other European countries not elsewhere classified.

[28] See graphs on pp. 472–475 of H. K. Carroll, *The Religious Forces of the United States* (New York, 1893).

When he wrote of Romanism, the liquor power, and the extremes of wealth and poverty, when he related these themes to the antagonism between native Anglo-Saxons and foreign immigrants, between Protestants and Catholics, he was using the language of politics. Public and personal conduct of individuals, religion, patriotism, clean government, distaste for ostentation and rampant wealth in the face of suffering, support for reform causes from good government to temperance, and above all the service of all these ideals in building a better America—these were the sentiments of morality, but they were the most intense issues of politics as well, and Strong exploited them all.

The success of Strong's book may be attributed, finally, to his instinct for the taste of the book-reading public. The juxtaposition of an older rural America with an emerging urban civilization and the celebration of the virtues of the agrarian past were familiar and appealing literary themes. Romances of childhood were best-sellers—not merely *Tom Sawyer* but Margaret Sidney's *Five Little Peppers* and Miss Burnett's *Little Lord Fauntleroy*. Books romanticizing the virile virtues of the Christian faith—General Lew Wallace's *Ben Hur* and Thomas Hughes' *The Manliness of Christ*—were devoured; and novels concerned with the social and economic questions of the time—John Hay's *The Breadwinners,* Edward Bellamy's *Looking Backward*—were similarly popular.[29] *Our Country* succeeded in interweaving these themes, and infusing them with a radiant faith in America's future. It was a faith composed of the Protestant version of belief in the chosen people, a secular, science-supported theory of progress, and a nationalistic sense of manifest destiny.

Josiah Strong's *Our Country* conveys both a picture of rural America as seen from the home missionary's angle of vision and a sketch of urban America as it was emerging in the 1880's. In its ambiguity of focus, shifting back and forth between the rural West and the urban East, it reveals an uncertainty of

[29] See Alice P. Hackett, *Fifty Years of Best Sellers* (New York, 1945), and James D. Hart, *The Popular Book* (New York, 1950), chs. 10–12.

conception, but one characteristic of the time. Where was the strength and promise of America to be located? Torn between farm and city, between past and future, Americans sought reassurance in traditional verities: in the vision of a Protestant American republic as a model for the world. To reaffirm this vision Strong had exploited masterfully the rising prestige of social science, had perceptively handled his readers' desire for morality in politics and the nation's affairs, and had grasped unerringly his countrymen's taste in books. *Our Country* is a mirror of Protestant America in the 1880's, reflecting its image of the past, its sense of present realities, and its dreams of the future.

A Note on the Text and Acknowledgments

The present edition of *Our Country* reproduces exactly the revised edition of 1891, except for the forms of citation and quotations, which have been modernized; obvious errors in typesetting and transcription have been silently corrected. New material, added by the present editor, appears in footnotes enclosed in brackets.

The editor is grateful to Miss Elsie Strong of Tryon, North Carolina, for information about her father's life and work; to Mrs. Kathleen Witten, reference librarian at Wesleyan University, for her advice and help; and to Mrs. Dorothy Hay of Portland, Connecticut, for her painstaking labors in preparing typescript of the editor's introduction and footnotes. The editor wishes to acknowledge also the financial support received from the Research Committee of the Public Affairs Center of Wesleyan University and from the University's research fund.

OUR COUNTRY

ITS POSSIBLE FUTURE AND ITS PRESENT CRISIS.

BY

REV. JOSIAH STRONG, D.D.,
GENERAL SECRETARY OF THE EVANGELICAL ALLIANCE FOR THE UNITED STATES, NEW YORK.

WITH AN INTRODUCTION BY
PROF. AUSTIN PHELPS, D.D.

REVISED EDITION, BASED ON THE CENSUS OF 1890.

One Hundred and Fifty-Eighth Thousand.

PUBLISHED BY
THE BAKER & TAYLOR CO.
740 & 742 BROADWAY, NEW YORK.
FOR
THE AMERICAN HOME MISSIONARY SOCIETY.

[the title page of the 1891 edition]

PREFACE TO THE REVISED EDITION

LIVING issues have changing aspects. The first edition of *Our Country,* which was prepared for the American Home Missionary Society when the author was its representative in Ohio, appeared early in 1886, and most of the book was written a year earlier. Although I endeavored to apply to the subjects discussed fundamental principles, which remain equally applicable to-day, the statistical treatment of these living issues renders revision, after six years, quite essential to the further usefulness of the book. Moreover the census of 1890 marks the present as a favorable time for such revision. Although important results of the census will not be available for many months and even for years to come, the Superintendent, Hon. Robert P. Porter, has kindly furnished me with much valuable information.

The favorable reception accorded to the book would seem to be sufficient reason for its revision. Perhaps it may be of interest to state that in addition to the 130,000 copies which have passed into circulation, a large part, if not the whole of the book, has been reprinted by the daily press, prominent papers in the East, West, South and in Canada, each having printed from one to three chapters entire. Four chapters were re-published in London [1] and one in Glasgow. The book has been translated into one foreign language, and numerous prop-

[1] [Josiah Strong, *The United States and the Future of the Anglo-Saxon Race* (London, 1889). This volume includes chapters 2, 3, 12, and 13 of the 1885 edition (chapters 2, 3, 13, and 14 in the edition of 1891), and a paper by Michael G. Mulhall, "The Growth of American Industries and Wealth."—All notes enclosed in brackets have been supplied by the present editor.]

ositions have been received relative to translating it into others.

I am devoutly thankful to God that he has used the book to accomplish in some measure what was intended by it. No one, I am sure, can have been more sensible of its defects than myself.

This revised edition has the benefit of criticisms made on earlier editions. It surely is not strange that among some thousands of statements of fact a number of errors should have been found, due in most instances to having accepted statements or estimates from men eminent enough, but not authorities on the point quoted; e. g., Mr. Gladstone's estimate (p. 98.) that "manufacturing power, by the aid of machinery, doubles for the world once in seven years," which, it appears, is altogether extravagant. I may add that none of the errors referred to was essential to the argument, and therefore did not invalidate its conclusions.

Our Roman Catholic friends have objected, and quite justly, that the Pope's utterances were not quoted literally. That no injustice might be done, it was my intention in the first edition to take all statements of Roman Catholic teaching or policy from Roman Catholics themselves, but as I then had no access to original sources of information, I was obliged to take quotations second-hand from Protestant writers. Six years ago there was very little agitation of the Roman Catholic question and reliable information was then much more difficult to obtain. The utterances of the Pope quoted were taken from *Fate of Republics*,[2] in which the propositions of the "Syllabus of Errors," issued by Pius IX., December 8, 1864, were put in positive instead of negative form, which does to some extent change their force and perhaps their meaning.[3] Although I had

[2] [Written anonymously by Luther Tracy Townsend (1838–1922), professor of practical theology at the Boston Theological Seminary, and published in Boston in 1880.]

[3] [In the 1885 edition Strong quoted Proposition 42 thus: "In case of conflict between the ecclesiastical and civil powers, the ecclesiastical powers ought to prevail" (p. 50). In the revised edition of 1891 Strong rendered the same proposition as follows: "It is an error to hold that,

then no reason to doubt the literalness of the quotations, I made repeated but unsuccessful efforts to obtain the Latin original by which to verify them.

No Roman Catholic, however, will have occasion to criticise the revision on any such ground.

It having been decided that the book would bear some enlargement, explanatory notes have been added more freely than was practicable in the narrower limits of the earlier editions. Some short passages have been omitted to make room for new and more important matter, which has been added to every chapter but one. A chapter on Peril to the Public Schools has been added, the greater part of which was read before the seventh triennial session of the National Council of Congregational Churches at Worcester, Mass., October 14, 1889.[4] The chapter on Romanism is almost entirely new and much enlarged.

The map and most of the diagrams which appear in this revision are from *Leaves from 'Our Country,'* illustrated by Rev. C. C. Otis, of Springfield, Ill., published by the American Home Missionary Society in 1888, to which society I am indebted for their use. I desire also to express my thanks to the many gentlemen, too numerous to name, who have kindly aided me with courteous answers to my inquiries for information.

The outlook is distinctly brighter than it was a half dozen years ago, not because there are fewer perils to face, nor, with one or two exceptions, because they are any less threatening, but because the public mind is being aroused to some appreciation of them, and the Christian Church is beginning to awake to the magnitude of her opportunity and obligation. The awakening however, is only a beginning, and leaves very much to be desired.

---

in the case of conflicting laws between the two powers, the civil law ought to prevail" (p. 63). Similar changes in wording concerning Propositions 45 and 47 can be found on pages 49 and 73 of the 1885 and 1891 editions, respectively. For the sources used by Strong in the 1891 edition see Chapter V, n. 3.]

[4] [See *Minutes* of the Council, published in Boston, 1889, pp. 352–365.]

The difference in the situation to-day and five years ago is not such as to warrant the slightest relaxation of effort, but should rather stimulate endeavor with new courage.

This work is an attempt to present some of the perils which threaten our future, and to point out the magnitude of the issues which hang on the present. I have in preparation a work which is more constructive in character, and which will endeavor to show what action is demanded by existing conditions.[5] This book is for the most part, a diagnosis; the forthcoming one will venture to suggest some remedies. JOSIAH STRONG.

[5] [This reference is to Strong's *The New Era or the Coming Kingdom* (New York, 1893). In the preface to this work Strong restated his aim: "I have tried to lay hold of fundamental laws and principles and to apply them to the explanation of existing conditions and to the solution of the great problems of the age" (p. v).]

INTRODUCTION

This is a powerful book. It needs no introduction from other sources than its own. Its great strength lies in its facts. These are collated with rare skill, and verified by the testimony of men and of documents whose witness is authority. The book will speak for itself to every man who cares enough for the welfare of our country to read it, and who has intelligence enough to take in its portentous story.

It is worthy of note that almost all the thinking which thinking men have given to the subject for the last fifty years has been in the line of the leading idea which this volume enforces—the idea of *crisis* in the destiny of this country, and through it in the destiny of the world. The common sense of men puts into homely phrase the great principles which underlie great enterprises. One such phrase lies under the Christian civilization of our land. It is "the nick of time." The present hour is, and always has been, "the nick of time" in our history. The principle which underlies all probationary experience comes to view in organized society with more stupendous import than in individual destiny. This book puts the evidence of that in a form of cumulative force which is overwhelming.

Fifty years ago our watchful fathers discerned it in their forecast of the future of the Republic. The wisest among them even then began to doubt how long the original stock of American society could bear the interfusion of elements alien to our history and to the faith of our ancestry. The conviction was then often expressed that the case was hopeless on any theory of our national growth which did not take into account the eternal decrees of God. Good men were hopeful, only because they had faith in the *reserves* of might which God held secret from human view.

Those now living who were in their boyhood then, remember well how such men as Dr. Lyman Beecher, of Ohio,[1] and Dr. Wm. Blackburn, of Missouri,[2] used to return from their conflicts with the multiform varieties of Western infidelity to thrill the hearts of Christian assemblies at the East with their pictures of Western greatness, and Western perils. Those were the palmy days of "May Anniversaries." The ideas which the veterans of the platform set on fire and left to burn in our souls were three: The magnitude of the West in geographical area; the rapidity with which it was filling up with social elements, many of them hostile to each other, but nearly all conspiring against Christian institutions; and the certainty that Christianity must go down in the struggle, if Eastern enterprise was not prompt in seizing upon the then present opportunity, and resolute in preoccupying the land for Christ. Again and again Dr. Beecher said, in substance, on Eastern platforms: "Now is the nick of time. In matters which reach into eternity, now is always the nick of time. One man now is worth a hundred fifty years hence. One dollar now is worth a thousand then. Let us be up and doing before it is too late."

From that time to this the strain of appeal has been the same, but with accumulating volume and solemnity of warning. The fate of our country has been in what Edmund Burke describes as "a perilous and dancing balance." Human wisdom could at no time foresee which way the scales would turn.

[1] [Lyman Beecher (1775–1863) served as Presbyterian clergyman in Connecticut, Massachusetts, and Ohio. From 1832 to 1850 he was president of Lane Theological Seminary in Cincinnati, Ohio. He became widely known for his temperance agitation and revivalist preaching. For his anti-Catholicism and views on Protestant missions in the West see his *A Plea for the West* (Cincinnati, 1835).]

[2] [In all likelihood this reference is to William Maxwell Blackburn (1828–1898). Blackburn served as Presbyterian minister in Three Rivers, Michigan, and in Erie, Pennsylvania. He was a professor of theology at the McCormick Theological Seminary of the Northwest in Chicago, president of the Territorial University of North Dakota and, subsequently, of Pierre University in South Dakota.]

Every day has been a day of crisis. Every hour has been an hour of splendid destiny. Every minute has been "the nick of time." And this is the lesson which this volume emphasizes by an accumulated array of facts and testimonies and corollaries from them, the force of which can scarcely be overstated. Fifty years of most eventful history have been piling up the proofs of our national peril, till now they come down upon us with the weight of an avalanche. Such is the impression which the argument here elaborated will make upon one who comes to it as a novelty, or in whose mind the facts have become dim.

One is reminded by it of the judgment which has been expressed by almost all the great generals of the world, from Julius Cæsar to General Grant, that in every decisive battle there is a moment of crisis on which the fortunes of the day turn. The commander who seizes and holds that *ridge* of destiny wins the victory. The conflict for the world's salvation partakes of the same character. And the facts and their corollaries massed together in this book show that nowhere is it more portentously true than in this country. Our whole history is a succession of crises. Our national salvation demands in supreme exercise certain military virtues. Vigilance in watching opportunity; tact and daring in seizing upon opportunity; force and persistence in crowding opportunity to its utmost of possible achievement—these are the martial virtues which must command success.

This volume presents, also, with a power which can scarcely be exceeded—for it is the power of the simple facts—the truth that Christian enterprise for the moral conquest of this land needs to be conducted with the *self-abandonment* which determined men would throw into the critical moment in the critical battle of the critical campaign for a nation's endangered life. What the campaign in Pennsylvania was to the Civil War, what the battle of Gettysburg was to that campaign, what the fight for Cemetery Hill was to that battle, such is the present opportunity to the Christian civilization of this country.

Turn whichever way we will—South, West, North, East—we are confronted by the same element of crisis in the outlook upon the future. Everything seems, to human view, to depend on present and dissolving chances. Whatever can be done at all must be done with speed. The building of great states depends on one decade. The nationalizing of alien races must be the work of a period which, in a nation's life, is but an hour. The elements we work upon and the elements we must work with are fast precipitating themselves in fixed institutions and consolidated character. Nothing will await our convenience. Nothing is indulgent to a dilatory policy. Nothing is tolerant of a somnolent enterprise.

The climax of the argument appears in the view taken of the auxiliary relation of this country's evangelizing to the evangelizing of the world. One who studies even cursorily the beginnings of Christianity will not fail to detect a masterly *strategy* in apostolic policy. Christian enterprise at the outset took possession first of strategic localities, to be used as the centers of church-extension. The first successes of Christian preachers were in the great cities of the East. The attractive spots, to the divine eye, were those which were crowded with the densest masses of human beings. Not a trace do we find of labor thrown off at random in the apostolic tactics. As little do we discover of the spirit of romance. The early missions were not crusades for the conquest of holy places. They were not pilgrimages to sacred shrines. Martial ardor in the work was held well in hand by martial skill in the choice of methods and localities.

The same military forecast has ruled Christian missions from that day to this, so far as they have been crowned with great successes. How little of work and expenditure at haphazard has entered into the splendid structure of English and American missions to the heathen! How little has the spirit of romance or of æsthetic taste ever accomplished in evangelizing the nations! The two localities to which the romance of Christian enterprise would naturally turn are Palestine and Greece; the one as the home of our Lord, the other as the birthplace of art and culture. Yet how little, comparatively speaking, have Christian missions achieved in either land! Labor has been as faithful, and self-sacrifice as generous there as elsewhere; but in the comparison with other missions, where are the fruits?

Success in the work of the world's conversion has, with rare exceptions, followed the lines of human growth and prospective greatness. But a single exception occurs to one's memory —that of the Hawaiian Islands. Seldom has a nation been converted to Christ, only to die. The general law has been that Christianity should seat itself in the great metropolitan centers of population and of civilized progress. It has allied itself with the most virile races. It has taken possession of the most vigorous and enterprising nations. The colonizing races and nations have been its favorites. It has abandoned the dying for the nascent languages. Its affinities have always been for the youthful, the forceful, the progressive, the aspiring in human character, and for that stock of mind from which such character springs. By natural sequence, the *localities* where those elements of powerful manhood are, or are to be, in most vigorous development, have been the strategic points of which our religion has taken possession as by a masterly military genius.

The principles of such a strategic wisdom should lead us to look on these United States as first and foremost the chosen seat of enterprise for the world's conversion. Forecasting the future of Christianity, as statesmen forecast the destiny of nations, we must believe that it will be what the future of this country is to be. As goes America, so goes the world, in all that is vital to its moral welfare. In this view, this volume finds the superlative corollary of its argument.

AUSTIN PHELPS.[3]

[3] [Austin Phelps (1820–1890) served as Congregational minister in Boston from 1842 to 1848 and as chaplain of both houses of the Massachusetts General Court. As professor of sacred rhetoric and homiletics at Andover Seminary he belonged to the conservative wing of the Andover faculty. At the time of writing the preface to *Our Country* he was professor *emeritus*.]

CHAPTER I

THE TIME FACTOR IN THE PROBLEM

THERE are certain great focal points of history toward which the lines of past progress have converged, and from which have radiated the molding influences of the future. Such was the Incarnation, such was the German Reformation of the sixteenth century, and such are the *closing years of the nineteenth century,* second in importance to that only which must always remain first; viz., the birth of Christ.

Many are not aware that we are living in extraordinary times. Few suppose that these years of peaceful prosperity, in which we are quietly developing a continent, are the pivot on which is turning the nation's future. And fewer still imagine that the destinies of mankind, for centuries to come, can be seriously affected, much less determined, by the men of this generation in the United States. But no generation appreciates its own place in history. Several years ago Professor Austin Phelps [1] said: "Five hundred years of time in the process of the world's salvation may depend on the next twenty years of United States history." It is proposed in the following pages to show that such dependence of the world's future on this generation in America is not only credible, but in the highest degree probable.

To attribute such importance to the present hour may strike one who has given little or no study to the subject as quite

[1] [See note 3 of Introduction.]

extravagant. It is easy to see how a great battle may in a day prove decisive of a nation's future. A political revolution or a diplomatic act in some great crisis may cut the thread of destiny; but how is it possible that a few years of national growth, in time of peace, may be thus fateful? Great civilizations have been the product of ages. Their character is slowly developed, and changes therein are slowly wrought. What are twenty years in a nation's growth, that they should be so big with destiny?

It must not be forgotten that the pulse and the pace of the world have been marvelously quickened during the nineteenth century. Much as we boast its achievements, not every one appreciates how large a proportion of the world's progress in civilization has been made since the application of steam to travel, commerce, manufactures, and printing. At the beginning of this century there was very little travel. Men lived in isolated communities. Mutually ignorant, they naturally were mutually suspicious. In English villages a stranger was an enemy. Under such conditions there could be little exchange of ideas and less of commodities. Buxton[2] says: "Intercourse is the soul of progress." The impetus given to intercommunication of every sort by the application of steam was the beginning of a new life in the world. Crompton's spinning mule was invented in 1775; Cartwright's power-loom in 1787; and Whitney's cotton-gin in 1793; but they did not come into common use until the nineteenth century. At the outbreak of the Revolutionary War there were in use in English and American homes the same primitive means by which the world's wool and flax had been reduced to yarn for thousands of years; the same rude contrivance used in ancient Mycenæ and Troy by Homer's heroines. There are men alive to-day, whose mothers, like Solomon's virtuous woman, laid their hands to the spindle and distaff, and knew no other way. William Fairbairn, an eminent mechanic,[3] states

[2] [Sir Thomas Fowell Buxton (1786–1845), eminent British philanthropist and member of Parliament. He was active in prison reform movements and the antislavery cause.]

[3] [Sir William Fairbairn (1789–1874), a self-schooled engineer, pioneered in the construction of iron ships and bridges.]

that "in the beginning of the century the human hand performed all the work that was done, and performed it badly." Methods of travel and communication were as primitive as those of manufacture. "Toward the close of the [eighteenth] century Lord Campbell accomplished the journey from Edinburgh to London in three days and three nights. But judicious friends warned him of the dangers of this enterprise, and told him that several persons who had been so rash as to attempt it had actually died from the mere rapidity of the motion." [4] In August, 1888, the same journey was made by the Great Northern route (392 miles) in seven hours and thirty-two minutes. And that year the railways of Great Britain conveyed upwards of 742,000,000 passengers.[5] It took Dr. Atkinson eight months to go from New England to Oregon in 1847.[6] When he returned the journey occupied six days. When the battle of Waterloo was fought (1815) all haste delivered the thrilling dispatches in London three days later. The news of the bombardment of Alexandria (1882) was received in the English capital a few minutes after the first shell was thrown.

Any one as old as the nineteenth century has seen a very large proportion of all the progress in civilization made by the race. When seven years old he might have seen Fulton's steamboat on her trial trip up the Hudson. Until twenty years of age he could not have found in all the world an iron plow. At thirty he might have traveled on the first railway passenger train. In 1889 the world had 359,071 miles of railway.[7] For the first thirty-three years of his life he had to rely on the tinder-box for fire. He was thirty-eight when steam communication between Europe and America was established. He had arrived

[4] Robert Mackenzie, *The 19th Century: A History* (London, 1879), pp. 91–92.

[5] *The Statesman's Year Book, 1890* (London, 1890), p. 86.

[6] [George Henry Atkinson (1819–1889), Congregational clergyman, was commissioned by the American Home Missionary Society to act as its representative in the Pacific Northwest. His journey from Boston to Oregon in the winter of 1847–1848 took him around Cape Horn to the Hawaiian Islands, and from there to Oregon City.]

[7] *The World Almanac, 1890* (New York, 1890), p. 125.

at middle life (forty-four) when the first telegram was sent. Forty-three years later the world had 780,433 miles of telegraph lines, and the number of messages annually transmitted is estimated at 300,000,000.[8] Our century has been distinguished by a rising flood of inventions. The English government issued more patents during the twenty years succeeding 1850 than during the two hundred and fifty years preceding.

But this has not been simply a mechanical era of marvelous material progress. With the exception of astronomy, modern science, as we now know it, is almost wholly the creation of the nineteenth century. In this century, too, have the glorious fruits of modern missions all been gathered. Another evidence of progress which, if less obvious than material results, is more conclusive, is found in the *great ideas* which have become the fixed possession of men within the past hundred years. Among them is that of individual liberty, which is radically different from the ancient conception of freedom that lay at the foundation of the Greek and Roman republics, and later, of the free cities of Italy. Theirs was a liberty of class, or clan, or nation, not of the individual; he existed for the government. The idea that the government exists for the individual is modern.

From this idea of individual liberty follows logically the abolition of slavery. At the close of the eighteenth century slavery existed almost everywhere—in Russia, Hungary, Prussia, Austria, Scotland, in the British, French, and Spanish colonies, and in North and South America. It is said that during the first seven years of this century English ships conveyed across the Atlantic 280,000 Africans, one-half of whom perished amid the horrors of the "middle passage," or soon after landing. But this century has seen slavery practically destroyed in all Christendom.

Another idea, which, like that of individual liberty, finds its root in the teachings of Christ, and has grown up slowly through the ages to blossom in our own, is that of honor to womanhood, whose fruitage is woman's elevation. Early in this century it was not very uncommon for an Englishman to sell his wife

[8] *The World Almanac, 1890,* p. 127.

into servitude. "A gentleman in this country, in 1815, having access to not a very large number of English sources of information, found, in a single year, thirty-nine instances of wives exposed to public sale, like cattle, at Smithfield." [9] The amazement or incredulity with which such a statement is received by this generation is the best comment on it.

Another striking evidence of progress is found in the enhanced valuation of human life, which has served to humanize law and mitigate "man's inhumanity to man." At the beginning of this century nothing was cheaper than human life. In the eye of English law the life of a rabbit was worth more than that of a man; for even an attempt upon the former cost the sacrifice of the latter. The law recognized two hundred and twenty-three capital offences. "If a man injured Westminster Bridge, he was hanged. If he appeared disguised on a public road, he was hanged. If he cut down young trees; if he shot at rabbits; if he stole property valued at five shillings; if he stole anything at all from a bleach-field; if he wrote a threatening letter to extort money; if he returned prematurely from transportation—for any of these offences he was immediately hanged. . . . In 1816 there were at one time (in England) fifty-eight persons under sentence of death. One of these was a child ten years old." [10]

Space does not suffer even the mention of other noble ideas, the growth of which has enriched our civilization and elevated man. Our glance at the condition, fourscore years ago, of the most enlightened of the nations, hasty as it has been, suffices to remind us of the amazing changes which have taken place within a few years; and to show that if we reckon time by its

[9] Daniel Dorchester, *The Problem of Religious Progress* (New York and Cincinnati, 1881), p. 219. The London *New Monthly Magazine,* II, 8 (September 1, 1814), on p. 185 contains the following note: "Shropshire.—A well-looking woman, wife of John Hall, to whom she had been married only one month, was brought by him in a halter, and sold by public auction, in the market, for two shillings and sixpence, with the addition of sixpence for the rope in which she was led to the cross. In this sale the customary market fees were charged, viz., toll, one penny; pitching, threepence."

[10] Mackenzie, *The 19th Century,* p. 78.

results, twenty years of this century may out-measure a millennium of olden time.

As the traveler in Asia follows the sun westward around the world, he finds life growing ever more intense and time more potent.

> "Better fifty years of Europe than a cycle of Cathay."

And to carry the comparison between the East and the West a degree further, permit me to quote an intelligent Englishman who is a competent witness; viz., Mr. Joseph Hatton, who says: "Ten years in the history of America is half a century of European progress. Ten years ago the manufactures of America were too insignificant for consideration in the Old World. To-day England herself is successfully rivaled by American productions in her own markets." [11] But the comparison does not end here. Ten years in the New West are, in their results, fully equal to half a century east of the Mississippi. There is there a tremendous rush of events which is startling, even in the nineteenth century. That western world in its progress is gathering momentum like a falling body. Vast regions have been settled before, but never before under the mighty whip and spur of electricity and steam. Referring to the development of the West, the *London Times* remarks: "Unquestionably, this is the most important fact in contemporary history. It is a new fact; it cannot be compared with any cognate phenomenon in the past." And, as it is without a precedent, so it will remain without a parallel, for there are no more New Worlds.

[11] *To-day in America,* 2 vols. (London, 1881).

CHAPTER II

NATIONAL RESOURCES

IT is necessary to the argument to show that the United States is capable of sustaining a vast population.

The fathers on Massachusetts Bay once decided that population was never likely to be very dense west of Newton (a suburb of Boston), and the founders of Lynn, after exploring ten or fifteen miles, doubted whether the country was good for anything farther west than that. Until recent times, only less inadequate has been the popular conception of the trans-Missouri region and the millions destined to inhabit it. Of late years, home missionary writers and speakers have tried to astonish us into some appreciation of our national domain. Yet it may well be doubted whether even he who has pondered most upon its magnitude has a "realizing sense" of it. Though astonishing comparisons have ceased to astonish, I know of no means more effective or more just by which to present our physical basis of empire.

What, then, should we say of a republic of eighteen states, each as large as Spain; or one of thirty-one states, each as large as Italy; or one of sixty states, each as large as England and Wales? What a confederation of nations! Take five of the six first-class powers of Europe, Great Britain and Ireland, France, Germany, Austria, and Italy; then add Spain, Portugal, Switzerland, Denmark, and Greece. Let some greater than Napoleon weld them into one mighty empire, and you could lay it all down in the United States west of the Hudson River, once, and again, and again—three times. Well may Mr. Gladstone say that we have "a natural base for the greatest continuous empire ever established by man;" and well may the English premier add: "And the distinction between continuous empire and empire severed and dispersed over sea is vital." [1] With the exception of Alaska our territory is compact, and though so vast, is unified by railways and an unequaled system of rivers and lakes. The latter, occupying a larger area than Great Britain and Ireland, are said to contain nearly one-half of all the fresh water on the globe. We are told that east of the Rocky Mountains we have a river-flow of more than 40,000 miles (*i.e.*, 80,000 miles of river-bank), counting no stream less than a hundred miles in length; while Europe in a larger space has but 17,000 miles. It is estimated [2] that the Mississippi, with its affluents, affords 35,000 miles of navigation. A steamboat may pass up the Mississippi and Missouri 3,900 miles from the Gulf—"as far as from New York to Constantinople." [3] Thus a "vast system of natural canals" carries our seaboard into the very heart of the continent.

But what of the resources of this great empire which makes so brave a display on the map? Alaska is capable of producing great wealth, but not including this territory, the area of the United States, according to the census of 1880, is 2,970,000 square miles. According to the smallest estimate I have ever seen (and doubtless too small), we have 1,500,000 square miles of arable land. China proper, which, according to the latest estimates, supports a population of 383,000,000,[4] has an area of 1,297,999 [5] square miles, or considerably less than one-half of ours not including Alaska. The Chinese are essentially an agricultural people. This vast population, therefore, draws

[1] W. E. Gladstone, "Kin Beyond Sea," *North American Review*, 127 (September–October 1878), 180.

[2] *Encyclopedia Britannica*, 9th ed. (Boston, 1875–1888).

[3] Dr. Goodell. [This is a reference to the Reverend Constans L. Goodell of St. Louis, whom Strong quotes from his *One Million Dollars a Year for Home Missions*, Sermon in behalf of the American Home Missionary Society, preached in the Broadway Tabernacle Church, New York, May 8, 1881 (New York, 1881), p. 4.]

[4] *The Statesman's Year Book, 1890* (London, 1890), p. 410.

[5] *The Statesman's Year Book, 1890,* p. 410.

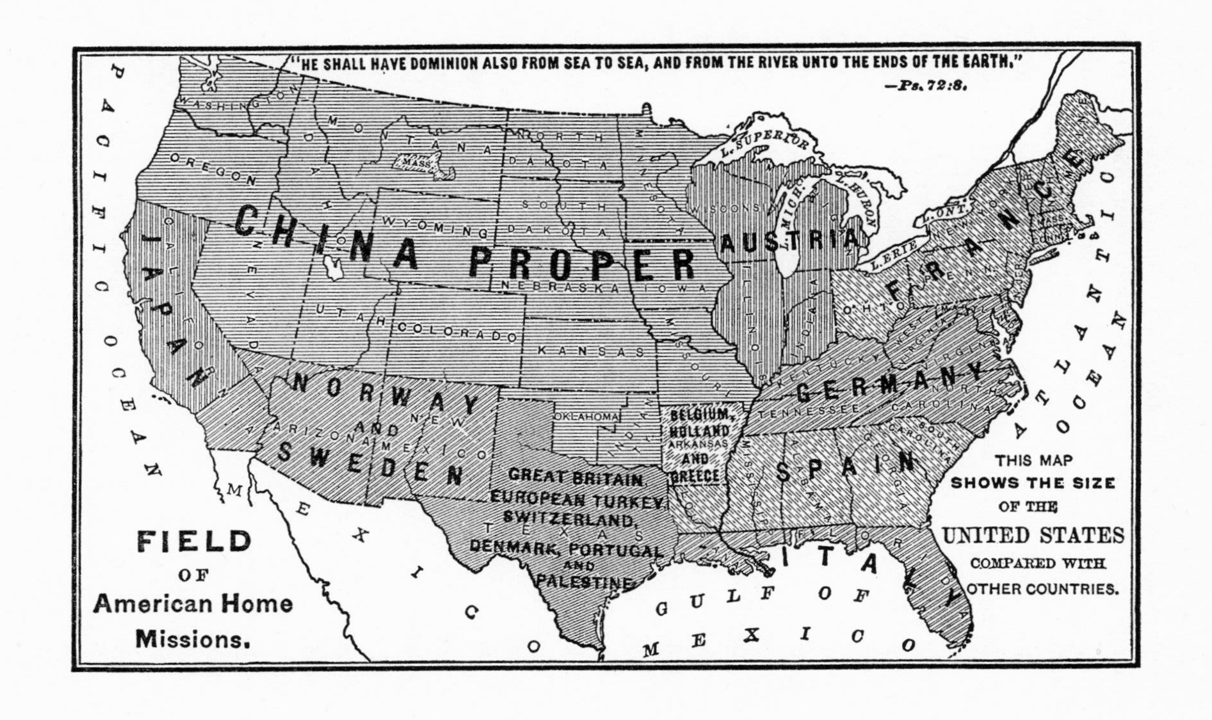
"HE SHALL HAVE DOMINION ALSO FROM SEA TO SEA, AND FROM THE RIVER UNTO THE ENDS OF THE EARTH."
—Ps. 72:8.
PACIFIC OCEAN
ATLANTIC OCEAN
GULF OF MEXICO
MEXICO
CHINA PROPER
AUSTRIA
FRANCE
GERMANY
SPAIN
ITALY
JAPAN
NORWAY AND SWEDEN
GREAT BRITAIN
EUROPEAN TURKEY
SWITZERLAND,
DENMARK, PORTUGAL
AND
PALESTINE
BELGIUM,
HOLLAND
ARKANSAS
AND
GREECE
WASHINGTON
OREGON
CALIFORNIA
NEVADA
IDAHO
MONTANA
MASS.
WYOMING
UTAH
COLORADO
ARIZONA
NEW MEXICO
NORTH DAKOTA
SOUTH DAKOTA
NEBRASKA
KANSAS
OKLAHOMA
INDIAN T.
TEXAS
MINNESOTA
IOWA
MISSOURI
WISCONSIN
ILLINOIS
INDIANA
MICHIGAN
OHIO
KENTUCKY
TENNESSEE
MISSISSIPPI
ALABAMA
GEORGIA
FLORIDA
LOUISIANA
WEST VIRGINIA
VIRGINIA
NORTH CAROLINA
SOUTH CAROLINA
PENN.
NEW YORK
N. JER.
MD.
MASS.
CONN.
L. SUPERIOR
L. MICH.
L. HURON
L. ERIE
L. ONT.
THIS MAP
SHOWS THE SIZE
OF THE
UNITED STATES
COMPARED WITH
OTHER COUNTRIES.
FIELD
OF
American Home
Missions.

nearly all of its support from the soil. The mountains of China occupy an area of more than 300,000 square miles, and some of her plains are barren. It would seem, then, that our arable lands, taking the lowest estimate, are in excess of those of China, by some hundreds of thousands of square miles. The fact, therefore, that Chinese agriculture feeds hundreds of millions ought, certainly, to be suggestive to Americans.

The area of the United States, excluding Alaska, is equal to that of Great Britain and Ireland, Norway, Sweden, Denmark, Germany, Austria, Holland, Belgium, France, Spain, Portugal, Switzerland, Italy, Greece, and European Turkey, together with that of Palestine, Japan and China proper (see map). These countries have a population of nearly or quite 650,000,000, and their aggregate resources are probably not equal to those of the United States. The crops of 1879, after feeding our 50,000,000 inhabitants in 1880, furnished more than 283,000,000 bushels of grain for export. The corn, wheat, oats, barley, rye, buckwheat and potatoes—that is, the food crops, were that year produced on 105,097,750 acres, or 164,215 square miles. But that is less than one-ninth of the smallest estimate of our arable lands. If, therefore, it were all brought under the plow, it would feed 450,000,000 and afford 2,554,000,000 bushels of grain for export. But this is not all. So excellent an authority as Mr. Edward Atkinson says that where we now support 50,000,000 people, "one hundred million could be sustained without increasing the area of a single farm, or adding one to their number, by merely bringing our product up to our *average standard of reasonably good agriculture;* and then there might remain for export twice the quantity we now send abroad to feed the hungry in foreign lands." [6] If this be true (and it will hardly be questioned by any one widely acquainted with our wasteful American farming), 1,500,000 square miles of cultivated land—less than one-half of our entire area this side of Alaska—are capable of feeding a population of 900,000,000,

[6] [Edward Atkinson, *Our National Domain* (a broadside; Boston, November 27, 1879). Atkinson (1827–1905), industrialist and statistician, was chief executive of the Boston Manufacturers Mutual Insurance Company.]

and of producing an excess of 5,100,000,000 bushels of grain for exportation; or, if the crops were all consumed at home, it would feed a population one-eighth larger; viz., 1,012,000,000. This corresponds very nearly with results obtained by an entirely different process from data afforded by the best scientific authority.[7] It need not, therefore, make a very severe draught on credulity to say that our agricultural resources, if fully developed, would sustain a thousand million souls.

But we have wonderful wealth under the soil as well as in it. From 1870 to 1880 we produced $746,613,792 of the precious metals, and during the nine succeeding years, $735,377,000; while the entire product from 1849 to 1889, inclusive, was $2,730,077,152.[8] The United States now raises one-half the gold and silver of the world's supply. Iron ore is to-day mined in twenty-three of our states. A number of them could singly supply the world's demand. Our coal measures are simply inexhaustible. English coal-pits, already deep, are being deepened, so that the cost of coal-mining in Great Britain is presumably increasing, while we have coal enough near the surface to supply us for centuries. When storing away the fuel for the ages, God knew the place and work to which he had appointed us, and gave to us twenty times as much of this concrete power as to all the peoples of Europe. Among the nations, ours is the youngest—the Benjamin—and Benjamin-like we have received a five-fold portion. Surely "He hath not dealt so with any people." Our mineral products are of unequaled richness and variety. The remarkable increase from 1870 to 1880 [9] placed us at the head of the nations. In 1880 our mining industries exceeded those of Great Britain three per

[7] See *Encyclopedia Britannica*, 9th ed., I (Boston, 1875), 717.

[8] From *Annual Report of the Director of the United States Mint, 1890* (Washington, D.C., 1890), p. 183.

[9] Michael G. Mulhall, [*Balance Sheet of the World* (London, 1881), p. 111.]

	1870	*1880*	*Increase*
Iron ore, tons	4,500,000	9,500,000	110 per cent
Copper "	12,700	20,300	60 " "
Coal "	33,000,000	55,000,000	66 " "
Petroleum, gallons	42,000,000	860,000,000	20-fold

cent, and were greater than those of all continental Europe, Asia, Africa, South America, Mexico, and the British Colonies collectively; while in 1888, the total mineral product of the United Kingdom was $289,601,385 [10] and that of the United States was $591,172,795 [11]; and as yet, we have hardly begun to develop these resources. Thousands of square miles of mineral wealth lie wholly untouched.

Let us glance at our manufactures, present and prospective. Our first great advantage is found in our superabounding coal. Our second lies in the fact that we have our raw material at hand. England must go at least 3,000 miles for every cotton boll she spins; we raise our own. And mills are now being built in the South which manufacture the cotton where it is grown. We produce also the wool, the woods, the hides, the metals of every sort, all that is required for nearly every variety of manufacture. The remaining advantage which crowns our opportunity is the quality of our labor; American operatives being, as a class, the most ingenious and intelligent in the world. Inventiveness has come to be a national trait. The United States Government issues four times as many patents as the English. From the Patent Office in Washington there were issued, during 1889, 21,518 patents. At the International Electrical Exposition in Paris, a few years ago, five gold medals were given for the greatest inventions or discoveries, all of which came to the United States. *The Mechanical World*, of London, says that the United States has the best machinery and tools in the world; and Mr. Lourdelot, who was sent over here a few years since by the French Minister of Commerce, says that the superiority of tools used here, and the attention to details too often neglected in Europe, are elements of danger to European industries. Herbert Spencer testifies that, "beyond question, in respect of mechanical appliances, the Americans are ahead of all nations." [12] The fact of superior tools would alone give us

[10] *The Statesman's Year Book, 1890.* [On p. 70 the total mineral product of the United Kingdom is listed at £59,834,997.]

[11] *The World Almanac, 1890* (New York, 1890), p. 110.

[12] For much additional and weighty testimony to the same point, see *The Tenth Annual Report of the Massachusetts Bureau of Statistics of Labor, January 1879* (Boston, 1879), pp. xiii–xiv.

no small advantage, but the possession of the best machinery implies much more; viz., that we have also the best mechanics in the world.

In close competition, any one of the three advantages enumerated ought to insure supremacy, provided labor were as cheap here as in Europe. The coincidence, then, of these three great essentials of manufactures, each in such signal measure as to constitute together a triple advantage, ought to offset the difference in the price of labor, and with favorable legislation ultimately deliver over to us the markets of the world. Already have we won the first rank as a manufacturing people, our products in 1880 having exceeded even those of Great Britain by $629,000,000. So soon is Mr. Gladstone's prophecy, uttered a few years ago, finding its fulfillment. Speaking of the United States, he said: "She will probably become what we are now, the head servant in the great household of the world, the employer of all employed, because her service will be the most and ablest." [13] And it is interesting to note not only our position, but our rate of progress. While the manufactures of France, from 1870 to 1880, increased $222,640,000, those of Germany $416,240,000, and those of Great Britain $561,440,000, those of the United States increased $997,040,000.[14] Moreover, the marked advantages which we now enjoy are to be enhanced. While England's coal is growing dearer, ours will be growing cheaper, and the development of our vast resources will greatly increase, and hence cheapen, raw materials.

And while our manufactures are growing, our markets are to be greatly extended. Steam and electricity have mightily compressed the earth. The elbows of the nations touch. Isolation —the mother of barbarism—is becoming impossible. The mysteries of Africa are being laid open, the pulse of her commerce is beginning to beat. South America is being quickened, and the dry bones of Asia are moving; the warm breath of the

[13] [Gladstone, "Kin Beyond Sea," p. 180.]

[14] Our total agricultural products for 1880 were $2,541,000,000; our manufactures for the same year were $4,297,920,000.—Mulhall. [On p. 108 of *Balance Sheet,* Mulhall gives these figures as £525,000,000 and £888,000,000, respectively.]

Nineteenth Century is breathing a living soul under her ribs of death. The world is to be Christianized and civilized. There are about 1,000,000,000 of the world's inhabitants who do not enjoy a Christian civilization. Two hundred millions of these are to be lifted out of savagery. Much has been accomplished in this direction during the past seventy-five years, but much more will be done during the next fifty. And what is the process of civilizing but *the creating of more and higher wants?* Commerce follows the missionary. Five hundred American plows went to the native Christians of Natal in one year. The millions of Africa and Asia are some day to have the wants of a Christian civilization. The beginnings of life in India demand $12,000,000 worth of iron manufactures, and $100,000,000 worth of cotton goods in a single year. During the last thirty years her foreign trade has nearly quadrupled. What will be the wants of Asia a century hence? A Christian civilization performs the miracle of the loaves and fishes, and feeds its thousands in a desert. It multiplies populations. A thousand civilized men thrive where a hundred savages starved. What, then, will be the population and what the wants of Africa, a century hence? And with these vast continents added to our market, with our natural advantages fully realized, what is to prevent the United States from becoming the mighty workshop of the world, and our people "the hands of mankind"?

If it is not unreasonable to believe that our agricultural resources alone, when fully developed, are capable of feeding 1,000,000,000, then surely, with our agricultural and mining and manufacturing industries all fully developed, the United States can sustain and *enrich* such a population. Truly has Matthew Arnold said: "America holds the future."

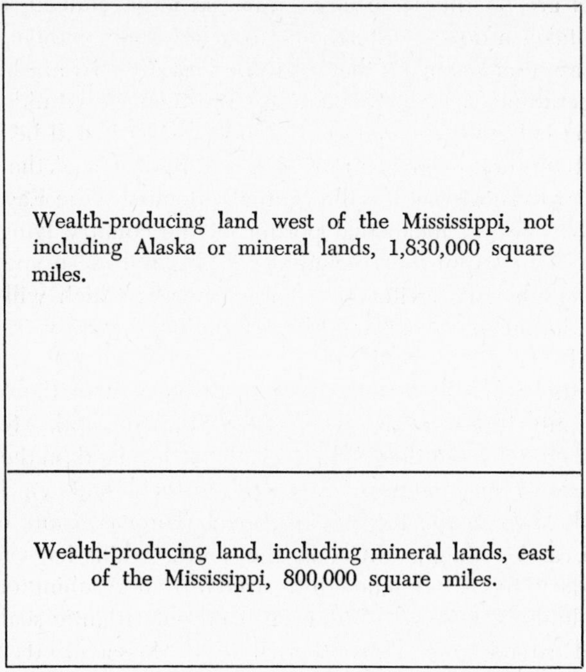

Wealth-producing land west of the Mississippi, not including Alaska or mineral lands, 1,830,000 square miles.
Wealth-producing land, including mineral lands, east of the Mississippi, 800,000 square miles.

CHAPTER III

WESTERN SUPREMACY

I NEVER felt as if I were out of doors before!" exclaimed a New Englander, as he stepped off the cars west of the Mississippi, for the first time.

The West is characterized by largeness. Mountains, rivers, railways, ranches, herds, crops, business transactions, ideas; even men's virtues and vices are cyclopean. All seem to have taken a touch of vastness from the mighty horizon. Western stories are on the same large scale, so large, indeed, that it often takes a dozen eastern men to believe one of them. They have a secret suspicion that even the best attested are inflated exaggerations, which, pricked by investigation, would burst, leaving behind a very small residuum of fact. It will be necessary, therefore, to glance rapidly at the resources of the West, in order to show that it will eventually dominate the East. And by "the West" I mean that portion of the country lying west of the Mississippi, not including Alaska, unless so specified; for, though that territory has vast resources which will some day add much to our wealth, the national destiny is to be settled this side of Alaska.

Of the twenty-two states and territories west of the Mississippi only three are as small as all New England. Montana would stretch from Boston on the east to Cleveland on the west, and extend far enough south to include Richmond, Va. Idaho, if laid down in the East, would touch Toronto, Can., on the north, and Raleigh, N.C., on the south, while its southern boundary line is long enough to stretch from Washington City to Columbus, O.; and California, if on our Atlantic seaboard, would extend from the southern line of Massachusetts to the lower part of South Carolina; or, in Europe, it would extend from London across France and well into Spain. New Mexico is larger than the United Kingdom of Great Britain and Ireland. The greatest measurement of Texas is nearly equal to the distance from New Orleans to Chicago, or from Chicago to Boston. Lay Texas on the face of Europe, and this giant, with his head resting on the mountains of Norway (directly east of the Orkney Islands), with one palm covering London, the other Warsaw, would stretch himself down across the kingdom of Denmark, across the empires of Germany and Austria, across Northern Italy, and lave his feet in the Mediterranean. The two Dakotas might be carved into a half-dozen kingdoms of Greece; or, if they were divided into twenty-six equal counties, we might lay down the two kingdoms of Judah and Israel in each.

Place the 50,000,000 inhabitants of the United States in 1880 all in Texas, and the population would not be as dense as that of Germany. Put them in the Dakotas, and the population would not be as dense as that of England and Wales. Place them in New Mexico, and the density of population would not be as great as that of Belgium. Those 50,000,000 might all have been comfortably sustained in Texas. After allowing, say 50,000 square miles for "desert," Texas could have produced all our food crops in 1879—grown, as we have seen, on 164,215 square miles of land—could have raised the world's supply of cotton, 12,000,000 bales, at one bale to the acre, on 19,000 square miles, and then have had remaining, for a cattle range, a territory larger than the State of New York. Place the population of the United States in 1890 all in Texas, and it would not be as dense as that of Italy; and if it were as crowded as England, this one state would contain 129,000,000 souls.

Accounting all of Minnesota and Louisiana west of the Mississippi, for convenience, we have, according to the census of 1880,[1] 2,115,135 square miles in the West, and 854,865 in the East. That is, for every acre east of the Mississippi we have nearly two and a half west of it. But what of the "Great American Desert," which occupied so much space on the map a generation ago? It is *nomadic* and elusive; it recedes before advancing civilization like the Indian and buffalo which once roamed it. There are extensive regions, which, because of rocks or lava-beds or alkali or altitude or lack of rain, are unfit for the plow; but they afford much of the finest grazing country in the world, much valuable timber, and mineral wealth which is enormous. Useless land, though much in the aggregate, is far less than is commonly supposed, and in comparison with wealth-producing lands is almost insignificant. The vast region east of the Rocky Mountains, though once the home of the "Great American Desert," really contains very little useless land. We have all heard of the "Bad Lands" of the Dakotas, but they comprise only about 75,000 acres out of 94,528,000 in the two states, and even these lands, are an excellent stock-range. Mr. E. V. Smalley says: "Cattle come out of the Bad Lands in

[1] The areas of the states given in the Ninth Census [1870] have been recomputed for the Tenth [1880].

the spring as fat as though they had been stall-fed all winter." [2] The United States Surveyor-General says: "The proportion of waste land in the territory (Dakota), owing to the absence of swamps, mountain ranges, overflowed and sandy tracts, is less than in any other state or territory in the Union." There are 20,000 square miles of "Bad Lands" in Northwestern Nebraska, rich in wonderful fossils, but economically worthless. It is often said that the Kansas lands near the Colorado border are alkaline; but Professor Mudge, State Geologist, says that, in fifteen years of exploration, he has found but two springs containing alkalies, and has never seen ten acres of land in one place which has been injured by it. There is perhaps as little waste land in Kansas as in Illinois. The "Staked Plain" of Texas is sometimes spoken of as a desert; but a Texan writer, who has lived there for years, says of it: "While it is true that this vast territory which we are describing is mainly a grazing country, it is also true that it abounds in fertile valleys and rich locations of large extent, which are as well watered and as fertile as any in the nation." That portion of the "Staked Plain" which is mountainous is rich in minerals.

Driven from the plains east of the Rocky Mountains, the "Great American Desert" seems to have become a fugitive and vagabond on the face of the earth. It was located for a time by the map makers in Utah, but being persecuted there, it fled to Arizona, Nevada and Southern California. I do not mean to imply that there are no waste lands in Utah. Portions of the territory are as worthless as some of its people. There are some deserts, one west of the Great Salt Lake, which contains several thousand square miles; but the Surveyor-General of the Territory says: "Notwithstanding the opinion of many who deem our lands 'arid, desert, and worthless,' these same lands, under proper tillage, produce forty to fifty bushels of wheat, seventy to eighty bushels of oats and barley, from two hundred to four hundred bushels of potatoes to the acre, and fruits and vegetables equal to any other state or territory in quantity and

[2] E. V. Smalley, "The New North-West," *Century*, 24 (August 1882), 510.

quality." [3] There are vast tracts which cannot be irrigated, but even such lands are not necessarily without agricultural value. Arizona has been considered a waste, and undoubtedly much land there is arid and irredeemable; but, on the other hand, there is much also which is wealth-producing. Gen. J. C. Fremont,[4] who, as Governor of the Territory for several years, had exceptional facilities for gaining information, in his official report in 1878, said: "So far as my present knowledge goes, the grazing and farming lands comprehend an area equal to that of the State of New York." And a writer in *Harper's Magazine* for March, 1883, says: "It is estimated by competent authority that, with irrigation, thirty-seven per cent can be redeemed for agriculture, and sixty per cent for pasturage." [5] Certain it is that when the Spaniards first visited the territory, in 1526, they found ruins of cities and irrigating canals, which indicated that it was once densely populated by a civilized race which subsisted by agriculture.

There is more barren land in Nevada than in any other state or territory of the West. The wealth of the state is not agricultural or pastoral, but mineral. Nevertheless the Surveyor-General of the State says: "In our sage-brush lands, alfalfa, the cereals, and all vegetables flourish in profusion where water can be obtained, and the state is speedily becoming one of the great stock-raising states of the Union." Below the Grand Cañon of the Colorado, with Nevada and California on the west and Arizona on the east, is a region of great aridity. Here date-palms, oranges, lemons, pomegranates, figs, sugar and cotton flourish where water can be applied, and "ultimately a region of country can be irrigated larger than was ever culti-

[3] A resident of Utah writes me that he has never heard of more than twenty-eight bushels of wheat or forty-five of oats to the acre.

[4] [John Charles Frémont (1813–1890), the 1856 presidential candidate of the Republican Party, was a noted explorer of the American West and served as territorial governor of Arizona from 1878 to 1883.]

[5] [William Henry Bishop, "Across Arizona," *Harper's Magazine*, 66 (March 1883), 490.] From all the information I can gather, this latter estimate seems to me too large. In my computation of the valuable lands of the West, page 32, I have called 26,700 square miles in Arizona, nearly one quarter of the territory, worthless.

vated along the Nile, and all the products of Egypt will flourish therein." [6]

The area in which occur, here and there, most of the worthless lands of the West, is pyramidal in shape, the base extending along the Mexican line into Texas, and the apex being found in the northern part of Idaho. That is, the proportion of useless lands decreases as you go north, until it seems to disappear entirely before reaching the Northern Pacific Railway. Mr. E. V. Smalley, who, in the summer of 1882, traveled the line of that road before its completion, writes: "The whole country traversed through the northern tier of territories, from Eastern Dakota to Washington, is a habitable region. . . . For the entire distance every square mile of the country is valuable either for farming, stock-raising, or timber-cutting. There is absolutely no waste land between the well-settled region of Dakota and the new wheat region of Washington Territory. Even on the tops of the Rocky Mountains there is good pasturage; and the vast timber belt enveloping Clark's Fork and Lake Pend d'Oreille, and the ranges of the Cabinet and Cœur d'Alene Mountains is more valuable than an equal extent of arable land." [7]

Much of the Rocky Mountain region is still unsurveyed. In the absence of exact knowledge, therefore, we must rely on the estimates of Surveyor-Generals, Governors, and others who have had opportunities to form intelligent opinions concerning the available lands of the West. In some cases official reports of surveys have afforded accurate information; but in most it has been necessary to rely on estimates which pretend to be only approximately correct. I believe they are temperate. According to these estimates, the region west of the Mississippi embraces 785,000 square miles of arable lands, 645,000 of grazing lands, 400,000 of timber lands, and 285,000 square miles which are useless, except so far as they are mineral lands. In weighing

[6] John Wesley Powell, "The Irrigable Lands of the Arid Region," *Century*, 39 (March 1890), 772. Mr. Powell was the director of the U.S. Geological Survey.

[7] Smalley in "The New North West," p. 872.

these figures several considerations should be borne in mind.

1. Generally speaking, those best acquainted with the West make the largest estimates of its resources and have the most faith in its future.

2. Land often appears worthless which experiment proves to be fertile. For instance, the "Great Columbia Plains" of Eastern Washington. The soil, which varies from one foot to twenty feet in depth, is, except in the bottom lands, a very light-colored loam, containing an unusually large percentage of alkalies and fixed acids. A few years ago, sowing wheat on that soil would have been deemed throwing it away; but the experiment resulted in a revelation; viz., that these 14,000,000 acres of peculiar soil are probably the best wheat fields in all the world. Other illustrations equally striking might be given. Rev. A. Blanchard, who is well acquainted with East Wyoming and Colorado, writes: "Nothing is more surprising than the material for supporting a population which continues to be developed in all this region of mountain and plain, which, twenty years ago, was considered an inhospitable desert, capable of supporting nothing but Indians."

3. Barren lands are often rendered fruitful. Frequently all that a sterile soil needs is treatment with some mineral which Nature has deposited near by; and water makes most of our western deserts blossom as the rose. In 1882, twelve Artesian wells were sunk in Tulare County, California, with astonishing results. They were found to flow from 200,000 to 1,500,000 gallons daily; and where once were barren plains, the fields are a succession of vineyards, orchards, and wheat fields. Since then many of these wells have been sunk in Arizona, Nevada, New Mexico and Colorado. Ultimately mountain torrents will be utilized for irrigation by means of great reservoirs and canals. Already more than 6,000,000 acres have been redeemed by such means and are now under cultivation. Major J. W. Powell, Director of the U.S. Geological Survey, has been engaged for more than twenty years in investigating the resources of the West and has commanded the best facilities for acquiring scientific knowledge of that region. This highest authority says:

"Arid lands are not lands of famine, and the sunny sky is not a firmament of devastation. Conquered rivers are better servants than wild clouds. The valleys and plains of the far West have all the elements of fertility that soil can have. . . . Abundant water and abundant sunshine are the chief conditions for vigorous plant growth, and that agriculture is the most successful which best secures these twin primal conditions; and they are obtained in the highest degree in lands watered by streams and domed by clear skies. For these reasons the arid lands are more productive under high cultivation than humid lands. The wheat fields of the desert, the corn fields, the vineyards, the orchards and the gardens of the far West far surpass those of the East in luxuriance and productiveness. . . . The arid lands of the West . . . . are the best agricultural lands of the continent." [8]

The total area of arid lands in the United States is 1,331,151 square miles, of which some 258,000 square miles are timbered lands. Much of the arid region is rich in minerals and much of it affords fine pasturage, while about 120,000,000 acres are capable of being redeemed for agriculture by irrigation. Major Powell says, "It has been fully demonstrated that the redemption of these lands is profitable to capital and labor. . . . When the waters are stored in the mountain lakes, and the canals are constructed to carry them to the lands below, a system of powers will be developed unparalleled in the history of the world. Here, then, factories can be established, and the rivers be made to do the work of fertilization, and the violence of mountain torrents can be transformed into electricity to illumine the villages, towns, and cities of all that land." [9]

It should be remarked that the rainfall seems to be increasing with the cultivation of the soil. And it is worthy of note that what rain there is usually falls in those months when it is most needed, and that there is little or none during harvest.

[8] Powell, "The Irrigable Lands," pp. 767–768.

[9] J. W. Powell, "The Non-Irrigable Lands of the Arid Region," *Century,* 39 (April 1890), 921.

4. The arable lands in the Rocky Mountains are mainly in valleys, which, like basins, have gathered the *detritus* of the mountains for ages. The soil is therefore very deep and strong, yielding much more than the same area in the East; and in the Southwest two crops a year from the same soil are very common, so that this land is equal to twice or three times the same area in the East. "Experiments in California, Nevada, Colorado, Utah, Arizona and other irrigating countries, show that eighty acres of irrigated land properly cultivated far exceed in productive capacity 160 acres watered by rainfall." [10]

5. The above estimate of arable lands in the West does not include the timber lands, a large proportion of which is of the finest quality. Of the 400,000 square miles of timber, 45,000 are in Texas, 26,000 in Arkansas, and 25,000 in Minnesota. A large proportion of the whole is in the Mississippi valley, and a good deal of the remainder is on fine soil, so that it is reasonable to infer that 100,000 square miles or more of this timber land would be arable, if cleared. Moreover, much of the 645,000 square miles of grazing land will prove to be arable. We may, therefore, expect the arable lands of the West ultimately to reach 900,000 square miles, and perhaps 1,000,000.

6. A considerable portion of the 854,865 square miles east of the Mississippi is not arable. In New England, New York and Pennsylvania, there are 94,500 square miles of unimproved lands.[11] It is a fair inference that in the old states where land has long been in demand, so much would not remain unimproved unless generally incapable of improvement. Throughout the many mountain ranges of the entire Appalachian system, there is much waste land and more that is not arable. In the absence of any exact data it would seem from the facts just given, that there must be not less than 50,000 or 60,000 square miles of waste land east of the Mississippi, and twice

[10] Senator W. M. Stewart, "Reclaiming the Western Deserts," *Forum*, 7 (April 1889), 204.

[11]

New England	has	28,468	square	miles	not	in	farms, 41,500	unimproved
New York	"	10,402	"	"	"	"	29,000	"
Pennsylvania	"	13,952	"	"	"	"	24,000	"

as much that is not fit for the plow. This reduces the arable lands of the East to about 700,000 square miles as against 785,000 in the West, with the probable eventual addition to the latter of one or two hundred thousand more. For every acre in the East, bad as well as good, there is another in the West capable of producing food; and in addition, a timber area of 400,000 square miles, not including the magnificent timber lands of Alaska, which William H. Seward [12] said would one day make that territory the ship-yard of the world. And besides all this, the West has grazing lands 50,000 square miles broader than the total area of all the Southern States east of the Mississippi. In 1880 there were in the West, 61,211,000 head of live stock, and those vast plains are probably capable of sustaining several times that number. The West, therefore, has 1,830,000 square miles of useful land (not including mineral lands) against 800,000 in the East, more than twice as much.

Nor have we finished our inventory of western wealth. Its mineral resources are simply inexhaustible. The precious metals have been found in most of the states and territories of our Western Empire. From the discovery of gold to June 30, 1881, California produced $1,170,000,000 of that metal. The annual product is now from eighteen to twenty-five millions. From 1863 to 1880, Idaho produced $90,000,000 of gold and silver, and Montana from 1861 to 1879, not less than $162,000,000. In twenty years, Nevada produced $448,545,000 of the precious metals. The production of Colorado, during the twenty-four years preceding 1883, was $167,000,000. Her out-put for 1882 was $27,000,000. In wealth-producing power a single rich mine represents a great area of arable land. For instance, the Comstock Lode, in 1877, produced $37,062,252. Those twelve insignificant looking holes in the side of the mountain yielded more wealth that year than 3,890,000 acres planted to corn the same year. That is, those few square rods on the surface in Nevada were as large as all the corn fields of New England, New York,

[12] [William Henry Seward (1801–1872), Secretary of State in President Lincoln's cabinet, negotiated the accession of Alaska in 1867.]

Pennsylvania, Michigan, Wisconsin and Minnesota, collectively. Rocky Mountain wealth, penetrating thousands of feet into the earth, compensates for large areas of barren surface. The agricultural resources of a country do not now as formerly determine its possible population. To-day, easy transportation makes regions populous and wealthy, which once were uninhabitable. Even if a blade of grass could not be made to grow in all the Rocky Mountain states, that region could sustain 100,000,000 souls, provided it has sufficient mineral wealth to exchange for the produce of the Mississippi valley. Quartz mines have been known in the Rockies for years, which could not be worked without heavy machinery. The inner chambers of God's great granite safes, where the silver and gold have been stored for ages to enrich this generation, are fastened with time locks, set for the advent of the railway. The projection of railway systems into the mountains will rapidly develop these mines. For the year ending May 31, 1880, the United States produced 55 tons 724 pounds (avoirdupois) of gold, and 1,090 tons 398 pounds of silver. "These huge figures may be better grasped, perhaps, by considering that the gold represents five ordinary car loads, while a train of 109 freight cars of the usual capacity would be required to transport the silver." [13] The total out-put of the precious metals for 1889 was $97,446,000 or nearly $23,000,000 more than in 1880.

But the precious metals constitute only a small part of the mineral wealth of the West. It has upwards of 200,000 square miles of coal measure, thirty-eight times the area of all the coal fields of Great Britain. Excepting Minnesota, coal has been found in every state and territory west of the Mississippi. And not one is without iron. California has superior ores. The iron of Oregon is equal to the very best Swedish and Russian metal. Wyoming has immense deposits. The supply of Utah is enormous. It is found in some form in every county of Missouri. Iron Mountain and Pilot Knob are estimated to contain 500,000,000 tons of the finest ore. There are great masses of iron in Texas, probably equal in quantity and quality to any de-

[13] *The Tenth Census of the United States, 1880.*

posits in the world. Lead is found in all the states and territories of the West, except Minnesota, Nebraska, and the Indian Territory. In many of them the ores are rich and abundant. The lead-producing area in Missouri is over 5,000 square miles. The product of that state in 1877 was over 63,000,000 pounds. Nebraska and Kansas alone are without copper. Rich ores and native metal abound in what seem inexhaustible quantities. The deposits of salt are without computation. Besides salt springs and lakes which yield great quantities, there are beds of unknown depth covering thousands of acres. Sulphur also is exceedingly abundant. In Idaho there is a mountain which is eighty-five per cent pure sulphur. A deposit in Louisiana, equally pure, is 112 feet thick. Nevada has borax enough to supply mankind. In Wyoming there are lakes in which the deposits of sulphate of soda are from ten to fifteen feet in thickness, and almost chemically pure. Gypsum abounds. Texas has the largest deposits known in the world,—"enough to supply the universe for centuries." The Colorado River of Texas cuts its way through mountains of solid marble. In many parts of the Rocky Mountains there are the finest building stones, granite, sandstone and marble, of all possible colors and shades, without end. It would be tiresome simply to enumerate the valuable minerals which swell the undeveloped wealth of the West.

Her unrivaled resources together with the unequaled enterprise of her citizens are a sure prophecy of superior wealth. Already have some of these young states outstripped older sisters at the East, as is seen by the following statement of wealth per caput according to the assessed valuation of property in 1880:

In South Carolina	$110	In Kansas	$161
" Illinois	255	" Minnesota	330
" Vermont	259	" Colorado	331
" New York	538	" California	674

From 1880 to 1890 the assessed valuation of property in these four states east of the Mississippi increased twenty-seven per cent while that in the four western states increased one hundred and seven. The aggregate increase of the former was $1,008,000,000; that of the latter, $1,160,000,000.[14] The West is destined to surpass in agriculture, stock-raising, mining, and eventually, in manufacturing. Already appears the superiority of her climate, which Montesquieu declares "is the most powerful of all empires, and gives guaranty alone of future development." Every advantage seems to be hers save only greater proximity to Europe, and if the East commands European commerce, the Golden Gate opens upon Asia, and is yet to receive

——"the wealth of Ormus and of Ind,"

and send her argosies to all the ports of the broad Pacific.

Beyond a peradventure, the West is to dominate the East. With more than twice the room and resources of the East, the West will have probably twice the population and wealth of the East, together with the superior power and influence which, under popular government accompany them. The West will elect the executive and control legislation. When the center of population crosses the Mississippi, the West will have a majority in the lower House, and sooner or later the partition of her great territories, and probably some of the states, will give to the West the control of the Senate.[15] When Texas is as densely peopled as New England, it is hardly to be supposed her millions will be content to see the 62,000 square miles east of the Hudson send twelve senators to the seat of government, while her territory of 262,000 sends only two. The West will direct the policy of the Government, and by virtue of her preponderating population and influence will determine our national character and, therefore, destiny.

Since prehistoric times, populations have moved steadily

[14] *The World Almanac, 1890,* pp. 116–117.

[15] The movement of population and of power westward is shown by the census of 1890. If under this census the apportionment for representatives in Congress is made so that the total membership of the House remains the same plus eight members from the six new states, the states east of the Mississippi will lose nine representatives and those west of it will gain nine in addition to those from the six states. That is, the East will be nine members weaker and the West seventeen stronger.

westward, as De Tocqueville said, "as if driven by the mighty hand of God." And following their migrations, the course of empire, which Bishop Berkeley sang, has westward taken its way. The world's scepter passed from Persia to Greece, from Greece to Italy, from Italy to Great Britain, and from Great Britain the scepter is to-day departing. It is passing on to "Greater Britain," to our Mighty West, there to remain, for there is no further West; beyond is the Orient. Like the star in the East which guided the three kings with their treasures westward until at length it stood still over the cradle of the young Christ, so the star of empire, rising in the East, has ever beckoned the wealth and power of the nations westward, until to-day it stands still over the cradle of the young empire of the West, to which the nations are bringing their offerings.

The West is to-day an infant, but shall one day be a giant, in each of whose limbs shall unite the strength of many nations.

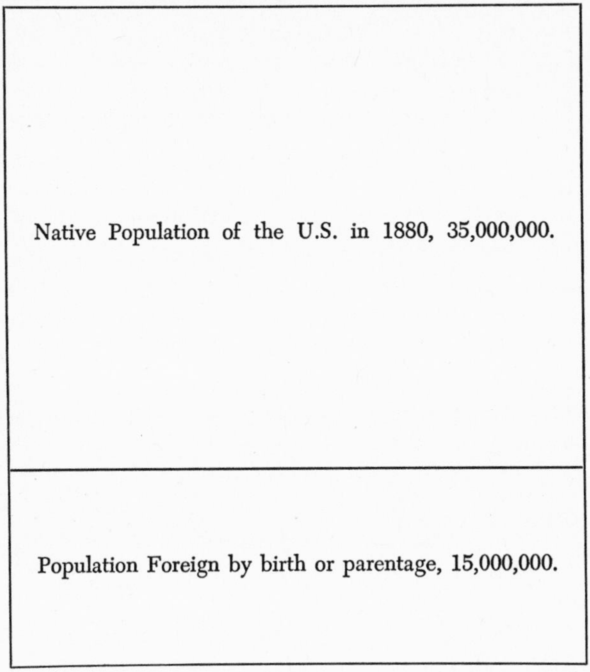

Native Population of the U.S. in 1880, 35,000,000.

Population Foreign by birth or parentage, 15,000,000.

CHAPTER IV

PERILS—IMMIGRATION

POLITICAL optimism is one of the vices of the American people. There is a popular faith that "God takes care of children, fools, and the United States." We deem ourselves a chosen people, and incline to the belief that the Almighty stands pledged to our prosperity. Until within a few years probably not one in a hundred of our population has ever questioned the security of our future. Such optimism is as senseless as pessimism is faithless. The one is as foolish as the other is wicked.

Thoughtful men see perils on our national horizon. Our argument is concerned not with all of them, but *only with those which peculiarly threaten the West.*

America, as the land of promise to all the world, is the destination of the most remarkable migration of which we have any record. During the last ten years we have suffered a peaceful invasion by an army more than four times as vast as the estimated number of Goths and Vandals that swept over Southern Europe and overwhelmed Rome. During the past hundred years fifteen million foreigners have made their homes in the United States, and three-quarters of them have come since 1850, while 5,248,000 have arrived since 1880. A study of the causes of this great world movement indicates that perhaps as yet we have seen only beginnings. These controlling causes are threefold. 1. The attracting influences of the United States. 2. The expellent influences of the Old World. 3. Facilities for travel.

1. The attracting influences of the United States. We have already seen that for every one inhabitant in 1880 the land is capable of sustaining twenty. This largeness of room and opportunity constitutes an urgent invitation to the crowded peoples of Europe. The prospect of proprietorship in the soil is a powerful attraction to the European peasant. In England only one person in twenty is an owner of land; in Scotland, one in twenty-five; in Ireland, one in seventy-nine, and the great majority of land-holders in Great Britain own less than one acre each. More than three-fifths of the United Kingdom is in the hands of the landlords, who own, each one, a thousand acres or more.[1] One man rides in a straight line a hundred miles on his own estate. Another owns a county extending across Scotland. A gentleman in Scotland a few years since, appropriated three hundred square miles of land, extending from sea to sea, to a deer forest, evicting many families to make room for the deer. "Scotland official figures show that one-third of the families live in a single room, and more than another third

[1] *Encyclopedia Britannica,* 9th ed., VIII (Boston, 1878), 223.

in only two rooms."[2] What must free land mean to such a people?

This, moreover, is the land of plenty. The following table, giving the average amount of food annually consumed per inhabitant, shows how much better the people of the United States are fed than any people of Europe. All kinds of grain are included, as what is fed to cattle serves ultimately to produce food for the population. Potatoes are estimated as grain, at the rate of four bushels to one of wheat.[3]

	Grain (*bushels*)	*Meat* (*pounds*)
France	24.02	81.88
Germany	23.71	84.51
Belgium	22.84	57.10
Great Britain	20.02	119.10
Russia	17.97	54.05
Spain	17.68	25.04
Austria	13.57	56.03
Sweden and Norway	12.05	51.10
Italy	9.62	20.80
Europe	17.66	57.50
United States	40.66	120.00

John Rae[4] says that in Prussia, nearly one-half of the population have to live on an annual income of $105 to a family. Is it strange that they look longingly toward the United States?

Immigration rises and falls with our prosperity. A financial crisis here operates at once as a check, but numbers increase again with the revival of business. We shall have, as heretofore, an occasional crash, followed by commercial depression, but it can hardly be questioned that the development of our wonderful resources will insure a high degree of material prosperity for many years to come. And the brightening blaze of our riches will attract increased immigration. Equal rights also and free schools are operative. We expend for education nearly six times as much, per caput, as Europe. Parents know that

[2] Henry George, "Democracy in England," in Chas. F. Wingate, ed., *Twilight Club Tracts* (New York, 1886), p. 37.

[3] Michael G. Mulhall, *Balance Sheet of the World, 1870–1880* (London, 1881), p. 39.

[4] [John Rae (1796–1872), a self-taught American economist, opposed the laissez-faire views of Adam Smith and, not unlike Mathew Carey and George F. List, favored a protectionist national economic policy.]

their children will have a better chance here, and come for their sake. These facts are becoming more widely known in other lands. Every foreigner who comes to us and wins success, as most of them do under more favorable conditions, becomes an advertiser of our land; he strongly attracts his relatives and friends, and very likely sends them money for their passage. Our consul at Frankfort writes: "Not less than one-half of the German emigrants to the United States emigrate by the advice and assistance of friends residing there." Says Prof. R. M. Smith, "The Inman Steamship Company has 3500 agents in Europe, and an equal number in this country, selling prepaid tickets to be sent to friends and relatives of persons already here in order to provide them with passage." [5] Of course other companies pursue a like policy.

2. The expellent influences of Europe. Social or political upheavals send new waves of immigration to our shores. A glance at the situation shows that the prospect for the next fifteen or twenty years is not pacific.

France. The French are fickle. From the Revolution down to 1870, no political *régime* had continued for twenty consecutive years. The fact, therefore, that the Third Republic has survived this period, which seems to constitute the necessary political probation of a French government, is a favorable augury of its permanence. Boulangism [6] expressed whatever dissatisfaction existed in various classes, with the republic; and its utter collapse justifies the hope that the French will enjoy a settled government for years to come. And if the Republic becomes permanent, which now seems likely, it will operate as a constant thorn in the sides of European monarchies, by stirring up popular discontent.

Germany. The Revolution of 1848 showed that the German

[5] Richard Mayo Smith, *Emigration and Immigration* (New York, 1890), p. 46.

[6] [A radical, antiparliamentarian movement, based in Paris and led by General George E. J. M. Boulanger (1837–1891). Boulanger, a popular hero, was removed from the army in 1888, entered the Chamber of Deputies from Paris, fled the country and in 1889 was tried for treason *in absentia.*]

people, always lovers of freedom, had grasped the principles of civil liberty; but it also showed that they had no practical knowledge of self-government. During those forty-two succeeding years of increasing acquaintance with our free institutions, their love of liberty has been growing, but in the science of self-government they have gained no experience. Germany presents the anomaly of a modern industrial civilization under a mediæval military government; a people characterized by a strong love of independence, ruled by an emperor who says, "Those who oppose me, I dash to pieces." Such a condition can hardly be one of stable equilibrium. Whether this young ruler is capable of adapting himself and his government to modern conditions remains to be seen. Meanwhile, emigration will probably increase with popular dissatisfaction, which latter is indicated by the rapid growth of socialism.

During the last twelve years, nearly three-quarters of a million of German subjects have emigrated to the United States, and the number is not likely to decrease under increasing burdens. A few years ago, a member of the Reichstag exclaimed: "The German people have now but one want—money enough to get to America."

Austria. Immigration from this quarter shows a marked increase; and the Minister of War calls for a considerable addition to the army, which will involve an increased expenditure of 80,000,000 or 100,000,000 florins.

Italy. The Italians are worse fed than any other people in Europe, save the Portuguese. The tax-collector takes thirty-one per cent of the people's earnings! Many thousands of small proprietors have been evicted from the crown-lands because unable to pay the taxes. The burden of taxation has become intolerable. Notwithstanding the industrial advance made by Italy from 1870 to 1880, the national debt increased so much more rapidly that the nation was $200,000,000 poorer in 1880 than ten years before. For the financial year ending in 1888 there was a deficit in the national treasury of 57,000,000 lire; and for the two years ending in 1890 the budget estimates showed a deficit of 248,000,000 lire. Growing population and increasing taxation are resulting in increased emigration. The total number of emigrants, which in 1884 was 147,000, had increased in 1888 to 290,000. At present this stream is mercifully being deflected in large measure to South America, but our portion of it tends to increase, and Italy, pressed by want as severe as that of Ireland, may yet send a like flood upon us.

Russia. The throne of the Czar stands on a volcano. Alexander III. seems fully committed to imperialism, and the Revolutionists are fully determined that the people shall assist in the work of government. They are wholly unrestrained by any religious scruples, and do not hesitate to sacrifice themselves as well as their enemies in the execution of their plans. "The Government may continue to arrest and hang as long as it likes, and may succeed in oppressing single revolutionary bodies. . . . But this will not change the state of things. Revolutionists will be created by events; by the general discontent of the whole of the people; by the tendency of Russia toward new social forms. An entire nation cannot be suppressed." [7] The utterly lawless warfare of the Nihilists naturally prevents the Czar from making any concessions, while his arbitrary and oppressive acts deepen popular discontent. Apparently, the repressive policy of the Government and popular agitation will serve each to intensify the other, until there results a spasmodic convulsion throughout Russia. And revolution in Russia means increased emigration.

Great Britain. There is much popular discontent in the United Kingdom, which will increase as England loses her manufacturing supremacy. The late Mr. Fawcett says that local expenditure, if it increases during the next quarter of a century as during the last, will exceed that of the Imperial Government.[8] Local authorities raise $200,000,000 a year for local purposes, and have an annual deficit of $100,000,000,

[7] "Address of the Executive Committee" of the Revolutionary Socialist Party to Czar Alexander III, March 10, 1881, reprinted in Stepniak (pseudonym for Sergei M. Kravchinskii), *Underground Russia* (New York, 1883), p. 267.

[8] Henry Fawcett, *Manual of Political Economy*, 6th ed. (London, 1883), p. 596.

which is met by borrowing. Local indebtedness increased from $165,000,000 in 1867 to $600,000,000 in 1884. In 1880 the amount of mortgage on landed property in Great Britain and Ireland was 58 per cent of its full value. Thomas Hughes [9] says: "We may despise the present advocates of social democracy, and make light of their sayings and doings; but there is no man who knows what is really going on in England but will admit that there will have to be a serious reckoning with them at no distant day." There is but one Gladstone, and he is an old man. A writer in *The British Quarterly* says: "The retirement of Mr. Gladstone will be the breaking up of the great deep in English politics." [10] And social and political disturbances in Great Britain mean increased emigration.

The progress of civilization is in the direction of popular government. All kings and their armies cannot reverse the wheels of human progress. I think it was Victor Hugo, who, with prophetic ear, heard a European of some coming generation say: "Why, we once had kings over here!" All the races of Europe will one day enjoy the civil liberty which now seems the peculiar birthright of the Anglo-Saxon. De Tocqueville, whom Mr. Gladstone calls the Edmund Burke of his generation, said he regarded the progress of democratic principles in government as a providential fact, the result of a divine decree. Matthew Arnold, after his last visit to America, speaking of the republican form of government, said: "It is the only eventual form of government for all people." Great revolutions, then, are to take place in Europe, why not within the next twenty-five years—some of them? And judging the future by the past, they will not be peaceful. The giant is blind and grinding in his prison house, howbeit his locks are growing, and we know not how soon he may bow himself between the pillars of despotism.

[9] [Thomas Hughes (1822–1896), the English author of *Tom Brown's School Days* and of the best-selling *The Manliness of Christ,* visited New York City in 1870 and there gave an address on the labor question from which, presumably, the quotation is taken.]

[10] Robert J. Griffiths, "The Future of English Politics," *British Quarterly Review,* 154 (April 1, 1883), 429.

Besides the great political revolutions which may reasonably be expected within a generation, men are fearing the tremendous conflict of arms which General Von Moltke[11] has seen for years pending "like the sword of Damocles," and which he and many others regard as inevitable. Silent, but profound influences are at work to revise the map of Europe. The common people are learning to read, and history and poetry kindle patriotism. With the growth of popular intelligence, the identity of language and of blood is exerting an increasing influence, and the fragments of nationalities, long since dismembered and thought dead, are seeking each other like the dry bones in Ezekiel's vision, to be followed by a resurrection of the old national spirit and life. The Eastern question of to-day springs from the fact that many fragments of different races, held together only by the arbitrary bond of force, are seeking a rearrangement based on a common origin and language. It looks as if this tendency would sooner or later disturb the existing balance of power, and so precipitate a great, and perhaps general, conflict.

In preparation for this crisis each nation is seeking to outdo its rivals. The following table[12] indicates in some measure what a European war might mean.

Countries	*Peace-Footing*	*War-Footing*	*Total, Including All Reserves*
Austria–Hungary	323,000	1,631,000	4,000,000
France	555,000	2,500,000	3,750,000
Germany	492,000	2,232,000	3,000,000
Italy	255,000	588,000	2,765,000
Russia	814,000	1,715,000	7,511,000 *
TOTAL	2,439,000	8,666,000	21,026,000

* *The World Almanac, 1890,* p. 192.

[11] [General Field Marshall Helmuth von Moltke (1800–1891), served as chief of the Prussian and later of the Imperial German General Staff from 1857 to 1888.]

[12] Compiled from *The Statesman's Year Book, 1890, passim.*

Of course readiness for war is something relative. Whatever its army may be, a nation becomes ill-prepared as soon as its enemy is better prepared. Hence the ever-increasing equipment and the growth of militarism, which, as Mr. Gladstone says, "lies like a vampire over Europe."

In Continental Europe generally the best years of all able-bodied men are demanded for military duty. Germans must be seven years in the army, and give three of them to active service; the French, nine years in the army and five years in active service; Austrians, ten years in the army and three in active service; Russians, fifteen years in the army and six in active service. When not in active service they are under certain restrictions. In addition to all this, when no longer members of the army, they are liable to be called on to do military duty for a period varying from two to five years. This robbery of a man's life, together with the common expectation that war must come sooner or later, will continue to be a powerful stimulus to emigration; [13] and the "blood tax" which is required to support these millions of men during unproductive years is steadily increasing. While aggregate taxation decreased in the United States, from 1870 to 1880, 9.15 per cent, it increased in Europe 28.01 per cent. The increase in Great Britain was 20.17 per cent; in France, 36.13 per cent; in Russia, 37.83 per cent; in Sweden and Norway, 50.10 per cent; in Germany, 57.81 per cent. And while the burden of taxation is so heavy and so rapidly increasing, the public debts of Continental Europe are making frightful growth. They increased 71.75 per cent from 1870 to 1880, since which time they have been enlarged by nearly three thousand million dollars and now reach a total of $20,580,000,000, entailing an annual burden of $1,000,000,000 for interest. The cost of government rose fifty per cent from 1875 to 1885. If existing tendencies continue a quarter of a century longer, they are likely to precipitate a terrible financial

[13] "During 1872 and 1873, which were good years for the working classes of Germany, there were not less than 10,000 processes annually for evasion of military duty by emigration." Smith, *Emigration and Immigration,* p. 27.

catastrophe and perhaps a great social crisis. Moreover, the pressure of a dense population is increasing; 22,225,000 souls having been added to the population of Europe during the ten years preceding 1880. Europe could send us an unceasing stream of 2,000,000 emigrants a year for a century, and yet steadily increase her population.

We find, therefore, the prospect of political commotions, the fear of war, the thumb-screw of taxation given a frequent turn, and a dense population becoming more crowded, all uniting their influence to swell European emigration for years to come.

3. Facilities of travel are increasing. From 1870 to 1880, 39,857 miles of railway were built in Europe, only two thousand less than in the United States during the same period; and from 1880 to 1888 there were 26,478 miles built. Thus, interior populations are enabled more easily to reach the seaboard. Instead of a long and tedious passage by sailship, the steamer lands the immigrant in a week or ten days. We find that steamships, in a single year, make 741 trips from nine European ports to New York, and 144 from other ports of Europe. And some of these ships carry upwards of a thousand steerage passengers. Improvements in steam navigation are making the ocean passage easier, quicker and cheaper. In 1825 the cheapest passage from Europe to America was about $100. Now the rates from continental ports to New York are from $23 to $26. Steerage passage from Hamburg to New York has been as low as seven dollars.[14] There are great multitudes in Europe who look westward with longing eyes, but who do not come, only because they cannot gather the passage money and keep soul and body together. The reduction of rates, even a few dollars, makes America possible to added thousands.

The threefold influences, therefore, which regulate immigration all co-operate to increase it and indicate that for years to

[14] Testimony before Ford Committee, p. 5. [The Ford Committee was the House Committee on Immigration, 50th Congress, 2nd session (1888–1889).]

come this great "gulf-stream of humanity" with here and there an eddy, will flow on with a rising flood.

Furthermore, labor-saving machinery has entered upon a campaign of world-wide conquest. This fact will render still more operative each of the three classes of influences enumerated above. Wherever man labors labor-saving machinery is destined ultimately to go; and the people of the United States are to make most of it for the world. We have mountains of iron and inexhaustible measures of coal, together with a genius for invention. In fifty-three years, 1837–1889, our Patent Office has issued 449,928 patents. Already are we sending our machines over the civilized world. And what does this mean? Sending a machine to Europe that does the work of a hundred men, temporarily throws a hundred men out of employment. That machine is useful because it renders useless the skill or strength of a hundred men. They cannot easily, in a crowded population, adjust themselves to this new condition of things. The making of this machinery in the United States increases the demand for labor here, and its exportation decreases the demand for labor in the Old World. That means immigration to this country. We are to send our labor-saving machinery around the globe, and in a sense, equivalents in bone and muscle are to be sent back to us.

In view of the fact that Europe is able to send us six times as many immigrants during the next thirty years as during the thirty years past, without any diminution of her population, and in view of all the powerful influences co-operating to stimulate the movement, is it not reasonable to expect a rising tide of immigration unless Congress takes effective measures to check it?

The Tenth Census gave our total foreign-born population as 6,679,943; but we must not forget their children of the first generation, who, as we shall see, present a more serious problem than their parents, the immigrants. This class numbered in 1880, 8,276,053, making a total population of nearly 15,000,000 which was foreign by birth or parentage.

We are not yet informed by the Eleventh Census what is the present foreign-born population. But knowing what it was in 1880 and knowing what immigration has been since then, we can estimate it approximately. If the death rate among the foreign-born population was the same from 1880 to 1890 as from 1870 to 1880 and if the same percentage returned to Europe, that population now numbers 9,590,000; and if the proportion of foreign-born to those of foreign-parentage is the same now as in 1880, our population which is foreign by birth or parentage numbers 21,385,000, or 33.94 per cent of the whole.[15]

So immense a foreign element must have a profound influence on our national life and character. Immigration brings unquestioned benefits, but these do not concern our argument. It complicates almost every home missionary problem and furnishes the soil which feeds the life of several of the most noxious growths of our civilization. I have, therefore, dwelt at some length upon its future that we may the more accurately measure the dangers which threaten us.

Consider briefly the moral and political influence of immigration. 1. Influence on morals. Let me hasten to recognize the high worth of many of our citizens of foreign birth, not a few of whom are eminent in the pulpit and in all the learned professions. Many come to us in full sympathy with our free institutions, and desiring to aid us in promoting a Christian civilization. But no one knows better than these same intelligent

[15] [Strong slightly overestimated his figures. According to the Census of 1890, the foreign-born population came to 9,249,547, and the population foreign by birth or parentage came to 20,676,046, or 33.02 per cent of the whole.]

In the first edition, it was estimated that in view of all the influences calculated to stimulate immigration the annual average from 1880 to 1900 would very likely reach 800,000 which was in round numbers the immigration in 1882. The annual average for the past ten years has been 524,800. Immigration for the next ten years, if unrestrained by a financial panic or hostile legislation, might be large enough to raise the average for the twenty years to 800,000 but the very general feeling of opposition to unrestricted immigration, which has manifested itself in recent years, would doubtless lead Congress to take action which would restrict it before it could assume such proportions.

and Christian foreigners that they do not represent the mass of immigrants. The typical immigrant is a European peasant, whose horizon has been narrow, whose moral and religious training has been meager or false, and whose ideas of life are low. Not a few belong to the pauper and criminal classes. "From a late report of the Howard Society of London, it appears that 'seventy-four per cent of the Irish discharged convicts have found their way to the United States.'"[16] "Every detective in New York knows that there is scarcely a ship landing immigrants that does not bring English, French, German, or Italian 'crooks.'"[17] Moreover, immigration is demoralizing. No man is held upright simply by the strength of his own roots; his branches interlock with those of other men, and thus society is formed, with all its laws and customs and force of public opinion. Few men appreciate the extent to which they are indebted to their surroundings for the strength with which they resist, or do, or suffer. All this strength the emigrant leaves behind him. He is isolated in a strange land, perhaps doubly so by reason of a strange speech. He is transplanted from a forest to an open prairie, where, before he is rooted, he is smitten with the blasts of temptation.

We have a good deal of piety in our churches that will not bear transportation. It cannot endure even the slight change of climate involved in spending a few summer weeks at a watering place, and is commonly left at home. American travelers in Europe often grant themselves license, on which, if at home, they would frown. Very many church-members, when they go west, seem to think they have left their Christian obligations with their church-membership in the East. And a considerable element of our American-born population are apparently under the impression that the Ten Commandments are not binding west of the Missouri. Is it strange, then, that those who come from other lands, whose old associations are all broken and

[16] Daniel Dorchester, *The Problem of Religious Progress* (New York, 1881), p. 423.

[17] W. M. F. Round, "Immigration and Crime," *Forum,* 8 (December 1889), 435.

whose reputations are left behind, should sink to a lower moral level? Across the sea they suffered many restraints which are here removed. Better wages afford larger means of self-indulgence; often the back is not strong enough to bear prosperity, and liberty too often lapses into license. Our population of foreign extraction is sadly conspicuous in our criminal records. This element constituted in 1870 twenty per cent of the population of New England, and furnished seventy-five per cent of the crime. That is, it was twelve times as much disposed to crime as the native stock. The hoodlums and roughs of our cities are, most of them, American-born of foreign parentage. Of the 680 discharged convicts who applied to the Prison Association of New York for aid, during the year ending June 30, 1882, 442 were born in the United States, against 238 foreign-born; while only 144 reported native parentage against 536 who reported foreign parentage.

The Rhode Island Work-house and House of Correction had received, to December 31, 1882, 6,202 persons on commitment. Of this number, fifty-two per cent were native-born and seventy-six per cent were born of foreign parentage.[18] Of the 182 prisoners committed to the Massachusetts Reformatory for Women in 1880–1881, eighty-one per cent were of foreign birth or parentage. While in 1880 the foreign-born were only thirteen per cent of the entire population, they furnished nineteen per cent of the convicts in our penitentiaries, and forty-three per cent of the inmates of work-houses and houses of correction. And it must be borne in mind that a very large proportion of the native-born prisoners were of foreign parentage, and this foreign-born element, while it constituted less than one-seventh of our population, furnished more than one-third of our paupers, and five-eighths of our suicides.

Moreover, immigration not only furnishes the greater portion of our criminals, it is also seriously affecting the morals of the native population. It is disease and not health which is

[18] For additional statistics on this point see Edward Self, "Evils Incident to Immigration," *North American Review*, 138 (January 1884), 78–88.

contagious. Most foreigners bring with them continental ideas of the Sabbath, and the result is sadly manifest in all our cities, where it is being transformed from a holy day into a holiday. But by far the most effective instrumentality for debauching popular morals is the liquor traffic, and this is chiefly carried on by foreigners. In 1880, of the "Traders and dealers in liquors and wines,"[19] (I suppose this means wholesale dealers) sixty-three per cent were foreign-born, and of the brewers and maltsters seventy-five per cent while a large proportion of the remainder were of foreign parentage. Of saloon-keepers about sixty per cent were foreign-born, while many of the remaining forty per cent of these corrupters of youth, these western Arabs, whose hand is against every man, were of foreign extraction.

2. We can only glance at the political aspects of immigration. As we have already seen, it is immigration which has fed fat the liquor power; and there is a liquor vote. Immigration furnishes most of the victims of Mormonism; and there is a Mormon vote. Immigration is the strength of the Catholic church; and there is a Catholic vote. Immigration is the mother and nurse of American socialism; and there is to be a socialist vote. Immigration tends strongly to the cities, and gives to them their political complexion. And there is no more serious menace to our civilization than our rabble-ruled cities. These several perils, all of which are enhanced by immigration, will be considered in succeeding chapters.

Many American citizens are not Americanized. It is as unfortunate as it is natural, that foreigners in this country should cherish their own language and peculiar customs, and carry their nationality, as a distinct factor, into our politics. Immigration has created the "German vote" and the "Irish vote," for which politicians bid, and which have already been decisive of state elections, and might easily determine national. A mass of men but little acquainted with our institutions, who will act in concert and who are controlled largely by their appetites and prejudices, constitute a very paradise for demagogues.

We have seen that immigration is detrimental to popular

[19] *The Tenth Census* (1880).

morals. It has a like influence upon popular intelligence, for the percentage of illiteracy among the foreign-born population is thirty-eight per cent greater than among the native-born whites. Thus immigration complicates our moral and political problems by swelling our dangerous classes. And as immigration will probably increase more rapidly than the population, we may infer that the dangerous classes will probably increase more rapidly than hitherto.[20] It goes without saying, that there is a dead-line of ignorance and vice in every republic, and when it is touched by the average citizen, free institutions perish; for intelligence and virtue are as essential to the life of a republic as are brain and heart to the life of a man.

A severe strain upon a bridge may be borne with safety if evenly distributed, which, if concentrated, would ruin the whole structure. There is among our population of alien birth an unhappy tendency toward aggregation, which concentrates the strain upon portions of our social and political fabric. Certain quarters of many of the cities, are, in language, customs and costumes, essentially foreign. Many colonies have bought up lands and so set themselves apart from Americanizing influences. In 1845, New Glarus, in southern Wisconsin, was settled by a colony of 108 persons from one of the cantons of Switzerland. In 1880 they numbered 1,060 souls; and in 1885 it was said, "No Yankee lives within a ring of six miles round the first built dug-out." This Helvetian settlement, founded three years before Wisconsin became a state, has preserved its race, its language, its worship, and its customs in their integrity. Similar colonies are now being planted in the West. In some cases 100,000 or 200,000 acres in one block, have been purchased by foreigners of one nationality and religion; thus building up states within a state, having different languages, different antecedents, different religions, different ideas and habits, prepar-

[20] From 1870 to 1880 the population increased 30.06 per cent. During the same period the number of criminals increased 82.33 per cent. In 1850, there were 290 prisoners to every million of the population; in 1860, there were 607 to each million; in 1870, there were 853, and in 1880, there were 1169. That is, in thirty years the proportion of criminals increased fourfold.

ing mutual jealousies, and perpetuating race antipathies. In New England, conventions are held to which only French Canadian Catholics are admitted. At such a convention in Nashua in 1888, attended by eighty priests, the following mottoes were displayed: "Our tongue, our nationality, and our religion." "Before everything else let us remain French." If our noble domain were tenfold larger than it is, it would still be too small to embrace with safety to our national future, little Germanies here, little Scandinavias there, and little Irelands yonder. A strong centralized government, like that of Rome under the Cæsars, can control heterogeneous populations, but local self-government implies close relations between man and man, a measure of sympathy, and, to a certain extent, community of ideas. Our safety demands the assimilation of these strange populations, and the process of assimilation will become slower and more difficult as the proportion of foreigners increases.

When we consider the influence of immigration, it is by no means reassuring to reflect that so large a share of it is pouring into the formative West. Already is the proportion of foreigners in the territories from two to three times greater than in the states east of the Mississippi. In the East, institutions have been long established and are, therefore, less easily modified by foreign influence, but in the West, where institutions are formative, that influence is far more powerful. We may well ask—and with special reference to the West—whether this in-sweeping immigration is to foreignize us, or we are to Americanize it. Mr. Beecher once said, "When the lion eats an ox, the ox becomes lion, not the lion, ox." The illustration would be very neat if it only illustrated. The lion happily has an instinct controlled by an unfailing law which determines what, and when, and how much he shall eat. If that instinct should fail, and he should some day eat a badly diseased ox, or should very much over-eat, we might have on our hands a very sick lion. I can even conceive that under such conditions the ignoble ox might slay the king of beasts. Foreigners are not coming to the United States in answer to any appetite of ours, controlled by an unfailing moral or political instinct. They naturally consult their own interests in coming, not ours. The lion, without being consulted as to time, quantity or quality, is having the food thrust down his throat, and his only alternative is, digest or die.

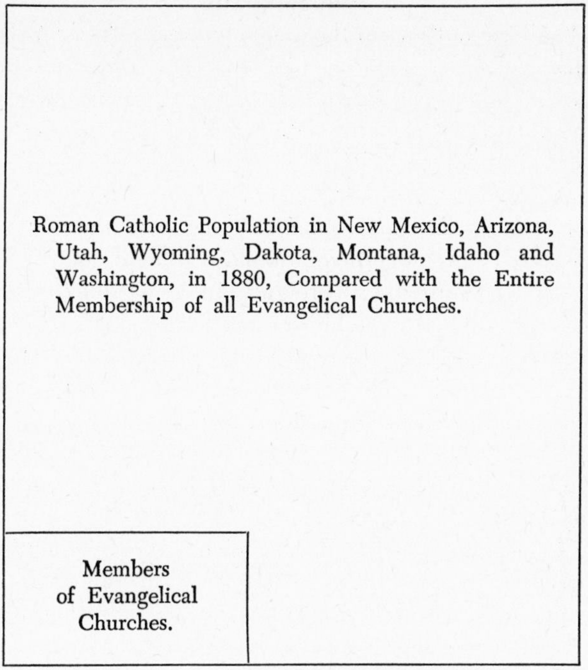

Roman Catholic Population in New Mexico, Arizona, Utah, Wyoming, Dakota, Montana, Idaho and Washington, in 1880, Compared with the Entire Membership of all Evangelical Churches.

Members of Evangelical Churches.

CHAPTER V

PERILS—ROMANISM

THE perils which threaten the nation and peculiarly menace the West demand, for their adequate presentation, much more space than the narrow limits of this work allow. We can touch only salient points.

ROMANISM

There are many who are disposed to attribute any fear of Roman Catholicism in the United States to bigotry or childishness. Such see nothing in the character and attitude of Romanism that is hostile to our free institutions, or find nothing portentous in its growth. Let us, then, first, compare some of the fundamental principles of our free institutions with those of the Roman Catholic church.

I. *The Declaration of Independence teaches Popular Sovereignty. It says that "governments derive their just powers from the consent of the governed."* Roman Catholic doctrine invests the Pope with supreme sovereignty. In *Essays on Religion and Literature,* edited by Archbishop Manning, 1867, we read, p. 416; "Moreover, the right of deposing kings is inherent in the supreme sovereignty which the Popes, as vicegerents of Christ, exercise over all Christian nations." [1]

In Art. VI., Sec. 2 of the Constitution we find: *"This Constitution and the laws of the United States which shall be made in pursuance thereof . . . . shall be the supreme law of the land."* The Canon Law of the Church of Rome is essentially the constitution of that church, binding upon Roman Catholics everywhere. The bull, *Pastoralis Regiminis,* published by Benedict XIV., is a part of the Canon Law and decrees that those who refuse to obey *any* "commands of the Court of Rome, if they be ecclesiastics, are *ipso facto* suspended from their orders and offices; and, if they be laymen, are smitten with excommunication."

The bull *Unam Sanctam* of Boniface VIII., which is also a part of the Canon Law, and acknowledged by Cardinal Manning as an "Article of Faith," says: "It is necessary that one sword should be under another, and that the temporal authority should be subject to the spiritual power. And thus the prophecy of Jeremiah is fulfilled in the church and the ecclesiastical power, 'Behold, I have set thee over the kingdoms, to root out, and to pull down, and to destroy, and to throw down, to build and to plant!' Therefore, if the earthly power go astray, it must be judged by the spiritual power; but if the spiritual power go astray, it must be judged by God alone.

[1] [Edmund Sheridan Purcell, "On Church and State," in H. E. Manning, ed., *Essays on Religion and Literature,* 2nd series (London).]

Moreover, we declare, say, define, and pronounce it to be altogether necessary to salvation that every human creature should be subject to the Roman Pontiff."[2] Bishop Gilmour, of Cleveland, Ohio, in his Lenten Letter, March, 1873, said: "Nationalities must be subordinate to religion, and we must learn that we are Catholics first and citizens next. God is above man, and the church above the state."

Here is a distinct issue touching the highest allegiance of the Roman Catholic citizens of the United States, whether it is due to the Pope or to the constitution and the laws of the land. In his Syllabus of Errors, Proposition 42, issued December 8, 1864, Pius IX. said: "It is an error to hold that, In the case of conflicting laws between the two powers, the civil law ought to prevail."[3] The reigning pontiff, in an encyclical issued January 10, 1890, says: "It is wrong to break the law of Jesus Christ in order to obey the magistrate, or under pretence of civil rights to transgress the laws of the church." Again Leo XIII. says: "But if the laws of the state are openly at variance with the law of God—if they inflict injury upon the church. . . . or set at naught the authority of Jesus Christ which is vested in the Supreme Pontiff, then indeed it becomes a duty to resist them, a sin to render obedience."[4]

We must not imagine that the two spheres, religious and secular, are so distinct as to prevent all conflict of authorities. Why does Pius IX. say that it is an error to hold that, "In the case of conflicting laws between the two powers, the civil law ought to prevail," unless there is some possibility of conflict?

[2] *Corpus Juris Canonici,* ed. A. L. Richter, II (Leipzig, 1839), 1160.

[3] See also Apostolic Letter, *Ad Apostolicae* (August 22, 1851). [Strong took the quotation from p. 119 of a volume containing four separate works bound as one: William Ewart Gladstone, *The Vatican Decrees in Their Bearing on Civil Allegiance;* Philip Schaff, *A History of the Vatican Council;* both the Latin and English texts of *The Papal Syllabus,* and of *The Vatican Decrees.* The book was published in New York in 1875, and Strong quoted from it repeatedly. Hereafter the volume will be cited as Gladstone, *Vatican Decrees.*]

[4] Authorized translation of Encyclical, pp. 3–4. [The translation used by Strong has not been identified. Strong's text, however, agrees with that in Joseph Husslein, ed., *Social Wellsprings* (Milwaukee, 1940), p. 146.]

Says Mr. Gladstone: "Even in the United States, where the severance between church and state is supposed to be complete, a long catalogue might be drawn of subjects belonging to the domain and competency of the State, but also undeniably affecting the government of the Church; such as, by way of example, marriage, burial, education, prison discipline, blasphemy, poor-relief, incorporation, mortmain, religious endowments, vows of celibacy, and obedience." [5] The Pope might declare that any or all of these are "things which belong to faith and morals" or "that pertain to the discipline and government of the church," over which matters the Vatican Council decreed him to be possessed of "all the fulness of supreme power." [6]

The word "morals" is quite broad enough to overlap politics. Cardinal Manning says: "Why should the Holy Father touch any matter in politics at all? For this plain reason, because politics are a part of morals. . . . .Politics are morals on the widest scale." [7] Leo XIII. in his encyclical of January 10, 1890, declares that "*politics . . . . are inseparably bound up with the laws of morality and religious duties.*" [8] This declaration is *ex cathedra* and, therefore, "infallible," the end of controversy to all good Roman Catholics. It renders every utterance which the Pope may hereafter make concerning politics absolutely binding on the conscience of every Romanist, at the peril of salvation. This is perhaps the most important word that has come from Rome since 1870 when the Vatican Council "put the top-stone to the pyramid of the Roman hierarchy." Not that papal interference in politics is anything new in doctrine [9] or practice, but it has often been denied, and Roman Catholics commonly profess entire loyalty both to the civil power and

[5] Gladstone, *Vatican Decrees*, p. 30.

[6] See "The First Dogmatic Constitution on the Church of Christ," ch. iii. [In Gladstone, *Vatican Decrees*, pp. 159–163.]

[7] Henry E. Manning, *Sermons on Ecclesiastical Subjects*, III (Dublin and London, 1873), 83.

[8] [Leo XIII, "Duties of the Christian Citizen."] *Pilot*, 53 (Boston, February 15, 1890), 2.

[9] See "Syllabus of Errors," of Pius IX (December 8, 1864), Proposition No. 27. Allocution *Maxima Quidem* (June 9, 1862). [In Gladstone, *Vatican Decrees*, p. 116.]

to the Pope, thus implying that the two spheres, secular and religious, are quite distinct; while moderate Romanists have sometimes expressly said: "We will take our religion but not our politics from Rome." It is, therefore, of the highest importance that we have here a perfectly clear and irreversible declaration, which no good Roman Catholic will dispute, that politics is not *possibly* or *incidentally* but *"inseparably,"* bound up with morality and religion. That is, the connection between the two spheres is necessary, and the Pope has "full and supreme power" over politics as one of the "things which belong to faith and morals;" and he who denies this must rest under the *"anathema sit"* of the Vatican Council.[10]

Said Vicar-General Preston, in a sermon preached in New York, January 1, 1888, "Every word that Leo speaks from his high chair is the voice of the Holy Ghost and must be obeyed. To every Catholic heart comes no thought but obedience. It is said that politics is not within the province of the church, and that the church has only jurisdiction in matters of faith. You say, 'I will receive my faith from the Pontiff, but I will not receive my politics from him.' This assertion is disloyal and untruthful. . . . You must not think as you choose; you must think as Catholics. The man who says, 'I will take my faith from Peter, but I will not take my politics from Peter,' is not a true Catholic. The Church teaches that the supreme Pontiff must be obeyed, because he is the vicar of the Lord. Christ speaks through him." The claims of the Ultramontanes are quite logical. Christ is King of kings and Lord of lords. His right to rule is absolute and his authority unlimited. If, now, Christ has a vicegerent on earth, if there is a vicar of God among men, his sovereignty is absolute, his authority unlimited. The Roman Catholic must, as Leo XIII. says, render as "perfect submission and obedience of will to the Church and the Sovereign Pontiff, AS TO GOD HIMSELF."[11] He who would divide the authority

[10] See "The First Dogmatic Constitution on the Church of Christ," ch. iii. [In Gladstone, *Vatican Decrees,* pp. 159–163.]

[11] [Leo XIII, "Duties of the Christian Citizen."] *Pilot,* 53 (February 15, 1890), 2. [The small capital letters are Strong's.]

of the Pope, accept a part and reject a part, is as poor a Romanist as he is logician. If, then, as Vicar-General Preston says, such a man "is not a true Catholic," how can a "true Catholic" be a loyal citizen? He can be such only until some issue arises which compels him to choose between the two masters. And as an eminent writer has said: "We can scarce hope that the time will not come when our Catholic fellow citizens will be put to the strain of electing between the allegiance due to the state and that due to the church." [12]

Cardinal Manning in his reply to Mr. Gladstone says: "That the civil allegiance of no man is unlimited, and therefore the civil allegiance of all men who believe in God, or are governed by conscience, is in that sense divided. In this sense, and in no other, can it be said with truth that the civil allegiance of Catholics is divided." [13] This is the best answer that can be made, but it is not adequate. Of course the civil allegiance of no man is absolutely unlimited. If divine and human laws are in conflict, "we ought to obey God rather than man." But just here appears the radical difference between a Roman Catholic and a Protestant. The latter accepts the will of God, revealed in the Bible and in his own conscience, *as interpreted by himself*. If the requirements of government are inconsistent with the Word of God (which is scarcely possible with our constitutional guarantees of religious liberty), or if he believes that they are, his understanding may be informed, his conscience may be enlightened, he is at liberty to change his views. And even if he does not, he stands alone, and cannot possibly be a menace to the peace of society.

The Romanist, on the other hand, accepts the will of God, *as interpreted by the Pope,* who, as we have seen, claims that his sphere of authority is "inseparably bound up" with that of the civil government and who, therefore, cannot be disinterested. If now, the requirements of government are inconsistent

[12] Henry Charles Lea, "Key Notes from Rome," *Forum,* 8 (February 1890), 635.

[13] Henry E. Manning, *The Vatican Decrees in Their Bearing on Civil Allegiance* (New York, 1875), p. 9.

with the will of the Pope, the Roman Catholic is not at liberty to weigh the Pope's judgment, to try his commands by his own conscience and the Word of God—to do this would be to become a Protestant. There can be no appeal to his reason or conscience, the decision is final and his duty absolute. And, moreover, he stands not alone, but with many millions more, who are bound by the most dreadful penalties to act as one man in obedience to the will of a foreign potentate and in disregard of the laws of the land. *This,* I claim, *is a very possible menace to the peace of society.*

If it seems to any that I have exaggerated the surrender of reason and conscience required of a good Roman Catholic, weigh these words of Cardinal Bellarmine, one of the most celebrated theologians of the Roman Church: "If the Pope should err by enjoining vices or forbidding virtues, the Church would be obliged to believe vices to be good and virtues bad, unless it would sin against conscience." [14]

The revised Statutes of the United States declare:—"*The alien seeking citizenship must make oath to renounce forever all allegiance and fidelity to any foreign prince, potentate, state*

[14] Ch. 5, book IV, of "De Summo Pontifice," in Roberto Bellarmino, *De Controversiis Christianae Fidei,* I (Venice, 1721), 398. Bishop Kain, of Wheeling, West Virginia, devoted his Lenten lecture, April 14, 1889, to Chapter V. of *Our Country.* In it he said that Bellarmine was here using the argument *reductio ad absurdum* to prove the inerrancy of the Pope, and that he, (Bellarmine) "draws the absurd and even blasphemous conclusion that would result from such a denial of his thesis." Does the Bishop forget that the whole force of a *reductio ad absurdum* lies in the *necessity* of the sequence? Of course the absurdity of the conclusion does not prove the absurdity of the premise unless the one follows necessarily from the other. The argument of Bellarmine has no force with a Protestant because he sees that the declared sequence is not only not necessary, but is impossible. The fact that such an argument can have weight with a Catholic, the fact that Bellarmine could use it, shows that in such minds the sequence is necessary, which, as was remarked in the First Edition, affords a most excellent illustration of the "utter degradation of reason, and the stifling of conscience."

The writer did not imagine that good Catholics would believe the Pope capable of error and, therefore, fear that they might some day be "obliged to believe vices to be good and virtues bad." The point of the quotation, which is missed by Bishop Kain, lies in the sequence which is affirmed by Bellarmine.

or sovereignty, in particular that to which he has been subject." The Roman Catholic profession of faith, having the sanction of the Council which met at Baltimore in 1884, contains the following oath of allegiance to the Pope:—"And I pledge and swear true obedience to the Roman Pontiff, vicar of Jesus Christ, and successor of the blessed Peter, prince of the Apostles."[15] We have already seen how broad is the obligation which the oath lays on the Romanists. Here, then, are men who have sworn allegiance to two different powers, each claiming to be supreme, whose spheres of authority are "inseparably" bound together and which, therefore, afford abundant opportunity for the rise of conflicting interests and irreconcilable requirements.

By way of throwing light on such a situation, it is interesting to read in the Canon Law: "No oaths are to be kept if they are against the interests of the Church of Rome."[16] And again: "Oaths which are against the Church of Rome, are not to be called oaths, but perjuries."[17] An American ecclesiastic, Bishop English, of Charleston, S.C., quotes this canon, and defending it says: "These are the principles which I have been taught from Roman Catholic authors, by Roman Catholic professors; they are the principles which I find recognized in all enactments and interpretations of councils in the Roman Catholic church, from the Council at Jerusalem, held by the Apostles, down to the present day."[18] In a work prepared by Rev. F. X.

[15] *"Romanoque Pontifici, beati Petri Apostolorum Principis successori ac Jesu Christi vicario veram obedientiam spondeo ac juro." Acta et Decreta Concilii Plenarii Baltimorensis Tertii A.D. MDCCCLXXXIV* (Baltimore, 1886), p. liii.

[16] *Corpus Juris Canonici,* ed. Richter, II, 1159.

[17] *Ibid.,* p. 358.

[18] Richard Fuller and John England, *Letters Concerning the Roman Chancery* (Baltimore, n.d.), pp. 162–163. [The quotation is from Bishop England's letter of September 16, 1839. In a passage immediately preceding the quoted sentence Bishop England defines the principles he refers to: ". . . the first obligation of every citizen is the law of God; the second is the constitution of his state, and as no form of oath could bind him to the violation of the divine law, so except the constitution of his state should conflict with the divine law, no form of oath could bind him to violate that constitution; and should there be such a conflict,

Schouppe for Roman Catholic schools and colleges and bearing the imprimatur of Cardinal Manning, we read (p. 278), "The civil laws are binding on the conscience only so long as they are conformable to the rights of the Catholic Church."[19]

When a man has placed his conscience and will in the keeping of another for life, and on pain of eternal damnation, how can he make unconditional pledges touching anything? Or, having made them, how can they be of any value, if he accepts such doctrine as the above? Is his oath of allegiance to the government worthy of respect? Ought we not to place the same estimate on it that Cardinal Newman did when he said that no pledge from Catholics was of any value to which Rome was not a party?[20]

The two greatest living statesmen, Gladstone and Bismarck, hold that the allegiance demanded by the Pope is inconsistent with good citizenship. Says the former: "—the Pope demands for himself the right to determine the province of his own rights, and has so defined it in formal documents as to warrant any and every invasion of the civil sphere; and that this new version of the principles of the Papal church inexorably binds its members to the admission of these exorbitant claims, without any refuge or reservation on behalf of their duty to the Crown."[21] He also says: "That Rome requires a convert who now joins her to forfeit his moral and mental freedom, and to

---

he is bound to the state in every other point save that in which the conflict exists; and his exemption in this instance arises from that sound maxim of legal interpretation that where two laws are in irreconcilable conflict, that of the first or higher authority must prevail . . ." (p. 162).]

[19] [Rev. Father F. X. Schouppe, *A Course of Religious Instruction*, new ed. (London, n.d.), p. 278. Strong here shortened the sentence to give it a more stringent import than it bears in the original. There it reads as follows: "The civil laws are binding in conscience so long as they are conformable to the constitution of the state, and also are not contrary to justice, religion, or the rights of the Catholic Church."]

[20] John Henry Newman, *A Letter Addressed to His Grace the Duke of Norfolk on Occasion of Mr. Gladstone's Recent Expostulations* (London, 1875), p. 14. [In the New York edition the quotation may be found on p. 18.]

[21] Gladstone, *Vatican Decrees*, p. 31.

place his loyalty and civil duty at the mercy of another." [22]

The constitution of the United States guarantees *Liberty of Conscience.* Nothing is dearer or more fundamental. The first amendment to the constitution says: "*Congress shall make no law respecting an establishment of religion or prohibiting the free exercise thereof.*" Pius IX. declared it to be an error that, "Every man is free to embrace and profess the religion he shall believe true, guided by the light of reason." [23] And from this dictum no good Roman Catholic can differ. The same Pope in his encyclical of December 8, 1864, said: "Contrary to the teaching of the Holy Scriptures, of the Church, and of the Holy Fathers, these persons do not hesitate to assert that 'the best condition of human society is that wherein no duty is recognized by the government *of correcting by enacted penalties the violators of the Catholic Religion,* except when the maintenance of the public peace requires it.' From this totally false notion of social government, they fear not to uphold that erroneous opinion most pernicious to the Catholic Church, and to the salvation of souls, which was called by our predecessor, Gregory XVI., the insanity (deliramentum), namely, that 'liberty of conscience and of worship is the right of every man; and that this right ought, in every well-governed state, to be proclaimed and asserted by the law.'" Much more to the same effect might be quoted from Pius IX. and Leo XIII.

"When, in May, 1851, New Granada proclaimed religious toleration and subjected the clergy to the secular courts, Pius IX., in the allocution '*Acerbissimum,*' of September 27, 1852, pronounced the laws to be null and void, and threatened heavy ecclesiastical penalties on all who should dare to enforce them. . . . . When, in 1855, Mexico adopted a constitution embodying the same principles, Pius, in the allocution '*Nunquam fore,*' December 15, 1856, annulled the Constitution and forbade obedience to it. When, about the same time Spain made an

[22] *Ibid.,* p. 8.

[23] See "Syllabus of Errors" of Pius IX (December 8, 1864), Proposition No. 15. Allocution *Maxima Quidem* (June 9, 1882). [In Gladstone, *Vatican Decrees,* p. 113.]

effort in the same direction, the allocution *'Nemo vestrum,'* of July 24, 1855, similarly abrogated the obnoxious provisions. Even a powerful empire like that of Austria fared no better when, in December, 1867, it decreed liberty of conscience and of the press, and in May, 1868, adopted a law of civil marriage; for the allocution *'Nunquam certe,'* of June 22, 1868, denounced all these as atrocious laws, and declared them to be void and of no effect."[24] And all this, be it remembered, transpired in modern times.

In *Essays on Religion and Literature,* edited by Cardinal Manning we read: "That neither the church nor the state, whensoever they are united on the true basis of divine right, have any cognizance of tolerance. . . . . The Church [of course the Roman Church] has the right in virtue of her divine commission, to require of every one to accept her doctrine. Whosoever obstinately refuses, or obstinately insists upon the election out of it of what is pleasing to himself is against her. But were the Church to tolerate such an opponent, she must tolerate another. If she tolerate one sect, she must tolerate every sect, and thereby give herself up."[25] For the Roman Church to grant liberty of conscience would be, as is here said, to "give herself up." What that high American Roman Catholic authority, Dr. O. A. Brownson, says is quite too true; viz.: "Protestantism of every form has not, and never can have any right where Catholicity is triumphant."[26] (An odd kind of *catholicity,* isn't it?) Again he says: "Heresy [that is, any doctrine in conflict with Romanism] and infidelity have not, and never had, and never can have, any rights, being, as they undeniably are, contrary to the law of God."[27]

[24] Lea, "Key Notes from Rome," pp. 630–631.
[25] [Purcell, "On Church and State," p. 403.]
[26] Brownson's *Catholic Review* (June 1857). [Strong erred in this citation. In the 1885 edition of *Our Country* (p. 47) he attributed the quotation to an unnamed writer in *The Catholic Review,* a New York paper which did not appear before 1872. Brownson's periodical was called *Brownson's Quarterly Review.* Its New York Series (1856–1859) did not publish a June edition.]
[27] *Brownson's Quarterly Review,* n.s. 6 (January 1852), 26.

In the *Pontificale Romanum* [28] is the bishop's oath, in which occur these words: "Heretics, schismatics and rebels against our said Lord or his successors I will to my utmost persecute (persequar) and oppose." What if Methodist and Episcopal bishops took an oath to *persecute* Roman Catholics and all others who refuse to accept the standards of their respective churches! If Romanists were persecuted in Protestant countries, would they not demand the religious liberty for themselves which they refuse to others? Their policy is very frankly stated by M. Louis Venillot, a distinguished French Roman Catholic writer, highly esteemed at Rome, who says: "When there is a Protestant majority we claim religious liberty because such is their principle; but when we are in majority we refuse it because that is ours."

Another of our principles closely related to that of religious liberty is *Freedom of Speech and of the Press,* which is guaranteed to us by the First Amendment to the Constitution. "*Congress shall make no law . . . . abridging the freedom of speech or of the press.*" Leo XIII., in a letter, June 17, 1885, said, "Such a duty (obedience), while incumbent upon all without exception, *is most strictly so on journalists* who, if they were not animated with the *spirit of docility and submission* so necessary to every Catholic, would help to extend and greatly aggravate the evils we deplore." A writer for the *Catholic World* in an article entitled "The Catholic of the Nineteenth Century," shows us what would become of free speech and the freedom of the press in the event of Roman ascendency

[28] This is a book on rites and ceremonies, issued by order of Clement VIII. and Urban VIII. This form of the bishop's oath is quoted from the edition printed in Mechlin, 1845. In it we find this Papal utterance: "We command this our Pontifical, so restored and reformed, to be received and observed in all churches of the *whole world; decreeing that the aforesaid Pontifical must never, at any time, be altered in whole or in part, nor anything at all be added to, or detracted from, the same.*" Bishop Kain of Wheeling, if correctly reported by the press, states that the word *persequar,* is now omitted by American bishops when taking the oath. How much weight should be allowed to this statement when we set over against it the above "infallible" and irrevocable command of a Supreme Pontiff, the reader can judge as well as I.

in the United States. He says: "The supremacy asserted for the Church in matters of education implies the additional and cognate function of the censorship of ideas, and the right to examine and approve or disapprove all books, publications, writings and utterances intended for public instruction, enlightenment, or entertainment, and the supervision of places of amusement. This is the principle upon which the Church has acted in handing over to the civil authorities for punishment *criminals in the world of ideas.*" [29]

Again, none of our fundamental principles is more distinctly American than that of the *Complete Separation of Church and State,* which is required in the First Amendment to the Constitution, already quoted. Pius IX. teaches the exact opposite. He says it is an error to hold that, "The Church ought to be separated from the State, and the State from the Church." [30] He also declares it to be an error that, "The Church has not the power of availing herself of force, or any direct or indirect temporal power." [31]

Another foundation stone of our free institutions is the *Public School,* of which the state has and should have the entire direction without any ecclesiastical interference whatever. Touching this point, Pius IX. says it is an error to hold that, "The entire direction of public schools . . . . may and must appertain to the civil power, and belong to it so far that no other authority whatsoever shall be recognized as having any right to interfere in the discipline of the schools, the arrangement of the studies . . . . or the choice and approval of the teachers." [32] And again the same Pope: It is an error that, "The best theory of civil society requires that popular schools . . . . should be freed from all ecclesiastical authority, government,

[29] Anonymous author in vol. 11 (July 1870), p. 442.

[30] "Syllabus of Errors," of Pius IX (December 8, 1864), Proposition No. 55. Allocution *Acerbissimum* (September 27, 1852). [In Gladstone, *Vatican Decrees,* p. 123.]

[31] *Ibid.,* Proposition No. 24. Apostolic Letter, *Ad Apostolicae* (August 22, 1851). [In Gladstone, *Vatican Decrees,* p. 115.]

[32] *Ibid.,* Proposition No. 45. Allocution, *In Consistoriali* (November 1, 1850). [In Gladstone, *Vatican Decrees,* p. 120.]

and interference, and should be fully subject to the civil and political power, in conformity with the will of rulers and the prevalent opinions of the age." [33] Again he says: It is an error, that, "This system of instructing youth, which consists in separating it from the Catholic faith and from the power of the church . . . . may be approved by Catholics." [34] Bishop McQuaid in a lecture at Horticultural Hall, Boston, February 13, 1876, declared: "The state has no right to educate, and when the state undertakes the work of education it is usurping the powers of the church."

If there remains in any mind a lingering doubt as to the irreconcilable hostility of the Roman hierarchy toward our public school system it would be dissipated by reading, *The Judges of Faith vs. Godless Schools,* a little book written by a Roman Catholic priest and "Addressed to Catholic Parents." [35] It bears the indorsements of Cardinals Gibbons and Newman, and of various dignitaries of that church. The prefatory note states that the book contains, "the conciliar or single rulings of no less than three hundred and eighty of the high and highest church dignitaries. There are brought forward, twenty-one plenary and provincial councils; six or seven diocesan synods; two Roman pontiffs; two sacred congregations of some twenty cardinals and pontifical officials; seven single cardinals, who with thirty-three archbishops, make forty primates and metropolitans; finally, nearly eighty single bishops and archbishops, deceased or living, in the United States." All this mass of authority is against our public schools; and the animus of these ecclesiastics toward this cherished institution is indicated by such epithets and appellations as the following: "mischievous," "baneful to society," "a social plague," "Godless," "pestilential," "scandalous," "filthy," "vicious," "diabolical," places of "unre-

[33] *Ibid.,* Proposition No. 47. Letter to the Archbishop of Fribourg, *Quum non sine* (July 14, 1864). [In Gladstone, *Vatican Decrees,* p. 121.]

[34] *Ibid.,* Proposition No. 48. Letter to the Archbishop of Fribourg, *Quum non sine* (July 14, 1864). [In Gladstone, *Vatican Decrees,* p. 121.]

[35] [The correct title is Thomas J. Jenkins, *The Judges of Faith: Christian vs. Godless Schools,* rewritten ed. (Baltimore, 1886).]

strained immorality," where things are done the recital of which would "curdle the blood in your veins."

Rome has never favored popular education. In Protestant countries like Germany and the United States, where there is a strong sentiment in favor of it, she has been compelled in self-defence to open schools of her own. But her real attitude toward the education of the masses should be inferred from her course in those countries where she has, or has had, undisputed sway; and there she has kept the people in besotted ignorance. *The Cyclopedia of Education,* 1877, in its article on "Illiteracy," gives a table containing the statistics of thirty countries. Of these, five are starred as "nearly free from illiteracy," and all of them are Protestant. The highest percentage of illiteracy given for any Protestant country in the world is thirty-three. In all those countries where fifty per cent or more are illiterate the religion is Roman Catholic, Greek or heathen, viz.: Argentine Republic, eighty-three per cent; China, fifty per cent; Greece, eighty-two per cent; Hungary, fifty-one; India, ninety-five; Italy, seventy-three; Mexico, ninety-three; Poland, ninety-one; Russia, ninety-one; Spain, eighty. Here, six Roman Catholic countries, including Italy, the home of the Pope, where until recent years, the church has had undisputed sway, are far more illiterate than heathen China.[36] Touching the education of the masses—except in Protestant countries as explained above—we are forced to infer either the indifference or the incompetence of the Church of Rome.

We have made a brief comparison of some of the fundamental principles of Romanism with those of the Republic. And,

1. We have seen the supreme sovereignty of the Pope opposed to the sovereignty of the people.

[36] Edited by Henry Kiddle and Alexander J. Schem, Superintendent and Assistant Superintendent of Public Schools, New York City. [The five countries "nearly free from illiteracy" are Denmark, Hawaii, Norway, Sweden, Switzerland. England is the Protestant country with the highest illiteracy rate of 33 per cent (p. 452).]

2. We have seen that the commands of the Pope, instead of the constitution and laws of the land, demand the highest allegiance of Roman Catholics in the United States.

3. We have seen that the alien Romanist who seeks citizenship swears true obedience to the Pope instead of "renouncing forever all allegiance to any foreign prince, potentate, state or sovereignty," as required by our laws.

4. We have seen that Romanism teaches religious intolerance instead of religious liberty.

5. We have seen that Rome demands the censorship of ideas and of the press, instead of the freedom of the press and of speech.

6. We have seen that she approves the union of church and state instead of their entire separation.

7. We have seen that she is opposed to our public school system.

Manifestly there is an irreconcilable difference between papal principles and the fundamental principles of our free institutions. Popular government is self-government. A nation is capable of self-government only so far as the individuals who compose it are capable of self-government. To place one's conscience, therefore, in the keeping of another, and to disavow all personal responsibility in obeying the dictation of another, is as far as possible from *self*-government, and, therefore, wholly inconsistent with republican institutions, and, if sufficiently common, dangerous to their stability. It is the theory of absolutism in the state, that man exists for the state. It is the theory of absolutism in the church that man exists for the church. But in republican and Protestant America it is believed that church and state exist for the people and are to be administered by them. Our fundamental ideas of society, therefore, are as radically opposed to Vaticanism as to imperialism, and it is as inconsistent with our liberties for Americans to yield allegiance to the Pope as to the Czar. It is true the Third Plenary Council in Baltimore denied that there is any antagonism between the laws, institutions and spirit of the Roman church and those of our country, and in so doing illustrated the French proverb that "To deny is to confess." No Protestant church makes any such denials.

History fully justifies the teaching of philosophers that civil and political society tends to take the form of religious society. Absolutism in religion cannot fail in time to have an undermining influence on political equality. Already do we see its baneful influence in our large cities. It is for the most part the voters who accept absolutism in their faith who accept the dictation of their petty political popes, and suffer themselves to be led to the polls like so many sheep.

Says the eminent Professor de Laveleye: "To-day we can prove to demonstration that which men of intellect in the eighteenth century were only beginning to perceive. The decisive influence which forms of worship bring to bear on political life and political economy had not hitherto been apparent. Now it breaks forth in the light, and is more and more closely seen in contemporary events." "Representative government is the natural government of Protestant populations. Despotic government is the congenial government of Catholic populations." [37]

II. Look now very briefly at the attitude or purpose of Romanism in this country. In an encyclical letter of November 7, 1885, Leo XIII., as reported by cable to the *New York Herald*, said: "We exhort all Catholics to devote careful attention to public matters, and take part in all municipal affairs and elections, and all public services, meetings and gatherings. All Catholics must make themselves felt as active elements in daily political life in countries where they live. All Catholics should exert their power to cause the constitutions of states to be modeled on the principles of the true church." "If Catholics are idle," says the same Pope, "the reins of power will easily be gained by persons whose opinions can surely afford little prospect of welfare. Hence, Catholics have just reason to enter

[37] Emile de Laveleye, *Protestantism and Catholicism in Their Bearing upon the Liberty and Prosperity of Nations* (London, 1875), pp. 32, 33.

into political life; . . . . having in mind the purpose of introducing the wholesome life-blood of Catholic wisdom and virtue into the whole system of the state. All Catholics who are worthy of the name must . . . . work to the end, that every state be made conformable to the Christian model we have described."[38] That Catholic authority, Dr. Brownson, in his Review for July, 1864, declared: "Undoubtedly it is the intention of the Pope to possess this country. In this intention he is aided by the Jesuits and all the Catholic prelates and priests."[39] And in some cases expectation is as eager as desire. Father Hecker in his last work, published in 1887, says: "The Catholics will out-number, before the close of this century, all other believers in Christianity put together in the republic."[40]

III. Many of our Roman Catholic fellow citizens undoubtedly love the country, and believe that in seeking to Romanize it they are serving its highest interests, but when we remember, as has been shown, that the fundamental principles of Romanism are opposed to those of the Republic, that the difference between them does not admit of adjustment, but is diametric and utter, it becomes evident that it would be *impossible to "make America Catholic,"* (which the archbishop of St. Paul declared at the late Baltimore Congress to be the mission of Roman Catholics in this country) *without bringing the principles of that church into active conflict with those of our government, thus compelling Roman Catholics to choose between them, and in that event, every Romanist who remained obedient to the Pope, that is, who continued to be a Romanist, would necessarily become disloyal to our free institutions.*

IV. It is said, and truly, that there are two types of Roman Catholics in the United States. They may be distinguished as those who are "more Catholic than Roman," and those who are

[38] Quoted by Michael Müller in his Roman Catholic Catechism, *Familiar Explanation of Catholic Doctrine,* No. 4 (New York, 1888), pp. 250–252.

[39] [The editor could not find this quotation in *Brownson's Quarterly Review* of July 1864.]

[40] Isaac Thomas Hecker, *The Church and the Age* (New York, 1887), p. 56.

more Roman than Catholic. The former have felt the influence of modern thought, have been liberalized, and come into a large measure of sympathy with American institutions. Many are disposed to think that men of this class will control the Roman church in this country and already talk of an "American Catholic Church." But there is no such thing as an American or Mexican or Spanish Catholic Church. It is the Roman Catholic Church in America, Mexico and Spain, having one and the same head, whose word is law, as absolute and as unquestioned among Roman Catholics here as in Spain or Mexico. "The archbishops and bishops of the United States, in Third Plenary Council assembled," in their Pastoral Letter "to their clergy and faithful people," declare: "We glory that we are, and, with God's blessing, shall continue to be, not the American Church, nor the Church in the United States, nor a Church in any other sense, exclusive or limited, but an integral part of the one, holy, Catholic and Apostolic Church of Jesus Christ." [41]

The Roman Catholics of the United States have repudiated none of the utterances of Leo XIII. or of Pius IX., nor have they declared their political independence of the Vatican. On the contrary, the most liberal leaders of the church here vehemently affirm their enthusiastic loyalty to the Pope. The Pastoral Letter issued by the Third Plenary Council of Baltimore (December 7, 1884), and signed by Cardinal Gibbons, "In his own name and in the name of all the Fathers," says: "Nor are there in the world more devoted adherents of the Catholic Church, the See of Peter, and the Vicar of Christ, than the Catholics of the United States." [42] Says a writer on the recent Roman Catholic Congress at Baltimore: "It was well that Masonic pseudo-Catholics, compromisers of the papal authority, persecutors of the clergy, anti-Jesuits, social revolutionalists, legal robbers of church property, lay educationists, anti-clericals, should learn once for all, that the *Catholic laymen of America are proud of being pro-papal without compromise;* that they are proud of the Jesuits from whose chaste

[41] *Acta et Decreta,* p. lxxvi.
[42] *Acta et Decreta,* p. lxxvi.

loins the church in the United States drew its vigorous life." [43] This writer is not quoted as a representative of moderate Romanism, but, as one who very justly expresses the sentiment of loyalty to the Pope, which characterized the Baltimore Congress, and which, so far as we can judge, was shared by all alike.

It is undoubtedly safe to say that there is not a member of the hierarchy in America, who does not accept the infallibility of the Pope and who has not sworn to obey him.[44] Now this dogma of papal infallibility as defined by the Vatican Council and interpreted by Pius IX. and Leo XIII. carries with it logically all of the fundamental principles of Romanism which have been discussed. Infallibility is necessarily intolerant. It can no more compromise with a conflicting opinion than could a mathematical demonstration. Truth cannot make concessions to error. Infallibility represents absolute truth. It is as absolute as God himself, and can no more enter into compromise than God can compromise with sin. And if infallibility is as intolerant as the truth, it is also as authoritative. Truth may be rejected, but even on the scaffold it is king, and has the right and always must have the right to rule absolutely, to control utterly every reasoning being. If I believed the Pope to be the infallible vicar of Christ, I would surrender myself to him as unreservedly

[43] John A. Mooney, "Our Recent American Catholic Congress and Its Significance," *American Catholic Quarterly Review*, 15 (January 1890), 152. [The italics in the passage quoted are Strong's.]

[44] "Hence, that no one in future may craftily pretend not to know how and whence to ascertain what the Church officially teaches; above all, that no one may henceforth scatter the baneful seeds of false doctrine with impunity, under the mask of an appeal from the judgment of the Holy See (whether it be to learned universities, or state tribunals or future councils, particular or general, as was done by Luther and the Jansenists), the Church of the living God, through the Fathers of the Vatican Council, has unequivocally declared that her authentic spokesman is the successor of St. Peter in the Apostolic See of Rome, and that whatever he, as Head of the Church, defines *ex cathedra* is part of the Deposit of Faith intrusted to her keeping by Christ, Our Lord, and hence is subject to neither denial, doubt nor revision, but is to be implicitly received and believed by all." *Acta et Decreta*, p. lxxiii.

The oath of allegiance to the Pope prescribed by this same council has already been given. See p. 66.

as to God himself. How can a true Roman Catholic do otherwise? A man may have breathed the air of the nineteenth century and of free America enough to be out of sympathy with the absolutism and intolerance of Romanism, but if he accepts the Pope's right to dictate his beliefs and acts, of what avail are his liberal sympathies? He is simply the instrument of the absolute and intolerant papal will. His sympathies can assert themselves and control his life only as he breaks with the Pope, that is, ceases to be a Roman Catholic. I fear we have little ground to expect that many would thus break with the Pope, were a distinct issue raised. Everyone born a Roman Catholic is suckled on authority. His training affects every fiber of his mental constitution. He has been taught that he must not judge for himself, nor trust to his own convictions. If he finds his sympathies, his judgment and convictions in conflict with a papal decree, it is the perfectly natural result of his training for him to distrust himself. His will, accustomed all his life to yield to authority without question, is not equal to the conflict that would follow disobedience. How can he withstand a power able to inflict most serious punishment in this life, and infinite penalties in the next? Only now and then will one resist and suffer the consequences, in the spirit of the Captain in Beaumont and Fletcher's poem "The Sea Voyage." Juletta tells the Captain and his company:

> "Why, slaves, 'tis in our power to hang ye."

The Captain replies:

> "Very likely,
> 'Tis in our powers, then, to be hanged and scorn ye."

Modern times afford an excellent illustration of what may be expected when liberal prelates, strongly opposed to ultramontanism, are brought to the crucial test. Many members of the Vatican Council (1870) vigorously withstood the dogma of papal infallibility, among whom, says Professor Schaff, "were the prelates most distinguished for learning and position." Many of them spoke and wrote against the dogma. Archbishop Kendrick, of St. Louis, published in Naples an "irrefragable argument" against it.[45] The day before the decisive vote was to be taken, more than a hundred bishops and archbishops, members of the opposition, left the council and departed from Rome rather than face defeat. But these moderate and liberal Romanists, including the several American prelates who had belonged to the opposition, all submitted, and published to their respective flocks the obnoxious decree which some of them had shown to be contrary to history and to reason. It must be remembered that these men were the most liberal and among the most able in the church. In view of the fact that their opposition thus utterly collapsed, what reason have we to expect that liberal Romanists in this country, who have already assented to the infallibility of the Pope, will ever violate their oath of obedience to him? If the liberality of avowed opponents of ultramontanism yielded to papal authority, what reason is there to think the liberality of avowed ultramontanists will ever resist it?

Moreover it should be borne in mind that the more moderate Roman Catholics in the United States are generally those who in childhood had the benefit of our public schools, and their intelligence and liberality are due chiefly to the training there received. In the public schools they learned to think and were largely Americanized by associating with American children. But their children are being subjected to very different influences in the parochial schools. They are there given a training calculated to make them narrow and bigoted; and, being separated as much as possible from all Protestant children, they grow up suspicious of Protestants, and so thoroughly sectarianized and Romanized as to be well protected against the broadening and Americanizing influences of our civilization in after life.[46]

[45] Philip Schaff ["History of the Vatican Council," in Gladstone, *Vatican Decrees,* pp. 74–75, 80.]

[46] It is shown in the following chapter that the parochial school has come to stay. It is the avowed purpose of the hierarchy to bring all Roman Catholic children under its instruction. That instruction is thoroughly ultramontane and is well calculated to destroy all tendencies

We have seen the fundamental principles of our free institutions laid side by side with some of those of Romanism, expressed in the words of the highest possible authorities in the Roman Catholic Church; and thus presented they have de-

---

toward moderate or liberal Romanism in the rising generation. *Familiar Explanation of Catholic Doctrine,* by Rev. M. Müller (Benziger Brothers, 1888), is a Roman Catechism, used in the parochial schools, bearing the imprimatur of Cardinal Gibbons and strongly commended by many Roman prelates. The following extracts are from No. IV. of the series. "The Pope could not discharge his office as the teacher of all nations, unless he were able with *infallible certainty to proscribe and condemn doctrines, logical, scientific, physical, metaphysical, or political of any kind,* which are at variance with the Word of God, and imperil the integrity and purity of the faith, or the salvation of souls" (p. 126). The italics are in all cases Father Müller's. Note the words "political of any kind." "To be separated from the divine authority of the Pope, is to be separated from God, and to have no place in the Kingdom of Christ" (p. 126). "The church only can judge how far her authority goes . . . . where the boundary line is to be drawn, and in what attitude we have to place ourselves as to certain subjects, these things are altogether beyond our power or our right, and are wholly within the judgment of the Apostolic See" (p. 127). The writer devotes eighteen pages to inculcating the infallibility of the Pope.

Twenty-five pages are devoted to "Reasons why no salvation is possible outside the Roman Catholic Church." "Christ has solemnly declared that only those will be saved, who have done God's will on earth as explained, not by private interpretation, but by the infallible teaching of the Roman Catholic Church" (p. 163). "All those who wish to be saved, must die united to the Catholic Church; for out of her there is no salvation" (p. 164). "*Any one separated from her* (*the church*) *however praiseworthy a life he may think he leads, by this crime alone, i.e., by his separation from the unity of Christ, he will be debarred from life eternal, and the wrath of God will remain upon him*" (Appendix, p. 9). This doctrine is iterated and reiterated a dozen times on a single page (Appendix, p. 7). The Allocution of Pius IX. to the Cardinals, December 17, 1847, is quoted: "But quite recently—we shudder to say it,—certain men have not hesitated to slander us by saying that we share in *their folly,* favor that *most wicked system,* and think so benevolently of every class of mankind as to suppose that not only the sons of the church, but that the rest also, however *alienated from Catholic unity,* are alike in the way of salvation, and may arrive at everlasting life. We are at a loss, from horror, to find words to express our detestation of this new and atrocious injustice that is done us."

The writer continues: "Mark well, Pius IX. uttered these solemn words against 'certain men,' whom he calls the enemies of the Catholic Faith—he means liberal-minded Catholics, as is evident from his words, which, clared for themselves the inherent contradiction which exists between them.

It has been shown that it is the avowed purpose of Romanists to "make America Catholic."

It has been shown that this could not be done without bringing into active conflict the diametrically opposed principles of Romanism and of the Republic, thus forcing all Romanists in the United States to choose between the two masters, both of whom they now profess to serve.

It has been shown that Roman Catholic training, from childhood up, is calculated to disqualify the mind for independent action, and renders it highly improbable that any considerable number of even moderate and liberal Romanists would, in the supposed event, forsake their allegiance to the Pope.

V. The rate of growth, therefore, of Romanism in the United States becomes a matter of vital importance.

Many who are well acquainted with the true character of Romanism are indifferent to it because not aware of its rapid growth among us. They tell us, and truly, that Rome loses

---

on July 28, 1873, he addressed to the members of the Catholic Society of Quimper: 'Tell the members of the Catholic Society that, on the numerous occasions on which we have censured those who held liberal opinions, we did not mean those who hate the church, whom it would have been useless to reprove, but *those Catholics who have adopted so-called liberal opinions: who preserve and foster the hidden poison of liberal principles.*'" Pius continues: "To entertain opinions contrary to this Catholic faith is to *be an impious wretch*" (Appendix, p. 8). This is what the rising generation of Roman Catholics is being taught concerning "liberal Catholics."

I can prolong this note to quote only a few words from the instructions given concerning the relations of church and state. "Therefore, the church is not to accommodate her legislation to the legislation of the state, but that the state laws must not conflict with the laws of the church" (p. 199). After enumerating some laws which Romanists do not like, the writer continues: "Just here let us lay down an incontestable platform. We have a right to secure just legislation and wipe out unjust and scandalous laws. We have that right on the ground of citizenship and we mean to exercise every right in that category, whether the hordes and mobs howl, sneer and jeer, or quietly let us do so" (p. 200).

Such is the mold in which the Roman Catholic mind of the coming generation is being cast.

great numbers of adherents here through the influence of our free schools, free institutions, and the strong pervasive spirit of independence which is so hostile to priestly authority. But let us not congratulate ourselves too soon. The losses of Romanism in the United States are not necessarily the gains of Protestantism. When a man, born in the Roman Catholic Church, loses confidence in the only faith of which he has any knowledge, instead of examining Protestantism he probably sinks into skepticism, which is even worse than superstition. Romanism is chiefly responsible for German and French infidelity. For, when a mind to which thought and free inquiry have been forbidden as a crime attains its intellectual majority, the largeness of liberty is not enough; it reacts into license and excess. Skepticism and infidelity are the legitimate children of unreasoning and superstitious credulity, and the grandchildren of Rome. Apostate Romanists are swelling our most dangerous classes. Unaccustomed to think for themselves, and having thrown off authority, they become the easy victims of the wildest and most dangerous propagandists.

But, notwithstanding the great losses sustained by Romanism in the United States,[47] it is growing with great rapidity. No one knows what the present Roman Catholic population is, and estimates vary widely.[48] Cardinal Gibbons at the Baltimore Congress in 1889 placed it at 9,000,000. Many Roman Catholic writers think it is larger. Bishop Hogan, of Missouri, estimates it at 13,000,000. But this is wild. No doubt the figures of *Sadliers' Catholic Directory* (1890) are large enough. This gives the Romanist population as 8,277,039 (p. 408). These figures are probably as reliable as earlier ones from the same source, and, therefore, serve as a basis for comparison to estimate the rate of growth.

In 1800 the Roman Catholic population was 100,000. There was then in the United States one Romanist to every 53 of the

[47] According to Roman Catholic authorities, the members they have lost here, together with their descendants, now number upwards of ten millions—considerably more than the present Romanist population.

[48] A recent Census Bulletin gives the R.C. Church in the United States 6,250,045 members, excluding children under nine years.

whole population; in 1850, one to 14.3; in 1870, one to 8.3; in 1880, one to 7.7; in 1890, one to 7.5. Thus it appears that, wonderful as the growth of our population has been since 1800, that of the Roman Church in this country has been still more rapid. Dr. Dorchester in his valuable and inspiring work, *Problem of Religious Progress* (New York and Cincinnati, 1881), easily shows that the *actual* gains of Protestantism in the United States, during the century, have been much larger than those of Romanism, and seems disposed, in consequence, to dismiss all anxiety as to the issue of the race between them. But it is *relative* rather than actual gains which are prophetic. We find that for the first eighty years of the century the *rate* of growth of the Roman Catholic Church was greater than that of any one Protestant church or of all Protestant churches combined. From 1800 to 1880 the population increased ninefold, the membership of all evangelical churches twenty-sevenfold, and the Romanist population sixty-three-fold.[49] Not much importance, however, should be attached to this comparison, as the Roman Catholic population was insignificant in 1800, and a small addition sufficed to increase it several-fold. But in 1850 that population was nearly one-half as large as the membership of all evangelical churches. Let us, then, look at

[49] Some criticism has been offered on the writer's comparison of the Roman Catholic *population* with the evangelical *church membership* instead of evangelical population. But the comparison is of rates of increase, not of actual numbers, and if made with the evangelical population instead of membership, the result would have been identical.

The following tables, showing the actual increase of evangelical communicants and of Roman Catholics are compiled from Dr. Dorchester's *Problem of Religious Progress,* from the church statistics of *The Independent* for 1890 (July 31), and from the Eleventh Census.

Year	*Evangelical Churches or Congregations*	*Ordained Ministers*	*Communicants*	*Population of the United States*
1800	3,030	2,651	364,872	5,305,925
1850	43,072	25,555	3,529,988	23,191,876
1870	70,148	47,609	6,673,396	38,558,371
1880	97,090	69,870	10,065,963	50,152,866
1890	142,599	93,776	13,417,180	62,480,540

their relative progress since that time. From 1850 to 1880 the population increased 116 per cent, the communicants of evangelical churches 185 per cent, and the Romanist population 294 per cent. During the same period the number of evangelical churches increased 125 per cent, and the number of evangelical ministers 173 per cent, while Roman Catholic churches increased 447 per cent and priests 391 per cent.

In 1800 priests were 1.9 per cent of the number of evangelical ministers; in 1850, 5.0 per cent; in 1870, 8.3 per cent; and in 1880, 9.1 per cent. In 1850, Roman Catholic churches were 2.8 per cent of the number of evangelical churches; in 1870, 5.4 per cent; and in 1880, 6.8 per cent. In 1800 the Roman Catholic population was 21 per cent of the number of evangelical church members; in 1850, 45 per cent; in 1870, 68 per cent; and in 1880, 63 per cent.[50] Thus we see that for the first eighty years of the century the Roman Catholics gained rapidly both on the population and on the evangelical churches. But the latest statistics show that between 1880 and 1890 the tide turned. In 1880 the Romanist population was 63 per cent of the number of evangelical communicants; in 1890, 61 per cent. In 1880 their priests were 9.1 per cent of the number of evangelical ministers; in 1890, 8.8 per cent. In 1880 their churches

Year	*Roman Catholic Churches*	*Priests*	*Population*
1800	—	50	100,000
1850	1,222	1,302	1,614,000
1870	3,806	3,966	4,600,000
1880	6,622 *	6,402	6,367,330
1890	7,523	8,332	8,277,039

* Estimated.

[50] The relative loss from 1870 to 1880 is probably only apparent and due to an overestimate of the Roman Catholic population in 1870. It will be observed that the figures given for the Roman Catholic population that year in the foregoing table are "round numbers." It is far more probable that their population increased at about an even rate with their churches and priests from 1850 to 1880, than that it increased much more rapidly than churches and priests from 1850 to 1870 and much less rapidly from 1870 to 1880.

were 6.8 per cent of the number of evangelical churches; in 1890, 5.2 per cent. This relative loss since 1880 has not been due to any lack of vitality, for, as we have already seen, Romanism has gained on the population during these ten years, but to the more vigorous growth of the Protestant churches, which during this time have been not a little quickened.

Whether this relative loss, however, marks a permanent or only temporary turn in the tide does not yet appear. It must be remembered, first, that this loss is only slight; and, secondly, that the now pronounced parochial school policy can hardly fail to keep great numbers in the Roman communion, which through the broadening influence of the public school would have left it, thus greatly stimulating the rate of growth of that church in the future.

But this is not all. Rome, with characteristic foresight, is concentrating her strength in the western territories. As the West is to dominate the nation, she intends to dominate the West. In the United States a little more than one-eighth of the population is Catholic; in the territories taken together, more than one-third.[51] In the whole country there are not quite two-thirds as many Romanists as there are members of evangelical churches. Not including Arizona and New Mexico, which have a large native Roman Catholic population, the six remaining territories in 1880 had four times as many Romanists as there were members in all Protestant denominations collectively; and including Arizona and New Mexico, Rome had eighteen times as many as all Protestant bodies.[52] We are told that the native Romanists of Arizona and New Mexico are not as energetic as the Protestants who are pushing into those territories. True, but they are energetic enough to be counted. The

[51] These are the figures for 1880. On this point the statistics of the Eleventh Census (1890) are not yet available.

[52] The writer has been criticized at this point also for comparing Roman Catholic *population* with evangelical *church membership* instead of population (which latter is something not definitely known). But the critics miss the writer's point. The comparison is not between the strength of Romanism and Protestantism in the West, but between the relative strength of Romanism in the whole country and in the territories.

most wretched members of society count as much at the polls as the best, and often *much more*. It is poor consolation which is drawn from the ignorance of any portion of our population. Those degraded peoples are clay in the hands of the Jesuits. When the Jesuits were driven out of Berlin, they declared that they would plant themselves in the western territories of America. And they are there to-day with empires in their brains. Expelled for their intrigues even from Roman Catholic countries, Spain, Portugal, France, Italy, Austria, Mexico, Brazil, and other states, they are free to colonize in the great West, and are there, purposing to Romanize and control our western empire. Rev. J. H. Warren, D.D., writes from California, in which state there are four times as many Romanists as Protestant church members: "The Roman Catholic power is fast becoming an overwhelming evil. Their schools are everywhere, and number probably 2000 in the State. Their new college of St. Ignatius is, we are told, the largest, finest, best equipped of its kind in the United States. They blow no trumpets, are sparing of statistics, but are at work night and day to break down the institutions of the country, beginning with the public schools. As surely as we live, so surely will the conflict come, and it will be a hard one." [53]

Lafayette, born a Romanist, and knowing well the nature of Romanism and its antipathy to liberty, said: "If the liberties of the American people are ever destroyed, they will fall by the hands of the Romish clergy." [54]

[53] Quoted by Dr. E. P. Goodwin, in a sermon before the American Home Missionary Society, May 9, 1880. [Edward P. Goodwin's sermon, *Possessing the Land*, was preached in the Broadway Tabernacle Church in New York City, and subsequently was published in that city in pamphlet form. The quotation is from p. 24. It was reprinted in *Home Missionary*, 53 (August 1880), 96.]

[54] From the title page of Samuel F. B. Morse, ed., *Confessions of a French Catholic Priest* (New York, 1837). [Strong's quotation differs somewhat from that given in the 1837 edition printed by John S. Taylor. There it reads: "American liberty can be destroyed only by the Popish Clergy."] Professor Morse, who wrote the introduction to the book, says in it: "The declaration of Lafayette, which the author has placed as a motto in the title page of this book, is a beautiful evidence of the sagacity and vigilance of liberty's great friend. Lafayette, like a veteran mariner,

was ever watching the political horizon for the indications of danger to his beloved America, and the danger to which his latest warnings pointed was this very covert political attack, which is in full operation upon our soil at this moment; an attack the more dangerous because it shields itself under the mask of religion, and cries out 'persecution' at every attempt to expose its true, its *political* character." These words are as applicable to-day as they were when written a generation ago.

Prof. Morse, in a foot-note contained in the introduction quoted above, says; "It may not be amiss here to state that the declaration of Lafayette in the motto in question was repeated by him to more than one American. The very last interview which I had with Lafayette on the morning of my departure from Paris, full of his usual concern for America, he made use of the same warning, and in a letter which I received from him but a few days after at Havre, he alludes to the whole subject with the hope expressed that I would make known the real state of things in Europe to my countrymen; at the same time charging it upon me as a sacred duty as an American, to acquaint them with the fears which were entertained by the friends of republican liberty, in regard to our country. If I have labored with any success to arouse the attention of my countrymen to the dangers foreseen by Lafayette, I owe it in a great degree to having acted in conformity to his often repeated instructions." [Quoted from pp. viii–ix.]

Letters might be given from gentlemen quoting language of the same import, but stronger, which Lafayette had used to them. It seems worth while to quote from Prof. Morse at some length because the authenticity of the above saying of Lafayette has been denied by Bishop Kain, of Wheeling, W. Va., and by other Roman Catholics.

CHAPTER VI

PERILS—RELIGION AND THE PUBLIC SCHOOLS

DEMOCRACY necessitates the public school. Important as is the school to any civilized people, it is exceptionally so to us, for in the United States the common school has a function which is peculiar, viz., to Americanize the children of immigrants. The public school is the principal digestive organ of the body politic. By means of it the children of strange and dissimilar races which come to us are, in one generation, assimilated and made Americans. It is the heterogeneous character of our population (especially in cities) which threatens the integrity of our public school system and at the same time renders it supremely important to maintain that integrity. Moreover, apart from consequences to the school system, the policy which is finally adopted by the American people touching religion and the public schools concerns most intimately the welfare both of our youth and of the State.

Public opinion as to the true relations of the State to religious instruction is as yet much divided or unformed. The schools are criticized both on the ground that they are godless and on the ground that they are sectarian, because they have too little religion and again because they have too much. Two theories which threaten the well-being of the schools and of the State demand our attention:—

First, that of the Roman Catholic hierarchy, which holds that education should be distinctly religious, which of course means Roman Catholic. Vague or general instruction will not suffice, there must be inculcated the system of doctrine found in the Roman catechism. It holds that religious and secular education cannot be safely separated. Inasmuch, therefore, as the State will not teach Roman Catholic doctrine in the public schools, parochial schools become necessary.

It is held that the public schools are in fact Protestant, and that Catholics are taxed to support them while they carry the burden of their own parochial schools. They complain that this is an injustice which can be removed only by the division of the school fund, and that to divide this fund between the "Protestant" and Catholic schools *pro rata* would be only equitable. To secure such division is their avowed policy.

This position is to be regretted but not to be wondered at. It was inevitable that the parochial school should be opened and attendance upon it made obligatory. The hierarchy could not otherwise be true to the spirit and genius of their church. The conflict between the parochial and the public schools goes far deeper than the question of religious instruction. It involves the whole subject of education, its aim and methods. The object of the public school is to make good citizens. The object of the parochial school is to make good Catholics. The public school seeks to give both knowledge and discipline, not only truth but the power to find truth. The parochial school aims to lead, rather than to train the mind; to produce a spirit of submission rather than of independence. The one system is calculated to arouse, the other to repress, the spirit of inquiry. The one aims at self-control, the other at control by superiors. The one seeks to secure intelligent obedience to rightful authority; the other unquestioning obedience to arbitrary authority. In a trial held in one of the courts of New York City, November, 1888, Monsignor Preston, vicar-general of New York, was asked on the witness stand if Roman Catholics must obey their bishops, whether right or wrong. He replied, "Yes!" and, when the question was repeated, answered, "They must obey, right or wrong." (Notes of hearing before the Committee on Education and Labor, United States Senate, page 79.) The free school system is intended to build up society by developing in the pupil a strong individuality, while Catholic education strengthens the church at the expense of individuality. This is frankly admitted by the late Father Hecker, who was one of the ablest as well as most loyal writers of the Roman Catholic Church in the United States. In his recent work, published just before his death, he says: "The defense of the church and the salvation of the soul were ordinarily secured at the expense necessarily of those virtues which properly go to make up the strength of Christian manhood."[1] (The salvation of the soul at the expense of Christian virtues!) "In the principles above briefly stated," he continues, "may in a great measure be found the explanation why fifty million of Protestants have had generally a controlling influence, for a long period, over two hundred million Catholics in directing the movements and destinies of nations."[2]

But doubtless the decree of the Third Plenary Council in 1884, ordering the establishment of parochial schools, was due quite as much to a significant fact as to the Roman Catholic theory of education. That fact is the heavy loss sustained by the Roman Catholic Church among the descendants of immigrants in the United States. The editor of the *Irish World,* who is called by an intelligent Catholic writer "a master of statistics," has made an elaborate analysis of the population, from which he infers that there are now living in the United States ten million persons, who as descendants of Roman Catholics ought to be members of the Roman Church, but who are lost to it. This loss is commonly attributed to the influence of the public school. Says the *Catholic Review* of August 31, 1889: "The parochial school is necessary because Catholic children cannot be brought up Catholic and attend the public school. This is a recognized fact. . . . At the present moment the Catholic Church in America depends more on the faith of the Catholic immigrant than on the faith of the generation which

[1] Isaac Thomas Hecker, *The Church and the Age* (New York, 1887), p. 16.
[2] *Ibid.,* p. 17.

has received its education in the public schools. . . . We see no way of making them (young Americans) Catholics than by the parochial school. Our conscience forces us to take up the work" (p. 136).

Attention has been called to the ground of action on the part of the hierarchy to show that there is no possibility of compromise with it. If the Bible in the public school were the cause of the Catholic secession therefrom, its removal might stop the movement; but it is not the cause, and its removal would be a fruitless sacrifice. We may as well recognize the fact that the parochial school has come to stay, regardless of the treatment of religion in the public schools.[3] It is a necessary part of a great educational system, which, to provide for its 3,194[4] parochial schools, has its teaching brotherhoods and sisterhoods, its 102 colleges, its 35 theological seminaries, and to crown all its great Catholic American University at Washington, for which $1,000,000 have already been subscribed, and which, including the endowments of chairs, we are told will cost between $5,000,000 and $10,000,000.

Here, then, is a theory of education which can no more be harmonized with the American theory than water can be made to coalesce with oil; here is the discovery that it is absolutely necessary to act on this theory in order to prevent disastrous results to the Catholic Church; here is an elaborate educational system for whose equipment many millions of dollars have already been invested; and finally, the authoritative declarations of the Catholic Church referred to in the preceding chapter (p. 72) place beyond all doubt the attitude of the hierarchy toward the public schools, the permanence of the educational policy which they have adopted, and the impossibility of compromise.

We must not forget that there are many Roman Catholic

[3] "We must multiply them (parochial schools) till every Catholic child in the land shall have the means of education within its reach." From the pastoral letter reprinted in *Acta et Decreta Concilii Plenarii Baltimorensis Tertii A.D. MDCCCLXXXIV* (Baltimore, 1886), p. lxxxv.

[4] See *Sadlier's Catholic Directory, 1890* (New York, 1890), p. 408.

laymen who prefer, and who dare to patronize, the public schools, but they have no share in the authority of the Church. The hierarchy has thoroughly and irrevocably committed the Church against the public school, and infallibility cannot retreat; to do so would be to confess itself fallible.

It has seemed worth while to show that the educational policy of the Roman Catholic Church must needs remain fixed, because the recognition of this fact should aid the public toward a fixed policy touching religious instruction in the public schools.

This cleavage of the population along religious lines is greatly to be regretted. It is un-American. It carries the shadow on the dial of progress back from the nineteenth to the seventeenth century. Intercourse tends to eliminate differences and to make a population homogeneous. Non-intercourse nourishes suspicion, prejudice, and religious bitterness, of which the world has had quite enough already. There are many reasons why children of different religions and different races, of rich and poor, of all classes of society, should mingle in the public school. This segregation of the Catholic children, though well intended, inflicts injury upon society and a greater injury upon the Catholic children themselves. How can the evil results which must necessarily attend the establishment of parochial schools be minimized? Certainly not by secularizing the public schools. This remedy was tried to a considerable extent, when the question of the Bible in the public schools was so widely discussed some twenty years ago. Instead of conciliating the Catholic priesthood, it only put into their mouth the cry which they are using to-day, with the greatest effect upon their own people, viz., that the public schools are "godless."

There are Roman Catholics who, as has been said, are "more Catholic than Roman,"—men who have much of the American spirit, who have learned in large measure to think and act for themselves (and who are, therefore, rather "off color," as Romanists). Many such Catholics patronize the public school, and it is to be hoped will continue so to do. Only the more liberal-minded will dare to disregard the commands of the priests, and such, I take it, will not object to what little religious instruction their children receive in the public school.

Of course the mischief which the parochial schools do will be in proportion to the number of children they draw off. The best remedy is to make the public schools as good as possible, so manifestly and so vastly superior that many Catholic parents will refuse to sacrifice the interests of their children at the behest of the priest.

It may be remarked in passing that the action of the hierarchy in establishing parochial schools, and the arguments with which they have defended that action, may have an unexpected and unwelcome effect. The prelates of the Catholic Church have of late taken pains to assert that Romanism is thoroughly American in spirit, and in beautiful harmony with American institutions; but when they insist that our public schools, which are among the most cherished of our institutions, and deemed essential to the preservation of our liberties, are wholly unfit for Catholic children, and cannot be attended by such without sin, they unintentionally acknowledge and publicly declare that there is an inherent conflict between Romanism and free institutions. Every American recognizes the assimilating and Americanizing power of the public school. When, therefore, the Catholic hierarchy and press assert that the only way to make a good Catholic out of a child is to keep him out of the public school and separate him from American children, it is an acknowledgment that Romanism is un-American and represents an alien civilization.

When the full force of this acknowledgment is appreciated, it will tend to create a general distrust of the Church, and to alienate from it Catholics who have become in any considerable degree Americanized.

A few words concerning the Catholic claim for a division of the school funds, and we will leave this branch of our subject. If this claim were granted, a similar claim from Lutherans or Episcopalians, or the many parents who choose to send their children to private schools could not be denied. Such a concession would be liable, perhaps likely, to result in the depletion and final destruction of the public school.

But the question is not simply one of policy. To grant this claim would be to violate a principle in the hearty support of which Americans are singularly united, viz., the entire separation of Church and State. At this point the Catholics meet us with the argument that the public schools are Protestant. "Why should the State support Protestant schools and not Catholic? The support of the latter would be no more in violation of the aforesaid principle than the support of the former, and equity demands it." The argument is specious. Its fallacy lies in the fact that the public schools are not Protestant. What constitutes a school Protestant? The fact that the teacher is a Protestant does not make the school so any more than the fact that President Harrison is a Presbyterian constitutes the United States government Presbyterian. Nor does the fact that most of the pupils belong to Protestant families make the school denominational. If the religious preference of teachers or scholars gave denominational character to the school, the public schools, in many quarters of our large cities, would be emphatically Roman Catholic. But no Catholic would admit that any public school in the United States was Catholic, even though the teacher and every scholar were a Romanist, nor would it be, unless distinctively Roman Catholic doctrine were taught. The public schools are not Protestant, because *distinctively* Protestant doctrines are not taught in them.

When the public fully appreciates the fact that the Roman Catholic school policy is fixed, and that concessions are useless, it would not be strange if there were a tendency developed to Protestantize the public schools; but against this we must caution ourselves, if for no other reason, because in the eyes of the average voter it would make valid the Catholic argument for the division of the school fund; against which division every true American must set his face without variableness or the faintest shadow of turning. Remember the wise words of President Garfield: "It would be dangerous to our institutions to apply any portion of the revenues of the nation or of the

States to the support of sectarian schools;"[5] and those of General Grant, "Encourage free schools, and resolve that not one dollar appropriated to them shall be applied to the support of any sectarian school."[6]

The second theory touching religion and the public schools which demands our attention is that of the *secularists,* among whom are counted many Christian men as well as all Jews and agnostics.

According to this theory the province of the State is wholly secular; its true attitude is that of absolute neutrality toward all forms of religious belief and unbelief; to teach religion in any form is to do violence to the rights of certain classes of citizens.

The Jewish Exponent quotes Rabbi Calisch as saying: "The public schools are an outgrowth of our broad American republicanism, which, in the interest of freedom, forbids any union or partnership of Church and State. Hence, in the name of the Jewish brotherhood all over this country, and in the name of persons of differing views on religious matters everywhere, I wish to protest against the manner in which our public schools are conducted. It is a favorite claim of the churches," he continues, "that this is a Christian country, and this, so far as it is confined to the church instruction or family instruction, is unobjectionable and right. The idea of Christ, however, is not confined to such teaching. It is, with all its religious dependencies, made a part of our public-school instruction. It is to be denounced as in violation of the fundamental theory of our government. I demand in the name of justice that the principle of law designed to protect all in their religious freedom be recognized."[7]

[5] "Letter Accepting the Nomination for the Presidency, July 12, 1880." [In Burke A. Hinsdale, ed., *The Works of James Abram Garfield,* II (Boston, 1883), 783.]

[6] To the Army of the Tennessee, Des Moines, 1876. [*New York Times,* October 1, 1875, p. 4, col. 7.—The address was delivered in Des Moines, Iowa, on September 29. See also James S. Clarkson, "General Grant's Des Moines Speech," *Century Magazine,* 55 (March 1898), 788.]

[7] "Religion in the Public Schools," *Jewish Exponent,* 5 (Philadelphia, August 16, 1889), 2.

The platform of the Liberal League of the United States contains the following: "We demand that all religious services now sustained by the government shall be abolished, and especially that the use of the Bible in the public schools, whether ostensibly as a textbook or avowedly as a book of religious worship, shall be prohibited."

This theory of the secularists is built on a wrong application of a right principle, viz., the complete separation of Church and State. Of all the great experiments which are being tried in this New World, none is more distinctively American than the entire separation of Church and State, and none of our principles has more abundantly justified itself. We must be willing to follow it wherever logic shall require, but our secularist friends, being compelled to go with it one mile, go with it twain. They fail to distinguish, it seems to me, between *church* and *religion*. Rabbi Isaacs, in the *Forum*, referring to the readings of a proposed manual for use in the public schools, says, "They are distinctly religious, and the State cannot sanction religious teachings in its schools any more than in its governmental offices. Such action is entirely beyond its province. Church and State must be forever separate." [8] As if the use of religious readings in the public schools compromised that principle.

As a matter of fact our government is, and has always been, religious. Says Chief Justice Shea, "Our own government, and the laws by which it is administered, are in every part—legislative, judicial, and executive—Christian in nature, form, and purpose." [9] In his "Institutes of International Law," [10] Judge Story says, "One of the beautiful traits of our municipal jurisprudence is that Christianity is part of the common law from which it seeks the sanction of its rights, and by which it endeavors to regulate its doctrine." Says the great interpreter of

[8] Abram S. Isaacs, "What Shall the Public Schools Teach?" *Forum*, 6 (October 1888), 210.

[9] George Shea, *The Nature and Form of the American Government* (Boston and New York, 1882), p. 35.

[10] [This, presumably, is a reference to Joseph Story's *Commentaries on the Conflict of Laws.*]

the Constitution, Webster: "There is nothing that we look for with more certainty than the general principle, that Christianity is part of the law of the land . . . . general, tolerant Christianity, . . . independent of sects and parties." [11] Many other authorities to the same effect might be cited.

When the fathers added to the Constitution the principle of strict separation of *Church* and State, they did not intend to divorce the State from all *religion.* Says Judge Story, speaking of the time when the Constitution was adopted, "The attempt to level all religions, and make it a matter of State policy to hold all in utter indifference, would have created universal disapprobation, if not universal indignation." [12] The principle of the separation of Church and State undoubtedly forbids sectarian instruction in the State schools; but we have the highest legal and judicial authority for saying that it does not forbid undenominational religious teaching. "But," it will be asked, "does not the teaching of religious doctrine which is undenominational violate the rights of agnostics quite as much as inculcating the dogmas of one sect wrongs the adherents of others?" By no means; because the teaching of the three great fundamental doctrines which are common to all monotheistic religions is essential to the perpetuity of free institutions, while the inculcation of sectarian dogmas is not. These three doctrines are that of *the existence of God, the immortality of man* and *man's accountability.* These doctrines are held in common by all Protestants, Catholics and Jews. There are comparatively few in this country who do not hold them; and the children of these few should be taught these fundamental truths of religion, not because agnostics are in the minority, for questions of conscience can be settled neither by majorities nor by authority, but because the necessities of the State are above individual rights. The State, when its necessities require,

[11] *Works of Daniel Webster,* VI (Boston, 1851), 176. [The quotation is from a speech before the U.S. Supreme Court in Vidal v. Girard's Executors (2 Howard 205), February 22, 1844.]

[12] Joseph Story, *Commentaries on the Constitution of the United States,* III (Boston, 1833), 726. The subject is discussed at length on pp. 722–730.

does not hesitate to draft into the army a citizen who has conscientious scruples against war. The government, utterly disregarding individual conscience, inclinations and rights, forces him away from his occupation and family, and exposes him to injury and death.

The question is not, as some would seem to think, whether religion has a right to be taught in the public schools, but whether the government has a right to teach it. That right is beyond question, if the necessities of the State require. Let us look at this more closely.

"If there is any incontestable maxim on the rights of nations, it is that laid down by the illustrious Bossuet, in his defense of the declaration of the clergy of France, in 1682, that all sovereign power is sufficient to itself, and is provided by God with all the power that is necessary for its own preservation." [13] Self-preservation is the first law of states as of individuals. If the State has the right to exist, manifestly it has the right to do or require whatever is necessary to perpetuate its existence. To refuse this right to the State is to attack its life. As Shylock said:—

> "You take my house, when you do take the prop
> That doth sustain my house; you take my life
> When you do take the means whereby I live."

No one will deny that popular intelligence is essential to successful popular government; and popular morality is no less a political necessity than intelligence. These statements may be regarded as axiomatic. Here is the bed rock on which rest compulsory educational laws, the right of taxation for the public schools, and the right and duty of giving religious instruction in them.

Our common school system is not based on the doctrine that each child is *entitled* to an education. *So far as individual right is concerned,* under our theory of government a man is as much entitled to demand of the State capital on which to begin busi-

[13] *A Glimpse of the Great Secret Society,* 4th ed. (London, 1880), p. 43.

ness, as to demand for his children that intellectual capital which we call an education. Both might be done in a socialistic state, but our government is neither socialistic nor "paternal." Why does the State take money from your pocket to educate my child? *Not on the ground that an education is a good thing for him, but on the ground that his ignorance would be dangerous to the State.* This may be "low ground," but it is not marshy. In like manner, the State must teach in its schools fundamental religious truths, not because the child should know them in preparation for a future existence,—the State is not concerned with the eternal welfare of its citizens,—but because immorality is perilous to the State, and popular morality cannot be secured without the sanctions of religion. Of course the advocacy of religion on the ground that it serves as moral police is not very exalted; but if our ground is to be broad enough for upwards of 60,000,000 people to stand on, it must needs be low. The top of the pyramid is narrow.

Secularists deny that religious teaching is essential to moral instruction. It is claimed that it makes no practical difference whether happiness or utility or the will of God be the ground of morality; that whatever view is taken of the metaphysical ground of right, all theories end in adopting the same practical virtues, which may therefore be taught quite independently of religion. Yes, a child may be taught that this is wrong and that is right without any reference to God, but the child must have moral *training* as well as moral instruction; and moral training is addressed to the will, and the will must be influenced by motives. The lying that is done by children in this country is not due to ignorance of the fact that lying is wrong, but to the fact that their wills have not been sufficiently strengthened by motives to truthfulness. We do not claim that religion must be taught in connection with morals, on the ground that it affords the only adequate basis of the science of ethics, for the children are not taught the science of ethics; but on the ground that *religion alone affords adequate motives to the practice of moral precepts.* The philosopher Cousin, in a report upon Public Instruction in Germany, referring to the fact that it is based on the Bible, says, "Every wise man will rejoice in this; for, with three-fourths of the population, morality can be instilled only through the medium of religion." President Woolsey, in a paper on *The Bible in the Public Schools,*[14] said: "We can, in a system of morals, considered in the abstract, separate religion from it, but in the practical part, even of a book on ethics, there is an unavoidable necessity of bringing the two into connection." And Daniel Webster, in a Fourth of July oration, said: "To preserve the government we must also preserve morals. Morality rests on religion; if you destroy the foundation, the superstructure must fall. When the public mind becomes vitiated and corrupt, laws are a nullity and constitutions are waste paper."

There are of course individuals who are agnostics or atheists and yet moral in life, but many if not most of these had Christian training in childhood, under which their habits became fixed. This is a very different thing from teaching a child that there is no God or leaving him uninstructed. And though there are individual atheists who are moral, there are no moral infidel communities. Plutarch says, you remember, "There never was a state of atheists. You may travel all over the world, and you may find cities without walls, without king, without mint, without theater or gymnasium; but you will nowhere find a city without a god, without prayer, without oracle, without sacrifice. Sooner may a city stand without foundations than a state without belief in the gods. This is the bond of all society, and the pillar of all legislation." Permit me to add that oft-quoted passage from Washington's Farewell Address, "Whatever may be conceded to the influence of refined education on minds of peculiar structure, reason and experience both forbid us to expect that national morality can prevail in exclusion of religious principle."

All Christian secularists hold of course that the children should receive religious instruction, but tell us that it should

[14] Read before the National Council of Congregational Churches, 1877. [See Theodore Dwight Woolsey's paper in the *Minutes of the National Council* (Boston, 1877), p. 127.]

be furnished by the home and the Sunday school. But how are those children to be instructed who are in no Sunday school, most of whom doubtless have little or no religious training in their homes? Assuming that two-thirds of all the Catholic children are in their Sunday schools, it leaves about one-half of the children and youth in the United States of school age, who are in no Sunday school of any kind. Will the secularists tell us how these children are to be taught "reverence for God, reverence for man, reverence for woman, reverence for law, which," it is said, "are the pillars of the Republic," unless they are taught it in the public school? It is not enough that one-half our children be instructed in the knowledge of God; not enough that one-half only reverence divine, and therefore human, authority; not enough that one-half are instructed in morals whose motives include the solemn sanctions of religion. Such a division of our population would leave our destiny in a hesitating balance. Popular government is by majorities. Free institutions are safe only when the *great majority* of the people have that reverence for law which can spring only from reverence for God. The most striking defect of young America is the lack of reverence. The spirit of independence and sense of equality are unfriendly to it. Our youth have little reverence for their elders, for authority, for law, for rulers. Our irreverence as a people is noted by our critics. Says Matthew Arnold in his famous study of American civilization which appeared just before his death, in the *Nineteenth Century:* "If there be a discipline in which the Americans are wanting, it is the discipline of awe and respect. An austere and intense religion imposed on the Puritan founders the discipline of respect; . . . . but this religion is dying out." [15] An eminent English clergyman, the Rev. Dr. Dale, who visited this country some years ago, wrote on his return a little sketch of his impressions of America, in which, after referring to the fact that the children of Jonathan Edwards always rose from their seats when their

[15] [Matthew Arnold, "Civilization in the United States," *Nineteenth Century,* 23 (April 1888), 489. Also in *Civilization in the United States* (Boston, 1888), p. 176.]

father or mother came into the room, he gravely informs the British public that this custom does not exist in any of the families that showed him hospitality! There is little reverence, and therefore little authority, in many American homes, except that which is exercised by children over their parents. The spirit of self-assertion, which is characteristically American, easily becomes impatient of restraint and often grows lawless. There are no children in all Christendom who stand in so great need, *civil* need, of a sense of divine authority as American children. Many teachers and school officials whose positions afford exceptional opportunities of observation might be quoted to show how widespread among the young is the spirit of irreverence and lawlessness. A word from the school commissioner of Rhode Island must suffice. He says, "The spirit of self-assertion, of insubordination, of dislike to all restraint, of open antagonism to law,—all this is far more prevalent to-day than ever before."

All this most vitally concerns the State. Here is an evil which is great and prophetic of evil greater. How shall the State apply a remedy? The school is the place where she may touch the young with molding hand. Shall she inspire them with a spirit of reverence by secularizing the schools? by purging textbooks of every religious reference? by forbidding the children to know through their teachers that there be a God?

How shall our American youth be taught reverence, without which our future is insecure? From history? The present generation has become irreverent of the past. We are become, in the name of science, a race of iconoclasts. Whatever is "gray with time," so far from being "godlike" and therefore worthy of veneration, is subjected to the focal light of scientific methods of investigation. In thousands of instances the new has supplanted the old, simply because it deserved to, was incomparably better. So that in the popular mind there has sprung up a sort of contempt for the past.

Shall our youth learn reverence from the study of Nature? If Nature is studied not as a revelation of the Infinite One,—her processes his methods; her harmonies his reason; her beauties his thoughts; her wonders his wisdom; her forces his power; her laws his will; if Nature is studied not as the drapery which hides and yet reveals the Infinite, but simply as a magazine of supplies, whence we may enrich ourselves, a quarry from which we may hew a mighty materialistic civilization; if her laws are to be obeyed only that they may be mastered; if her forces are to be studied only that they may be conquered,—how are our youth to learn reverence from the study of Nature, and not rather learn proudly to glorify man as Nature's master?

In his *Wilhelm Meister,* Goethe expresses the opinion that reverence is not innate, but must be inculcated in order to exist. If reverence is to be taught, who shall do it, if not the State? And how can the State teach reverence to American children without teaching them of God and their accountability to him?

We are building a nation. We cannot build permanent institutions on mere intelligence, smartness, push, self-assertion. There must be a profound respect for law.

> "The keystone of the world's wide arch,
> The one sustaining and sustained by all;
> Which, if it fall, brings all in ruin down."
>
> *Schiller.*

There must be a fixed habit of obedience to rightful authority. Such obedience on the part of the many can never be secured by teaching a religionless morality; as well might we expect to run a locomotive with light or to propel an ocean steamer by means of her compass.

If, then, the State, which has the right to exist, has the right to perpetuate its existence, and if popular morality is essential to the perpetuity of free institutions, and if a knowledge of the fundamental truths of religion is essential to popular morality, then has the State the right to inculcate those truths.

As individuals we are of course bound to respect religious principles, however much they may differ from our own, and we must be patient with religious prejudices, however blind and bigoted; but if self-preservation be a duty as well as a right, then is it the duty of the State to teach these fundamental religious truths (not sectarian dogmas) to its children even though the agnostic parent objects, exactly as it is the right and duty of the State to take the boy from the plow, the mine or the mill and put him in school, if need be, against the protest of the parent, not for the good of the boy, not because the parent has no rights which we as individuals are bound to respect, but because the necessities of the State are superior to individual rights.

Sectarian dogmas are not essential to popular morality. The State, therefore, has no right to teach them, and to do so would be radically wrong in principle, and oppressive to many citizens.[16] It is objected by some that this distinction cannot be sustained. Archbishop Ireland, in his address to the National Educational Association (St. Paul, July, 1890), said: "There is and there can be no positive religious teaching where the principle of non-sectarianism rules." [17] But over against this opinion we will cite that of Daniel Webster, who says: "This objection to the multitude and difference of sects is but the old story, the old infidel argument. It is notorious that there are certain great religious truths which are admitted and believed by all Christians. All believe in the existence of a God. All believe in the immortality of the soul. All believe in the responsibility in another world for our conduct in this. . . . And cannot all these

[16] The writer has never heard of a public school in which a Protestant catechism was used or any distinctively Protestant doctrine was taught. But Rev. Dr. C. O. Brown, of Dubuque, Iowa, states that the Roman Catholic catechism is taught as a regular study, in school hours, in the public schools at Key West, New Malory, Prairie Creek, Bernard, Wilton, Holy Cross and Tete de Morte, all of that state.

"I myself," he says, "have seen it in two of these schools and heard a recitation at regular school hours." "At Spruce Creek, Spring Brook, La Motte, Otter Creek, Butler, District No. 3 and many other places in Jackson Co., a similar state of things exists."—*The Public Schools and Their Foes.* Fifth Address. [Dubuque, Iowa, 1890, 46 pp.]

[17] [John Ireland, "State Schools and Parish Schools—Is Union between them impossible?" *NEA Journal of Proceedings and Addresses, 1890* (Topeka, Kansas, 1890), p. 181.]

great truths be taught to children without their minds being perplexed with clashing doctrines and sectarian controversies? Most certainly they can." [18]

Such an amount of religious instruction would not be deemed adequate in an ideal society. But we must deal with society as it actually exists, and existing society is not ideal. As long as men think differently and have different and conflicting interests, society must be a compromise.

Of course parents and the Church may give as much added instruction as they wish, but for the State to go beyond the inculcation of the fundamental truths common to all monotheistic religions would probably lead to the division of the school fund, which would be a great calamity. On the other hand, to secularize the schools is to invite the corruption of popular morals and thus endanger the very foundations of our free institutions. Moreover, the secularists are unwittingly playing into the hands of those who desire a division of the school funds and the destruction of our existing school system. Most Protestant immigrants have been trained in denominational schools. The Lutherans, who number 1,000,000, naturally incline to them; and there are many other Protestants so deeply impressed with the necessity of religious instruction in the schools that rather than see them secularized, they would favor denominational schools supported by the State.

The great danger now is that between the upper and nether millstones of Romanism and Secularism, all religion will be ground out of our public schools. And this danger is greater in the West than in the East, for, as we have already seen, Romanism is relatively much stronger west of the Mississippi than east of it, and as we shall see later (Chap. XII.) evangelical church membership is much weaker.

[18] *Works of Daniel Webster*, VI, 161. [See above, n. 11.]

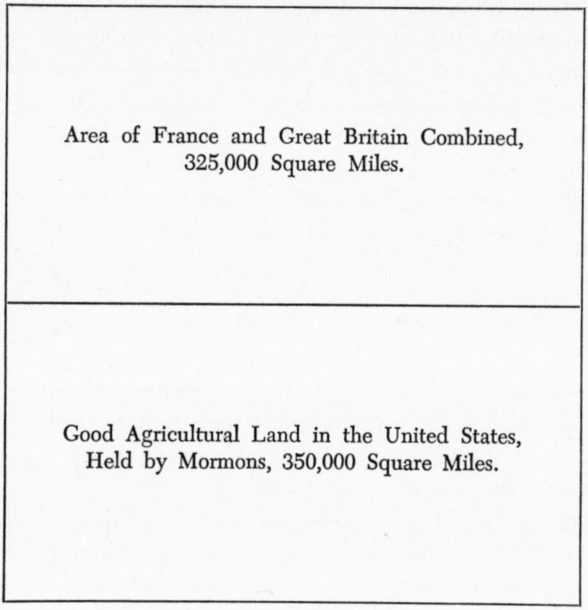

Area of France and Great Britain Combined, 325,000 Square Miles.
Good Agricultural Land in the United States, Held by Mormons, 350,000 Square Miles.

CHAPTER VII

PERILS—MORMONISM

The people of the United States are more sensible of the disgrace of Mormonism than of its danger. The civilized world wonders that such a hideous caricature of the Christian religion should have appeared in this most enlightened land; that such an anachronism should have been produced by the most progressive civilization; that the people who most honor womankind should be the ones to inflict on her this deep humiliation and outrageous wrong. Polygamy, as the most striking feature of the Mormon monster, attracts the public eye. It is this which at the same time arouses interest and indignation; and it is because of this that Europe points at us the finger of shame. Polygamy has been the issue between the Mormons and the United States government. It is this which has prevented the admission of Utah as a state. It is this against which Congress has legislated. And yet, polygamy is not an essential part of Mormonism; it was an after-thought; not a root, but a graft. There is a large and growing sect of the Mormons,[1] not located in Utah, which would excommunicate a member for practicing it. Nor is polygamy a very large part of Mormonism. Only a small minority practice it. Moreover, it can never become general among the "saints," for nature has legislated on that point, and her laws admit of no evasions. In Utah, as elsewhere, there are more males born than females; and, in the membership of the Mormon Church there are several thousand more men than women.

Polygamy might be utterly destroyed, without seriously weakening Mormonism. It has served to strengthen the system somewhat by thoroughly entangling its victim in the Mormon net; for a polygamist is not apt to apostatize. He has multiplied his "hostages to fortune;" he cannot abandon helpless wives and children as easily as he might turn away from pernicious doctrines. Moreover, he has arrayed himself against the government with law-breakers. Franklin's saying to the signers of the Declaration of Independence is appropriately put into the mouths of this class: "If we don't hang together, we shall all hang separately." Still, it may be questioned whether polygamy has added more of strength or weakness; for its evil results doubtless have often led the children of such marriages, and many others, to question the faith, and finally abandon it.

What, then, is the real strength of Mormonism? It is ecclesiastical despotism which holds it together, unifies it, and makes it strong. The Mormon Church is probably the most complete organization in the world. To look after a Mormon population

[1] The Josephites, scattered through the United States, are law-abiding citizens, deluded, but inoffensive. They are now said to number 25,000.

of 165,218 there are 31,577 officials, or one to every five persons.[2] And, so highly centralized is the power, that all of these threads of authority are gathered into one hand, that of the president. The priesthood, of which he is the head, claim the right to control in all things religious, social, industrial, and political. Brigham Young asserted his right to manage in every particular, "from the setting up of a stocking to the ribbons on a woman's bonnet." Here is a claim to absolute and universal rule, which is cheerfully conceded by every orthodox "saint." Mormonism therefore, is not simply a church, but a state; an "*imperium in imperio*" ruled by a man who is prophet, priest, king and pope, all in one—a pope, too, who is not one whit less infallible than he who wears the tiara. And, as one would naturally expect of an American pope, and especially of an enterprising Western pope, he out-popes the Roman by holding familiar conversations with the Almighty, and getting, to order, new revelations direct from heaven; and, another advantage which is more material, he keeps a firm hold of his temporal power. Indeed, it looks as if the spiritual were being subordinated to the temporal. Rev. W. M. Barrows, D.D., after a residence at the Mormon capital of nearly eight years, said: "There is no doubt that it is becoming less and less a religious power, and more and more a political power. The first Mormon preachers were ignorant fanatics, but most of them were honest, and their words carried a weight that sincerity always carries, even in a bad cause. The preachers now have the ravings of the Sibyl, but lack the inspiration. Their talk sounds hollow; the ring of sincerity is gone. But their eyes are dazzled now with the vision of an earthly empire. They have gone back to the old Jewish idea of a temporal kingdom, and they are endeavoring to set up such a kingdom in the valleys of Utah, and Idaho and

[2] In 1889 the Mormon Church officially reported its officers and membership in all the world as follows: Apostles, 12; patriarchs, 70; high priests, 3,919; elders, 11,805; priests, 2,069; teachers, 2,292; deacons, 11,610; families, 81,899; children under eight years of age, 49,303; total Mormon population (which does not include the "Josephites"), 165,218.

Montana, Wyoming, Colorado and New Mexico, Arizona and Nevada."[3]

If there be any doubt as to the designs of the Mormons, let the testimony of Bishop Lunt be conclusive on that point. He said in 1880: "Like a grain of mustard seed was the truth planted in Zion; and it is destined to spread through all the world. Our Church has been organized only fifty years, and yet behold its wealth and power. This is our year of jubilee. We look forward with perfect confidence to the day when we will hold the reins of the United States government. That is our present temporal aim; after that, we expect to control the continent." When told that such a scheme seemed rather visionary, in view of the fact that Utah cannot gain recognition as a state, the Bishop replied: "Do not be deceived; we are looking after that. We do not care for these territorial officials sent out to govern us. They are nobodies here. We do not recognize them, neither do we fear any practical interference by Congress. We intend to have Utah recognized as a state. To-day we hold the balance of political power in Idaho, we rule Utah absolutely, and in a very short time we will hold the balance of power in Arizona and Wyoming. A few months ago, President Snow of St. George, set out with a band of priests, for an extensive tour through Colorado, New Mexico, Wyoming, Montana, Idaho and Arizona to proselyte. We also expect to send missionaries to some parts of Nevada, and we design to plant colonies in Washington Territory.

"In the past six months we have sent more than 3,000 of our people down through the Sevier Valley to settle in Arizona, and the movement still progresses. All this will build up for us a political power, which will, in time, compel the homage of the demagogues of the country. Our vote is solid, and will remain so. It will be thrown where the most good will be accomplished for the church. Then, in some great political crisis, the two present political parties will bid for our support. Utah

[3] Address at the Home Missionary Anniversary, in Chicago, June 8, 1881. [Walter M. Barrows, "How Shall the Mormon Question Be Settled?" *Home Missionary,* 54 (October 1881), 165.]

will then be admitted as a polygamous state, and the other territories we have peacefully subjugated will be admitted also. We will then hold the balance of power, and will dictate to the country. In time, our principles, which are of sacred origin, will spread throughout the United States. We possess the ability to turn the political scale in any particular community we desire. Our people are obedient. When they are called by the Church, they promptly obey. They sell their houses, lands and stock, and remove to any part of the country the Church may direct them to. You can imagine the results which wisdom may bring about, with the assistance of a church organization like ours."

Since these words were uttered the United States government has made itself felt in "Zion," and its officers are no longer "nobodies" in Utah; but the astute bishop does not over-estimate the effectiveness of the Mormon Church as a colonizer. An order is issued by the authorities that a certain district shall furnish so many hundred emigrants for Arizona or Idaho. The families are drafted, so many from a ward; and each ward or district equips its own quota with wagons, animals, provisions, implements, seed and the like. Thus the Mormon president can mass voters here or there about as easily as a general can move his troops.

By means of this systematic colonization the Mormons have gained possession of vast tracts of land, and now "hold almost all the soil fit for agriculture from the Rocky Mountains to the Sierra Nevada, or an area not less than 500 miles by 700, making 350,000 square miles;" [4] that is one-sixth of the entire acreage between the Mississippi and Alaska. In this extended region it is designed to plant a Mormon population sufficiently numerous to control it. With this in view, the Church sends out from 200 to 400 missionaries a year, most of whom labor in Europe. They generally return after two years of service at their own charges. In 1849 the "Perpetual Emigration Fund" was founded for the purpose of assisting converts who were too

[4] Rev. D. L. Leonard, late Home Missionary Superintendent for Utah, Idaho, Montana, and West Wyoming.

poor to reach "Zion" unaided. During the first ten years after the founding of this fund the annual average was 750; for the next decade it was 2,000; from 1880 to 1885 the number ranged from 2,500 to 3,000; since 1885 it has gradually decreased. The losses by apostasy [5] are many, but are more than covered by the number of converts, while the natural increase of the Church by the growth of the family is exceedingly large. Furthermore, to the growing power of multiplying numbers is added that of rapidly increasing wealth. The Mormons are industrious—a lazy man cannot enter their heaven—and the tithing of the increase adds constantly to the vast sums already gathered in the grasping hands of the hierarchy. The Mormon delegate to Congress, who carries a hundred thousand votes in one hand, and millions of corruption money in the other, will prove a dangerous man in Washington, unless politicians grow strangely virtuous, and there are fewer itching palms twenty years hence.

Those best acquainted with Mormonism seem most sensible of the danger which it threatens. The pastors of churches and principals of schools in Salt Lake City, in an address to American citizens, say: "We recognize the fact that the so-called Mormon church, in its exercise of political power, is antagonistical to American institutions, and that there is an irrepressible conflict between Utah Mormonism and American republicanism; so much so that they can never abide together in harmony. We also believe that the growth of this anti-

[5] We may learn ere long that there is as little occasion for congratulation over Mormon apostasy as over Roman Catholic. The Mormon, in his mental make-up, is a distinct type. There are men in every community who were born for the Mormon Church. Let one of the missionaries of the "Saints" appear, and he attracts this class as naturally as a magnet attracts iron filings in a handful of sand. They are waiting to hear and believe some new thing; they are driven about by every wind of doctrine; they have probably been members of several different religious denominations; they are credulous and superstitious, and are easily led in the direction of their inclinations; they love reasoning, but hate reason; they are capable of a blind devotion, and strongly incline to fanaticism. In a word, they are *cranky*. A church largely made up of such material will, of course, multiply apostates. The Mormon Church is a machine which manufactures tinder for anarchistic fire.

republican power is such that, if not checked speedily, it will cause serious trouble in the near future. We fear that the nature and extent of this danger are not fully comprehended by the nation at large." [6]

If the Mormon power had its seat in an established commonwealth like Ohio, such an ignorant and fanatical population, rapidly increasing, and under the absolute control of unscrupulous leaders, who openly avowed their hostility to the State, and lived in contemptuous violation of its laws, would be a disturbing element which would certainly endanger the peace of society. Indeed, the Mormons, when much less powerful than they are to-day, could not be tolerated in Missouri or Illinois. And Mormonism is tenfold more dangerous in the new West, where its power is greater, because the "Gentile" population is less; where it has abundant room to expand; where, in a new and unorganized society, its complete organization is the more easily master of the situation; and where state constitutions and laws, yet unformed, and the institutions of society, yet plastic, are subject to its molding influence.

And what are we going to do about it? Something can be done by legislation, though it has proved less effective than was expected. From the first enactment of antipolygamy laws by Congress in 1882 down to September 1, 1889, only twenty-four convictions had been secured [7] while sixty-seven men are known to have entered into polygamy during the single year ending June, 1887. There were, however, 909 convictions for unlawful cohabitation, under the Edmunds Law, from 1882 to 1889. But this number is only five per cent of those known to be guilty.[8] The governor of the territory, Hon. A. L. Thomas, who is thoroughly acquainted with the situation, says, "The government has been for years well represented by able and efficient officers, and the result has been important, but not

[6] ["To the Patriotic Citizens of America,"] in J. M. Coyner, ed., *Hand-Book on Mormonism* (Hand-Book Publishing Co., Salt Lake City, Chicago and Cincinnati, 1882), p. 94.

[7] M. W. Montgomery, *The Mormon Delusion* (Boston, 1890), p. 292.

[8] Montgomery, *Mormon Delusion*, p. 293.

decisive. This course [vigorous prosecution] has not changed opinion, but has caused greater care in concealing offenses." [9]

Wilford Woodruff, the President of the Mormon Church has recently issued a proclamation in which he says: "Inasmuch as laws have been enacted by Congress forbidding plural marriages, which laws have been pronounced constitutional by the court of last resort, I do hereby declare my intention to submit to those laws and to use my influence with the members of the Church over which I preside to have them do likewise." [10]

If this declaration was made in good faith, it would probably mean that polygamy is to be abandoned, at least for a time. It is, however, the well-nigh universal opinion of Gentiles in Salt Lake City that this manifesto was a mere trick intended for obvious reasons to hoodwink the public. We have seen that polygamy might be destroyed without seriously weakening Mormonism; indeed, its destruction, by allaying suspicion, by creating the impression that the Mormon problem is solved, and by removing the obstacle to Utah's admission as a state, might materially strengthen Mormonism. Any blow to be really effective must be aimed at the priestly despotism.

The political power of the hierarchy has been in some measure curtailed by two decisions of the Supreme Court rendered February 3, 1890.[11] One decision [12] sustains the constitutionality of the law of Idaho which disfranchises all who are "members of any order, organization, or association which teaches, advises, counsels, or encourages its members or devotees or any other persons to commit the crime of bigamy or polygamy." A similar law in Utah would undoubtedly be sustained by the Supreme Court, but of course such a law can never be enacted so long as the Mormons control the territorial legislature.

[9] A. L. Thomas, *Report of the Governor of Utah, 1889* (Washington, D.C., 1889), p. 29.

[10] [*President W. Woodruff's Manifesto,* Proceedings at the Semi-Annual General Conference of the Church of Christ of Latter-Day Saints (Oct. 6, 1890), p. 2.]

[11] [Strong is in error here. The two cases to which he refers were decided on February 3, 1890, and on May 19, 1890, respectively.]

[12] [Davis v. Beason, 133 US 333.]

The other decision [13] of the Court sustained the constitutionality of an act of Congress, passed in 1887, by which the territorial charter of the Mormon Church was repealed, the corporation dissolved and its property, in excess of $50,000, escheated to the United States, to be used for the support of public schools in Utah. Under this law a receiver took possession of nearly $1,000,000 worth of property. The power of the hierarchy has been enhanced by the great wealth of the church. The sequestration of that wealth, therefore, must in some measure disable the hierarchy. But the power of the priesthood existed before that wealth was accumulated. It was their power which made such accumulation possible. This blow, therefore, does not go to the root of the matter. Indeed, it is liable to strengthen Mormonism as much on one side as it weakens it on another, for the public schools are taught almost wholly by Mormons, and this great sum of money will, therefore, be applied to teach Mormon doctrines unless Congress places the public schools of the territory under the control of the United States. If this were done and all Mormons were disfranchised as they should be (excepting of course the Josephites, who are loyal), much time and labor would yet be required to complete the work. "Let him who thinks that the Mormon problem is almost solved be undeceived. Even when Congress and the courts shall have done their utmost, it will take half a century yet of the gospel in the hands of missionaries and teachers to dig up the roots of this evil. The public has not yet grasped the proportions of this problem. The present laws and Christian forces at work in Utah still have a problem before them much like that which a single company of sappers and miners would have who should undertake to dig down the Wahsatch Mountain range with pick and spade." [14]

The secret power of the system is the people's belief in the divine inspiration, and hence infallibility of the priesthood. This is a veritable Pandora's box out of which may spring any pos-

[13] [The Late Corporation of the Church of Jesus Christ of Latter-Day Saints v. United States, 136 US 1.]
[14] Montgomery, *Mormon Delusion*, p. 349.

sible delusion or excess. Said Heber C. Kimball, formerly one of the Apostles:

"The word of our Leader and Prophet is the word of God to this people. We can not see God. We can not hold converse with him. But he has given us a man that we can talk to and thereby know his will, just as well as if God himself were present with us." Special "revelations" to the head of the church, even if directly contrary to the Scriptures, or the Book of Mormon, are absolutely binding. The latter says: "Wherefore I, the Lord God, will not suffer that this people do like unto them of old; wherefore, my brethren, hear me, and hearken to the word of the Lord. For there shall not any man among you have save it be one wife; and concubines he shall have none." [15] Yet a special "revelation" sufficed to establish polygamy. Mormon despotism, then, has its roots in the superstition of the people; and this Congress cannot legislate away. The people must be elevated and enlightened through the instrumentality of Christian education and the preaching of the gospel. This work is being effectively done by the various Christian denominations. It is *chiefly* to such agencies that we must look to break the Mormon power.

[15] Book of Jacob, ch. ii, verse 6.

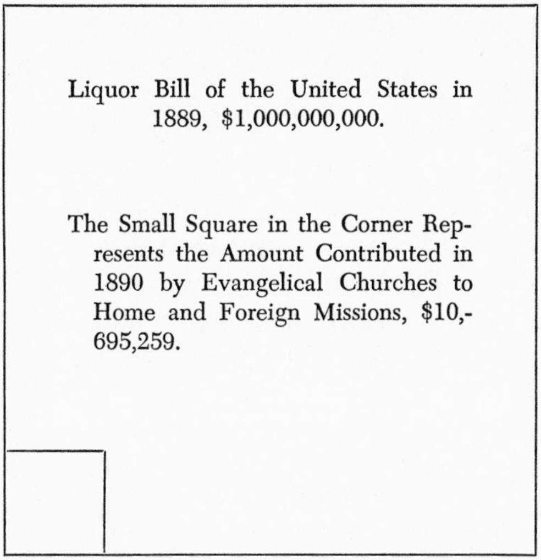

Liquor Bill of the United States in 1889, $1,000,000,000.

The Small Square in the Corner Represents the Amount Contributed in 1890 by Evangelical Churches to Home and Foreign Missions, $10,-695,259.

CHAPTER VIII

PERILS—INTEMPERANCE

To touch so vast a subject, and only touch it, is difficult. Let us consider briefly but two points—the danger of intemperance as enhanced by the progress of civilization, and the Liquor Power. I. The progress of civilization brings men into closer contact. The three great civilizing instrumentalities of the age, moral, mental and material, are Christianity, the press and steam, which respectively bring together men's hearts, minds and bodies into more intimate and multiplied relations. Christianity is slowly binding the race into a brotherhood. The press transforms the earth into an audience room; while the steam engine, so far as commerce is concerned, has annihilated, say, nine-tenths of space.

Observe how this bringing of men into closer and multiplied relations has served to increase the excitements of life, to quicken our rate of living. The Christian religion is an excitant. In proportion as it leads men to recognize and accept their responsibility for others, it arouses them to action in their behalf, under the stress of the most urgent motives. The press and telegraph, by bringing many minds into contact, have ministered marvelously to the activity of the popular intellect. Isolation tends to stagnation. Intercourse quickens thought, feeling, action. Steam has stimulated human activity almost to fury. By prodigiously lengthening the lever of human power, by bringing the country to the city, the inland cities to the seaboard, the seaports to each other, it has multiplied many-fold every form of intercourse. By establishing industries on an immense scale it has greatly complicated business; while severe and increasing competition demands closer study, a greater application of energy, a larger expenditure of mental power.

Thus it would seem that these three great forces of civilization move along parallel lines, and co-operate in stimulating the nations to an activity ever more intense and exciting; so that the progress of civilization seems to involve an increasing strain on the nervous system. These influences will be better appreciated if we compare, for a moment, ancient and modern civilization. Look at life in Athens, Jerusalem or Babylon, when they were centers of civilization, as compared with Paris, London, or New York. The chief men of an Oriental city might be found sitting in the gate gossiping, or possibly philosophizing. Those of an Occidental metropolis are deep in schemes of commerce, manufacture, politics or philanthropy, weaving plans whose threads reach out through all the land, and even to the ends of the earth. The Eastern merchant sits in his bazaar, as did his ancestor two or three thousand years ago, and chaffers with his customers by the hour over a trifle. The Western and modern business man is on his feet. The two attitudes are representative. Ancient civilization was sedentary and contemplative; ours is active and practical. "*Multum in parvo*" is its maxim. Immense results brought about in a few days, or even minutes, hurry the mind through a wide range of experience, and compress, it may be, years into hours. I am not at all sure that Abraham Lincoln did not live longer than Methuselah. In point of experience, results, acquisitions, enjoyment and sorrow—in all that makes up life, save the mere factor of time —I am not at all sure that the antediluvians were not the children, and the men of this generation the aged patriarchs. And life is fuller and more intense, activity is more eager and restless here in the United States than anywhere else in the world. We work more days in a year, more hours in a day, and do more work in an hour than the most active people of Europe.[1]

If we were quite unacquainted with the results of this feverish activity of modern civilization, and especially of American civilization, reason would enable us to anticipate those results. Such excitements, such restless energy, such continued stress of the nerves, must, in course of a few generations, decidedly change the nervous organization of men. We know that the progress of civilization has refined temperaments, has rendered men more susceptible and sensitive. A tragedy that is a nine days' horror with us would hardly have attracted more than a passing glance in old Rome, whose gentle matrons made a holiday by attending gladiatorial shows, and seeing men kill each other for Roman sport at the rate of 10,000 in a single reign. And when brothers met in the arena, and lacked the nerve to strike each other down, red-hot irons were pressed against their naked, quivering flesh to goad them on, while these same mothers shouted, "Kill!" We complain sometimes that modern life has become too largely one of feeling. It is true the many live lives of impulse, rather than of principle; but it is also true that the springs of human sympathy were never so easily touched as now. Such wide differences in men's sensibilities argue not only a difference of education, but a change in the world's nerves.[2]

[1] These statements could be abundantly confirmed, but it is presumed they will not be doubted. The point will be further developed in a later chapter.

[2] Since writing the above, I find the following sentence in George M. Beard, *American Nervousness* (New York, 1881), p. 118: "Fineness of

Physicians tell us that going from the equator north, and from the arctic regions south, nervous disorders increase until a climax is reached in the temperate zone. An eminent physician of New York, the late Dr. George M. Beard, who has made nervous diseases a speciality, says that they are comparatively rare in Spain, Italy and the northern portions of Europe, also in Canada and the Gulf States, but very common in our Northern States and in Central Europe. And this belt, it will be observed, coincides exactly with the zone of the world's greatest activity; and further, where this activity is greatest; viz., in the United States, these nervous disorders are the most frequent. Dr. Beard begins an exceedingly interesting work [3] on nervous exhaustion with these sentences: "There is a large family of functional nervous disorders that are increasingly frequent among the indoor classes of civilized countries, and that are especially frequent in the northern and eastern parts of the United States. The sufferers from these maladies are counted in this country by thousands and hundreds of thousands; in all the Northern and Eastern States they are found in nearly every brain-working household." After speaking of certain numerous and widespread nervous diseases among us, he adds: "In Europe these affections are but little known." They are all diseases of civilization, and of modern civilization, and mainly of the nineteenth century, and of the United States. "Neurasthenia," which is the name he gives to nervous exhaustion, "is," he says, "comparatively a modern disease, its symptoms surprisingly more frequent now than in the last century, and is an American disease, in this, that it is very much more common here than in any other part of the civilized world." [4]

When we consider that the increased activity of modern civilization is attended by new and increasing nervous disorders, that the belt of prevalent nervous diseases coincides

---

organization, which is essential to the development of the civilization of modern times, is accompanied by intensified mental susceptibility."

[3] Entitled Neurasthenia. [See n. 4.]

[4] [George M. Beard, *A Practical Treatise on Nervous Exhaustion* (*Neurasthenia*), 2nd and rev. ed. (New York, 1880), pp. 1–9, *passim.*]

exactly with that of the world's greatest activity, and further, that in this belt, where the activity is by far the most intense, nervous affections are by far the most common, it is evident that the intensity of modern life has already worked, and continues to work, important changes in men's nervous organization. The American people are rapidly becoming the most nervous, the most highly organized, in the world, if, indeed, they are not already such. And the causes, climatic and other, which have produced this result, continue operative.

Be it observed now that nervous people are exposed to a double danger from intoxicating liquors. In the first place, they are more likely than others to desire stimulants. Says Dr. Beard: "When the nervous system loses, through any cause, much of its nervous force, so that it cannot stand upright with ease and comfort, it leans on the nearest and most convenient artificial support that is capable of temporarily propping up the enfeebled frame. Anything that gives ease, sedation, oblivion, such as chloral, chloroform, opium or alcohol, may be resorted to at first as an incident, and finally as a habit. Such is the philosophy of opium and alcohol inebriety. Not only for the relief of pain, but for the relief of exhaustion, deeper and more distressing than pain, do both men and women resort to the drug shop. I count this one of the great causes of the recent increase of opium[5] and alcohol inebriety among women."[6]

As a nation grows more nervous, its use of intoxicating liquors increases. In Great Britain, Belgium, Holland and Germany, which are the European countries lying in the nervous belt, there has been a marked increase in the use of alcohol during the last half century. Since 1840, its consumption in Belgium has increased 238 per cent. In 1869 there were 120,000 saloons in Prussia; in 1880 there were 165,000. From 1831 to 1872, while the population (not including recent annexations) increased 53 per cent, whiskey saloons increased 91 per cent.

[5] There were imported into the United States in 1869, 90,997 pounds of opium; in 1874, 170,706 pounds; in 1877, 230,102 pounds; during the fiscal year ending 1880, 553,451 pounds; an increase of more than sixfold in eleven years.

[6] [Beard, *A Practical Treatise,* p. 49.]

For all Germany, the increase in consumption of spirituous liquors, per caput, from 1872 to 1875, was 23.5 per cent. It appears, however, that there was a decrease in the amount used per caput from 1.27 gallons in 1872 to 1.09 gallons in 1887. But during the same period the amount of beer consumed increased from 21.50 gallons per caput to 24.99 gallons.[7] In Great Britain, during the year 1800, a population of 15,000,000 consumed a little less than 12,000,000 gallons of spirits. Fifty years later, a population of 27,000,000 consumed 28,000,000 gallons. In 1874, a population of 32,000,000 consumed 41,000,000 gallons. That is, while the population increased 113 per cent, the consumption of spirituous liquors increased 241 per cent. From 1868 to 1877, while the population increased less than ten per cent, the amount of spirituous liquors consumed increased thirty-seven per cent. During the next ten years the amount of spirits used per caput somewhat decreased; but the Chancellor of the Exchequer in his statement of English finances in April, 1890, said that the revenue from alcoholic beverages showed a universal rush to the beer barrel, the spirit bottle and the wine decanter. "In 1888 the number of drams taken reached 245,000,000; in 1889, 275,000,000,"—an increase of twelve per cent.

The following table [8] shows the number of gallons of liquor consumed for all purposes in the United States in 1840, 1860 and in 1888:

	Distilled Spirits	*Wine*	*Malt Liquors*
1840	43,060,884	4,873,096	23,310,843
1860	89,968,651	11,059,141	101,346,669
1888	75,845,352	36,335,068	767,587,056

[7] See *The Cyclopedia of Temperance and Prohibition* (New York, 1891), p. 133, and *Statistisches Jahrbuch für das Deutsche Reich* (Berlin, 1880 ff.).

[8] From the *Quarterly Report of the Chief of the U.S. Bureau of Statistics, for the three months ending March 31, 1889* (Washington, D.C., 1889), p. 571, and from Spofford's *American Almanac for 1889* (New York, 1889), p. 51. [Strong took the 1840 and 1860 figures of gallons of liquor consumed from Spofford's *Almanac*. The figures for 1880 as well as those of the *per caput* consumption were taken from the *Quarterly Report*. The editor has made minor corrections of the *per caput* figures.]

Gallons consumed for all purposes, per caput:

	Spirits	*Wines*	*Malt Liquors*	*All*
1840	2.52	.29	1.36	4.17
1860	2.86	.35	3.22	6.43
1888	1.23	.59	12.48	14.30

The steady increase in the use of wine and beer per caput, since 1840 is very marked, and the decrease in the use of whiskey since 1860 is equally so. It has been argued by the brewers and others that beer and wine have proved a blessing by driving out to a great extent the use of spirituous liquors, and that there is now less alcohol used as a beverage per caput than there was half a century ago. Let us see if this position will bear examination.

Reducing these several liquors to alcohol, we find that the people of the United States consumed for all purposes, 1.51 gallons of alcohol per caput in 1840, 1.79 gallons in 1860, and 1.27 gallons in 1888. In order to a correct interpretation of these figures it must be remembered that formerly a large proportion of the whiskey consumed was used in manufactures. But after the heavy Internal Revenue tax was imposed, the price of whiskey per gallon rose seventeen-fold in three years, which drove it out of manufactures, for the most part. David A. Wells, as chairman of a commission to revise the whole Internal Revenue system, reported in 1866; "In some instances entire branches of business have been destroyed in consequence of the great advance in the price of alcohol." In other instances substitutes for alcohol were found. Mr. Wells estimates that in 1860, 25,000,000 gallons of proof spirits were consumed in the preparation of burning fluid. "Since 1862," he adds, "the production and consumption of burning fluid have almost entirely ceased." The commission said: "We are inclined to consider the estimate of a gallon and a half per head for the consumption of the United States (of spirits as a beverage) as somewhat exaggerated." [9] But taking this "exagger-

[9] [David A. Wells, *et al.*, *Reports of a Commission Appointed for a Revision of the Revenue System of the United States, 1865–66* (Washington, D.C., 1866), pp. 155–168, *passim.*]

ated estimate," we find that in 1840 there were .93 of a gallon of alcohol used per caput as a beverage and in 1860, 1.01 gallons. Most of the spirits now consumed in the United States are used as a beverage, but allowing ten per cent for use in the arts we, in 1888, consumed in our beverages 1.2 gallons of alcohol per caput. That is, the increased consumption of beer and wine has been accompanied by an increased use of alcohol.

Thus it appears that during the last half century or longer, in those countries lying in the nervous belt, the use of intoxicating drinks as a beverage has increased *per caput.* The full significance of this fact appears only when we remember that early in this century liquors were on every side-board, and conscientious scruples against their moderate use were almost unheard of, while to-day there are many millions of teetotalers both in this country and in Great Britain. Especially during the past twenty-five years, the temperance reform has made wonderful progress, and the proportion of teetotalers is much greater to-day than ever before. And yet there is more liquor used per caput now than formerly; showing, conclusively, that there is much more of excess now than then; declaring that, *as a nation grows nervous, those who drink at all are more apt to drink immoderately.*

Again, in the second place, men of nervous organization are not only more likely than others to use alcohol, and to use it to excess, but its effects in their case are worse and more rapid. The wide difference between a nervous and a phlegmatic temperament accounts for the fact that one man will kill himself with drink in four or five years, and another in forty or fifty. The phlegmatic man is but little sensitive to stimulus; hence, when its influence wears off, there is little reaction. He, accordingly, forms the appetite slowly, and the process of destruction is slow. Another man, of fine nervous organization, takes a glass of spirits, and every nerve in his body tingles and leaps. The reaction is severe, and the nerves cry out for more. The appetite, rapidly formed, soon becomes uncontrollable, and the miserable end is not long delayed. The higher development of the nervous system, which comes with the progress of civilization, renders men more sensitive to pain, more susceptible to the evil results which attend excess of any kind. Savages may, almost with impunity, transgress laws of health which would inflict on civilized men, for like transgression, penalties well-nigh or quite fatal. It would seem as if God intended that, as men sin against the greater light which comes with increasing civilization, they should suffer severer punishment.

It has been shown that the use of intoxicants is more dangerous for this generation than it has been for any preceding generation; that it is more dangerous for inhabitants of the nervous belt than for the remainder of mankind; that it is more dangerous for the people of the United States than for other inhabitants of this belt. It remains to be shown that it is more dangerous for the people of the West than for those of the East.

Among the principal causes which are operative to render the typical American temperament more nervous than the European is the greater dryness of our climate. "Dr. Max von Pettenkofer has concluded, from the investigations he has made into the comparative loss of heat experienced by a person breathing dry air and one breathing damp air, that with the dry air more heat is lost and more created, and, in consequence, the circulation is quicker and more intense, life is more energetic, and there is no opportunity for the excessive accumulation of fat or flesh, or for the development of a phlegmatically nervous temperament."[10] The mountain region of the West has by far the driest atmosphere of any portion of the country. The writer has often seen Long's Peak by moonlight at a distance of eighty miles. The wonderful transparency of that mountain air is due to the absence of moisture. Such a climate is itself a wine, and life in it is greatly intensified, with corresponding results in the nervous system. We should, accordingly, expect to find a marked increase of intemperance. And such is the case. In the Mississippi Valley, where the altitude is low, and the atmosphere moist there is much less intemperance than in the mountains, as appears from the ratio of voters to saloons.

[10] C. Edward Young, as quoted in the *Popular Science Monthly,* 17 (September 1880), 705.

Take the tier of states and territories next east of the Rocky Mountain range. In 1880, Dakota had 95 voters to every saloon;[11] Nebraska, 133; Kansas, 224; and Texas, 136. But notice the change as soon as we reach the high altitudes. Montana had only 28 voters to each saloon; Wyoming, 43; Colorado, 37; New Mexico, 26; Arizona, 25; Utah, 84; Idaho, 35; Washington, 68; Oregon, 58; California, 37; and Nevada, 32. The average for the states between the Mississippi and the Rocky Mountains was one saloon to every 112.5 voters. In the eleven mountain states and territories, the average was one saloon to every 43 voters. East of the Mississippi, the average was one saloon to every 107.7 voters. If our assumption that the ratio of saloons to voters correctly measures intemperance, is just, the people in the western third of the United States are two and one-half times as intemperate as those in the eastern two-thirds. There are several causes for this, some of which are more or less temporary; but one of the chief influences is climatic, which will continue operative.

We have seen that the progress of civilization brings men into more intimate relations, that closer contact quickens activity, that increased activity refines the nervous system, and that a highly nervous organization invites intemperance, and at the same time renders its destructive results swifter and more fatal. Thus the very progress of civilization renders men the easier victims of intemperance. We have also seen that under regulation the liquor traffic increases more rapidly than the population. The alternative, then, seems simple, clear, certain, that civilization must *destroy* the liquor traffic or be destroyed by it. Even here in the East, this death struggle is desperate, and no man looks for an easy victory over the dragon. What,

[11] Statistics compiled from Census of 1880, and Internal Revenue of same year. For this comparison the statistics of 1880 are preferable to those of 1890, because during this interval prohibitory laws have been adopted in several of these states. The number of saloons was doubtless much larger than was reported by the Census; but for comparison between the East and West, or the city and country, the Census statistics answer every purpose.

then, of the far West, where the relative power of the saloon is two and a half times greater?

II—THE LIQUOR POWER

The liquor traffic, of course, implies two parties, the buyer and the seller. The preceding discussion relates to the former, only a few words touching the latter. According to the Report of the Commissioner of Internal Revenue there were 184,889 liquor dealers and manufacturers in the United States in 1889. Their saloons, allowing twenty-two feet front to each, would reach in an unbroken line from Chicago to New York. There is invested in this business an immense capital. It is impossible to determine how much, but it certainly amounts to hundreds of millions of dollars. In an address in the House of Representatives, in favor of the Bonded Whiskey Bill, Hon. P. V. Deuster, of Wisconsin, member of Congress, and special champion of the liquor dealers, said that the total market value of the spirituous, malt, and vinous liquors produced in 1883 was $490,961,588. It is now estimated that the annual liquor bill of the nation is $1,000,000,000. So great wealth in the hands of one class, having common interests and a common purpose, is a mighty power.

And this power does not lack organization. Its success at Washington a few years since in securing legislation which granted to whiskey makers peculiar privileges, accorded to no other tax payers, is sufficient evidence of their influence. The United States Brewers' Association was organized in 1862. The object of the organization may be inferred from the introduction to their constitution, where we read: "That the owners of breweries, separately, are unable to exercise a proper influence in the interest of the craft in the legislature and public administration." How this "proper influence" is brought to bear upon legislatures will appear later. That it is potent there can be no doubt. At the Brewers' Congress, held in Buffalo, July 8, 1868, President Clausen, speaking of the action of the New York branch of the association, relative to the excise law of the state, said: "Neither means nor money were spared during the past twelve months to accomplish the repeal of this detested law. The entire German population were enlisted." "Editorials favorable to the repeal were published in sixty different English and German newspapers. Just before the election, 30,000 campaign circulars were distributed among the Germans of the different counties. A state convention of brewers, hop and malt dealers, hop growers, etc., was largely attended, and resolutions were adopted in which we pledged ourselves to support only such candidates who bound themselves to work for the repeal of the excise law, and thereby check the exertions of the temperance party. These resolutions were published, principally through the English press, in all the counties of the state. By these efforts the former minority in the Assembly was changed to a majority of twenty votes in our favor." The object of this association is not industrial, but avowedly political. The president said, at the Chicago Congress, in 1867: "Only by union in brotherly love it will be possible to attain such results, guard against oppressive laws, raise ourselves to be a large and wide-spread political power and with confidence anticipate complete success in all our undertakings." Again at Davenport, in 1870, President Clausen said: "Unity is necessary, and we must form an organization that not only controls a capital of two hundred million dollars, but which also commands thousands of votes, politically, through which our legislators will discern our power." At the Chicago Congress, the brewers resolved: "That we consider it absolutely necessary that our organization should exist in every state and county." The following resolution was passed by the Liquor Dealers and Manufacturers' Association of Illinois, in 1881: "*Resolved,* That the maintenance and perfection of our present State Association is absolutely necessary for the proper protection of our business interests; that the new Board of Trustees spare neither trouble nor expense to properly organize every senatorial district in the state, so that, by the time of the next election of members of the General Assembly, the business men engaged in the liquor trade may be thoroughly organized and disciplined." The liquor trade boasts that in New York City alone it controls 40,000 votes. That the saloons are the great centers of political activity is evident from the fact that out of 1,002 primary and other political meetings held in New York during the year preceding the November election of 1884, 633 were held in saloons and 96 were held next door to saloons, while only 283 were held apart from them.[12] These saloons and their keepers are controlled by a few strong men. In 1888, of the saloons in New York City, 4,710 were subject to chattel mortgages, which aggregated $4,959,578 in value. An overwhelming proportion of these mortgages were held by brewers, one firm holding upwards of 200, and another 600; which being interpreted means that two firms controlled upwards of 800 centers of political influence in New York.[13]

Let us now look at some of the methods of the Liquor Power. The brewers favor boycotting. The following resolution was passed at their seventh congress: "*Resolved,* That we find it necessary, in a business point of view, to patronize only such business men as will work hand in hand with us." They expend money freely to accomplish their purpose at the polls. "By direct testimony from the liquor campaign managers it has been ascertained that in the Rhode Island contest of 1889, $31,000 was paid for the single object of manipulating the newspapers." "It is known that in the Amendment campaign in Pennsylvania in 1889, $200,000 was contributed in the city of Philadelphia alone" by the liquor dealers, while the brewers of New York added $100,000 more.[14] The liquor lobby at Albany, New York, at the session of 1878–9, admitted before a legislative committee that they had expended about $100,000 to influence legislation. From the confessions of an old liquor dealer and lobbyist we learn by what methods legislation at Albany was "influenced" a quarter of a century ago. After the election and before the legislature convened, "Our correspond-

[12] [Robert Graham, *New York City and Its Masters* (New York, 1887), p. 38.] Graham was Secretary of the Church Temperance Society.

[13] Robert Graham, *Chattel Mortgages on Saloon Fixtures* (New York, 1888).

[14] *The Cyclopedia of Temperance and Prohibition,* p. 382.

ents throughout the state gave us special and truthful descriptions of every one of the opposition members, their mode of life, their habits, their eccentricities and their religious views; whether they were approachable; with a thorough analysis of their characters in every way, so that we might understand our subjects in advance." If the stiff-necked legislator could not be induced to vote directly against temperance measures, or persuaded to "dodge," he must be convinced that he was sick, threatened with diphtheria or something else, and unable to leave his room. A sworn affidavit of the doctor to this effect cost "anywhere from $25 to $100, according to the size of the lie sworn to." These cases of sickness never proved fatal, and recovery was always rapid. "I well remember a senator who was in great distress about a mortgage that was being foreclosed on his house, amounting to about $1,500. This man's trouble came to the knowledge of the lobby. Suddenly one of the lobbyists was missing, and a few days later the senator received his canceled mortgage through the post. He never forgot the favor, nor did his vote do us any harm afterwards." Sometimes a member found an elegant suit of clothes hanging over a chair by his bedside in the morning; and sometimes a relative would be presented with a neat little house. Another popular method was for a member to receive a package by express from Troy, or some other town near by. "This package always contained a certain sum of money, and it was always so arranged that one of the lobby should be with the gentleman when the package came to hand. No receipt was ever taken from the sender in his real name, but the receiver gave the express company one in his real name. So we had all the evidence we needed, and the receiver dared not go back on the compact the transaction covered. From that moment he was at the mercy of the lobby." "If our tactics failed in the legislature, and temperance laws were passed, we went home to defeat their execution. The officers designated to execute these laws were generally elected. If by ourselves, it was all right. If by our opponents, we had to buy them up, and but few were found who would not take a bribe." "Although the liquor lobby, during the last forty years.

has used *millions of dollars in corrupt bargaining and bribery,* and never has made a secret of the fact, yet no member was ever caught in the act, and, it is fair to presume, no one ever will be. There is no way so dark they cannot find their road through." [15] Thus does the Liquor Power corrupt public morals and defeat the popular will.

And this power, which does not hesitate to buy votes or intimidate voters, to defy the law or bribe its officers, comes to its kingdom through political partisanship, which enables it to make one of the two great parties its slave, and the other its minister. Even in the cities the citizens who desire clean government are in the majority; but, instead of uniting to make and enforce good laws, they permit politics to enter into the elections, thus throwing the power into the hands of the bad minority. "There are two things," said D'Alembert, "that can reach the top of the pyramid—the eagle and the reptile." Under the rum government of our cities, the reptile climbs. In 1883, of the twenty-four aldermen of the city of New York, ten were liquor dealers and two others, including the President of the Board, were ex-rumsellers. Important offices in the city government, which pay a salary of $12,000 or $15,000, have within a few years been occupied by men who kept "bucket shops" and "all night" dens; some have been prize fighters, and others had been tried for the crime of murder. Is it strange if the law in the hands of such men is a dead letter? Says Anthony Comstock: [16] "I have no doubt many of our influential city politicians are in receipt of a regular revenue in the way of hush money from gambling-saloons, brothels and groggeries, and the word is passed all the way down the line to let them alone." The late Dr. Howard Crosby [17] said: "One of the captains of police is

[15] C. B. Cotton in *Voice* (February 5, 1885). [*The Voice* was a prohibition newspaper founded by the New York publishing house of Funk and Wagnalls in 1884.]

[16] [Anthony Comstock (1844–1915), reformer, was best known for his crusade against obscene literature, and for his campaign to exclude such literature from the U.S. mails.]

[17] [Howard Crosby (1826–1891), a Presbyterian clergyman in New York City, who founded and served as first president of the Society for the Prevention of Crime.]

said to have made $70,000 in one year by his carefulness in leaving the law breakers alone. Anybody with half an eye can see that the exemption of the liquor-selling law breakers from prosecution is a system and not an accident." "From Police Headquarters" he continues "goes forth the order, not written but verbal, that the police are not to enforce the excise law. *I have had my man on the force,* and can speak with knowledge of the facts. If a man is arrested for violating an excise law, the next morning the one who arrested him is called up, reprimanded, and the man arrested is discharged, while the policeman is transferred to some far-off district, the twenty-fourth ward, for instance—that Botany Bay of the police force—if he is not immediately discharged by those four men we call Commissioners." Says the *New York Times:* "The great underlying evil, which paralyzes every effort to get good laws, and to secure the enforcement of such as we have, is the system of local politics, which gives the saloon-keepers more power over government than is possessed by all the religious and educational institutions in the city."

Our cities are growing much more rapidly than the whole population, as is the liquor power also. If this power continues to keep the cities under its heel, what of the nation, when the city dominates the country? Such a powerful organization, resorting to such unscrupulous methods in the interest of legitimate business—mining, railroading—would be exceedingly dangerous in a republic; and the whole outcome of this traffic, pushed by such wealth, such organized energy and such means, is the corrupting of the citizen and the embruting of the man.

And if the liquor power is a peril at the East, what of the Rocky Mountain region and beyond, where mammonism is more abject, where there is less of Christian principle to resist the bribe, and where the relative power of the liquor traffic is two and a half times greater than at the East?

Average Expenses of Working Men's Families in Mass., in 1883, $754.42.
Average Earnings of Working Men, $558.68.

CHAPTER IX

PERILS—SOCIALISM

SOCIALISM attempts to solve the problem of suffering without eliminating the factor of sin. It says: "From each according to his abilities; to each according to his wants." But this dictum of Louis Blanc[1] could be realized only in a perfect society.

[1] [Louis Blanc (1811–1832), French politician and historian, who in 1848 unsuccessfully sought to eradicate unemployment with the help of the short-lived *Commission du Luxembourg,* an assembly of delegates from the workers of Paris.]

Forgetting, as Herbert Spencer remarks, that "there is no political alchemy by which you can get golden conduct out of leaden instincts," [2] socialism thinks to regenerate society without first regenerating the individual; or, perhaps more accurately, it proposes to transform the individual by transforming society, and expects to work this regeneration by reorganizing society on a co-operative, instead of a competitive, basis. It talks much of fraternity, but forgets what Maurice [3] finely said, that "there is no fraternity without a common father." There is, however, an increasing number of men who believe devoutly in the Fatherhood of God and the brotherhood of man—Christian men, who are quite willing to let the public call them socialists, if the public will let them define the word. The amount of socialistic coloring found in current literature shows how large a place socialism has gained in the popular thought. It is quite obvious that the number of those who sympathize deeply with the struggles of the poor and who are inclined to look toward socialism for a remedy has largely increased during recent years. There are many of this class who are identified with no socialistic organization and who cannot be enumerated.

Socialism attracts very different classes of men: some, Christian philanthropists, large-hearted and self-sacrificing; others, who are discontented with their lot and see no way of bettering it under the existing industrial system; others, who are discouraged or are smarting under grievances; and others also are envious, selfish, vicious and lawless. Socialists of the latter class are generally immigrants.

The despotism of the few and the wretchedness of the many have produced European socialism. It has been supposed that its doctrines could never obtain in this land of freedom and plenty; but there may be a despotism which is not political, and a discontent which does not spring from hunger. We have discovered that German socialism has been largely imported,

[2] [Herbert Spencer, "The Coming Slavery," *Contemporary Review,* 65 (April 1884), 482.]

[3] [Frederick Denison Maurice (1805–1872), Anglican divine and leader of the English Christian Socialists, served as principal of the London Working Men's College.]

has taken root, and is making a vigorous growth. Let us look at it as it appears in this country.

The Socialistic Labor Party and the Internationalists differ widely and are strongly opposed to each other. The one is the thin, the other the thick, end of the socialistic wedge. Both seek to overthrow existing social and economic institutions; both propose a co-operative form of production and exchange, as a substitute for the existing capitalistic and competitive system; both expect a great and bloody revolution; but they differ widely as to policy and extreme doctrines. The platform of the Socialistic Labor Party [4] contains much that is reasonable, and is well calculated to disciple American workmen. It does not, as a party, attack the family or religion, and is opposed to anarchy.

The Internationalists are divided into two parties: the International Working People's Association and the International Workmen's Association. The latter, known as the "Reds," are somewhat less violent than the former, the "Blacks." The "Black" Internationalists are anarchists, while many of the "Reds" are state socialists. "The International Workmen's Association is composed chiefly of English-speaking laborers, and its main strength is west of the Mississippi." [5]

The ideals of the International Working People's Association are "common property, socialistic production and distribution, the grossest materialism, free love, in all social arrangements perfect individualism, or, in other words, anarchy. Negatively expressed—Away with private property! Away with all authority! Away with the state! Away with the family! Away with religion!" [6] In the manifesto unanimously adopted by the Internationals at Pittsburg, occurs the following: "The church finally seeks to make complete idiots of the mass, and to make them forego the paradise on earth by promising them a ficti-

[4] See the document in Joseph Cook, *Socialism,* Boston Monday Lectures (Boston, 1880), pp. 20–22, and in Richard T. Ely, *The Labor Movement in America* (New York, 1886), pp. 366–370.

[5] Ely, *Labor Movement,* p. 253. To this book I am indebted for many quotations from the socialistic press.

[6] Ely, *Labor Movement,* p. 244.

tious heaven." *Truth,* published in San Francisco, says: "When the laboring men understand that the heaven which they are promised hereafter is but a mirage, they will knock at the door of the wealthy robber, with a musket in hand, and demand their share of the goods of this life now." *Freiheit,* the blasphemous paper of Herr Most,[7] thus concludes an article on the "Fruits of the Belief in God": "Religion, authority and state, are all carved out of the same piece of wood—to the Devil with them all!" The same sheet "advocates a new genealogy, traced from mothers, whose names, and not those of the fathers, descend to the children, since it is never certain who the father is." "Public and common upbringing of children," says Prof. Ely, "is likewise favored in the *Freiheit,* in order that the old family may completely abandon the field to free love." [8]

Having lost all faith in the ballot, the Internationals propose to carry out their "reforms" by force. The following is from the Pittsburg manifesto: "Agitation for the purpose of organization; organization for the purpose of rebellion. In these few words the ways are marked, which the workers must take if they want to be rid of their chains. . . . We could show, by scores of illustrations, that all attempts in the past to reform this monstrous system by peaceable means, such as the ballot, have been futile, and all such efforts in the future must necessarily be so. . . . There remains but one recourse—force!" [9]

The *Vorbote,* published in Chicago, glorifies dynamite as "the power which, in our hands, shall make an end of tyranny." [10] *Truth* says: "War to the palace, peace to the cottage, death to luxurious idleness. We have no moment to waste. Arm! I say, to the teeth! for the revolution is upon you." [11] An article

[7] [Johann Joseph Most (1846–1906), German-born socialist, turned to anarchism, and in 1883 established himself and his newspaper in New York City. He was the chief author of the Pittsburgh Declaration of Principles of the "Black" anarchists.]

[8] [Ely, *Labor Movement,* pp. 242–244, *passim.*]

[9] [Ely, *Labor Movement,* p. 254.]

[10] [Ely, *Labor Movement,* p. 255.]

[11] [From *Truth* (November 17, 1883), as quoted in Ely, *Labor Movement,* p. 256.]

in the *Freiheit*, entitled "Revolutionary Principles," contained the following: "He [the revolutionist] is the irreconcilable enemy of this world, and, if he continues to live in it, it is only that he may thereby more certainly destroy it. He knows only one science—namely, destruction. For this purpose he studies day and night. For him everything is moral which favors the triumph of the revolution, everything is immoral and criminal which hinders it. Day and night may he cherish only one thought, only one purpose—namely, inexorable destruction. While he pursues this purpose, without rest and in cold blood, he must be ready to die, and equally ready to kill every one with his own hands who hinders him in the attainment of this purpose." [12] There has been formed in the United States a society called "The Black Hand," which, in its proclamation, urges "the propaganda of deed in every form," and cries: "War to the knife!" The explosions in the Houses of Parliament and Tower of London called forth the following declarations at a meeting of socialists in Chicago: "This explosion has demonstrated that socialists can safely go into large congregations in broad daylight and explode their bombs.

"A little hog's grease and a little nitric acid make a terrible explosion. Ten cents' worth would blow a building to atoms.

"Dynamite can be made out of the dead bodies of capitalists as well as out of hogs.

"All Chicago can be set ablaze in a minute by electricity.

"Private property must be abolished, if we have to use all the dynamite there is, and blow ninety-nine hundredths of the people off the face of the earth." Such teachings bore their legitimate fruits in the massacre of the Chicago Haymarket, May 4, 1886.

At the time of the railroad riots, in 1877, which cost many lives, and not less than a hundred million dollars of property, and to quell which ten states, reaching from the Atlantic to

[12] [From *Die Freiheit* (March 18, 1883), as quoted in Ely, *Labor Movement*, pp. 259–260. The first sentence, as given by Ely, ends with the phrase: ". . . it only happens in order to destroy it with greater certainty."]

the Pacific, called on the President of the United States for troops, there were but few socialists among us, and they seem to have been taken unawares by the outbreak; but they will be prepared to make the most of the next. The following are stock phrases, found in all their publications: "Get ready for another 1877;" "Buy a musket for a repetition of 1877;" "Buy dynamite for a second 1877;" "Organize companies and drill to be ready for a recurrence of the riots of 1877." [13]

As to the number of socialists in the United States we have no exact knowledge. Their press is numerous and is increasing. They now have nineteen journals, whose combined circulation is about 80,000. These papers are wholly devoted to the propagation of socialism, and there are many others which are more or less socialistically inclined. Some six years ago, or more, President Seelye, of Amherst College, said: "There are probably 100,000 men in the United States to-day whose animosity against all existing social institutions is hardly less than boundless." And Prof. Ely says: "If I wished to venture a guess,—a rash thing to do,—I should say that there might be half a million adherents of the general principles of moderate and peaceful socialism in the United States." [14] Since this opinion was expressed, some five years since, the class referred to has undoubtedly had a rapid growth.

There are many labor organizations, which are more or less socialistic in their sympathies and ideas, though not avowedly connected with any of the socialistic parties. The *Vorbote*, of Chicago, says: "You might as well suppose the military organizations of Europe were for play and parade, as to suppose labor organizations were for mere insurance and pacific helpfulness. They are organized to protect interests, for which, if the time comes, they would fight." But the present strength of socialistic organizations in the United States concerns us less than their prospective numbers. Let us look at the conditions favorable to the growth of socialism.

1. Most of the Internationals, the anarchic socialists, and

[13] [Ely, *Labor Movement*, p. 289.]
[14] Ely, *Labor Movement*, p. 282.

a larger proportion of the Socialistic Labor Party in this country are Germans, whose numbers are constantly being recruited by immigration. The rapid increase of socialism in Germany will, therefore, naturally influence its growth here. The following statistics of votes for members of the Reichstag show its increase in the last twenty years.

In 1871	124,655	In 1884	549,990
" 1874	351,952	" 1887	763,128
" 1877	493,288	" 1890	1,341,587
" 1881	311,961		

At the last election (1890) in Berlin the socialists cast 126,522 votes, over 20,000 more than all the other parties. "Professor Fawcett, in opening his present course of lectures at Oxford (1880), said that, if the growth of the socialistic political vote progressed in Germany and in the United States for the next fifty years as it has for the last fifty, capital can do nothing effectual against socialism." [15]

2. There are other influences, which, though obscure, are no less potent than immigration in fostering the growth of socialism in America. Among the deep currents of the centuries, flowing down through the last eighteen hundred years and rising to the surface in the great German Reformation of the sixteenth century, there has been an irresistible drift toward individualism. Guizot says that the "prime element in modern European civilization is the energy of individual life, the force of personal existence." The masses once existed for the state; the individual was nothing. When Christ said, "What shall it profit a man if he gain the whole world and lose his own soul?" thus teaching the priceless worth of every human being, he introduced a new idea into the world, which is leavening society. It has manumitted slaves, it has elevated woman, it has overthrown despotisms and written constitutions, it has swept away privileges and abolished caste. It is bearing Europe onward to popular government. Is it strange that the liberated pendulum should swing beyond the position of stable equi-

[15] Cook, *Socialism*, p. 17.

librium? Already are there signs of an excessive individualism among us; a certain self-assertion, a contempt of authority, which forgets that duties are co-extensive with rights. Anarchism is only "individualism gone mad." This powerful movement, therefore, toward individualism, and especially its perceptible tendency toward extremes, is favorable to the spread of socialism, as advocated by the Internationalists.

3. The prevalence of skepticism, also, is significant in this connection. A wide-spread infidelity preceded the French Revolution, and helped to prepare the way for it. A criminal in a prison on the Rhine left, a few years since, on the walls of his cell, the following message for his successors: "I will say a word to you. There is no heaven or hell. When once you are dead there is an end of everything. Therefore, ye scoundrels, grab whatever you can; only do not let yourselves be grabbed. Amen." Not only does irreligion remove all salutary fear of retribution hereafter, and thus give over low-minded men to violence and excess; but, when a man has lost all portion in another life, he is the more determined to have his proportion in this. There are Christian socialists; but the Internationalists are gross materialists. The socialist, Boruttau, says: "No man else is worthy of the name of socialist save he who, himself an atheist, devotes his exertions with all zeal to the spread of atheism." The great increase, therefore, of skepticism in this generation, and especially of doubt touching the sanctions of the divine law, has prepared a quick and fruitful soil for socialism, of the violent and godless sort.

4. Equality is one of the dreams of socialism. It protests against all class distinctions. The development of classes, therefore, in a republic, or the widening of the breach between them, is provocative of socialistic agitation and growth. Among the far-reaching influences of mechanical invention is a tendency, as yet unchecked, to heighten differences of condition, to establish social classes, and erect barriers between them. In a sense, classes do and must exist wherever there are resemblances and differences; but so long as the individual members

of social classes easily rise or fall from one to the other, by virtue of their own acts, such classes are neither unrepublican nor unsafe. But, when they become practically hereditary, differences are inherited and increased, antipathies are strengthened, the gulf between them is widened and they harden into casts which are both unrepublican and dangerous. Now the tendency of mechanical invention, under our present industrial system, is to separate classes more widely, and to render them hereditary.

Before the age of machinery, master, journeymen and apprentices worked together on familiar terms. The apprentice looked forward to the time when he should receive a journeyman's wages, and the journeyman might reasonably hope some day to have a shop of his own. Under this system there was little opportunity to develop class distinctions and jealousies.

Tools were not so expensive but that the workman might own them. And if he did not like his employer, he could leave; taking with him the means of earning a livelihood. If he did not easily find another employer, he could somewhere set up for himself. This single fact of owning his tools made him independent. But the introduction of machinery changed all this. It could not be carried from place to place like a kit of tools. It was too expensive for the workman to own. Without the machinery, owned by the employer, he was helpless. If he found himself out of a job, he could not set up for himself. He has lost his independence. Thus machinery has developed a dependent class.

Moreover machinery has rendered it vastly more difficult to rise from the condition of an employee to that of an employer, thus separating these classes more widely. Once they were only a step apart. That step could be taken by a workman's employing one other. They worked side by side, until the business demanded another "hand," and then another, until the little shop had grown into a large one. Thus gradually the workman acquired capital—a course open to every mechanic. But since the introduction of machinery, a considerable capital is necessary to make a beginning. It is found that other things being equal, the small factory cannot compete with the large one, hence fortunes are massed and factories become immense. A mechanic, by some happy invention or through remarkable abilities, may yet become a capitalist and an employer, but the condition of the average operative to-day is separated from that of his employer by an almost impassable gulf.

The immense production which has followed the advent of machinery has greatly raised the standard of living in all classes of society. There has not been a corresponding rise in wages, though they are much higher now than they were a hundred or fifty years ago. This discrepancy between wants and wages results in conditions which tend to form among operatives an hereditary class. In Massachusetts, where statistics of labor are the most elaborate published, the average working man is unable to support the average working man's family. In 1883 the average expenses of working men's families, in that state, were $754.42, while the earnings of workmen who were heads of families averaged $558.68.[16] This means that the average working man had to call on his wife and children to assist in earning their support. We accordingly find that, in the manufactures and mechanical industries of the state, in 1883, there were engaged 28,714 children under sixteen years of age. Of the average working man's family 32.44 per cent of the support fell upon the children and mother. I am not aware that the condition of the working man is at all exceptional in Massachusetts. "In their last report, the Illinois Commissioners of Labor Statistics say that their tables of wages and cost of living are representative only of intelligent working men, who make the most of their advantages, and do not reach 'the confines of that world of helpless ignorance and destitution in which multitudes in all large cities continually live, and whose only statistics are those of epidemics, pauperism, and crime.' Nevertheless, they go on to say, an examination of these tables will demonstrate that one-half of these intelligent working men of Illinois 'are not even able to earn enough for their daily

[16] *Fifteenth Annual Report of the* [*Massachusetts*] *Bureau of Statistics of Labor,* July 1884 (Boston, 1884), p. 464.

bread, and have to depend upon the labor of women and children to eke out their miserable existence.' "[17] In 1880, of persons engaged in all occupations in the United States, 1,118,356 were children fifteen years of age or under.[18] Their number, in ten years, increased 21 per cent more rapidly than the population. These children ought to be in the school instead of in the mill or the mine. How much longer will the operatives of the United States be distinguished for their intelligence if our children under sixteen are pressed into the factory? Child labor, which Professor Ely says is increasing with "alarming rapidity,"[19] tends to stunt the body and cramp the mind. In mills and factories children are put to feeding machines, and the narrow round of work prevents a natural development of either mind or body. Girls brought up in the factories, or whose mothers are there employed, make poor housekeepers, learn little of those arts of economy by which the handful of meal and the cruse of oil of a meager income waste not, neither fail. They make poor wives, and keep their husbands poor. Thus the children of another generation are forced into the factory. Hence the tendency to establish a class of hereditary operatives which class is already established in Europe, and will appear here in due time.

On the other hand machinery also tends to create a class of capitalists and monopolists.[20] Before the age of machinery, manufacturing power was, of course, muscular. That power belonged to the workmen, and could not be monopolized or centralized without their consent. Every man had a fair chance to compete with his fellow; no one enjoyed an immeasurable ad-

[17] George, *Social Problems* (New York, 1886), p. 100.

[18] *Compendium of the Tenth Census, 1880,* part II (Washington, D.C., 1883), p. 1358.

[19] Richard T. Ely, *An Introduction to Political Economy* (New York, 1889), p. 259.

[20] After discussing these tendencies of modern manufactures, De Tocqueville advises the friends of democracy to "keep their eyes anxiously fixed in this direction," and adds: "For if ever a permanent inequality of conditions and aristocracy again penetrate into the world, it may be predicted that this is the channel by which they will enter." *Democracy in America,* vol. II, ch. 20 (Cambridge, England, 1864), p. 193.

vantage; but machinery enables one man to own a power equal to that of a thousand or ten thousand men. Modern science and invention, in subjecting mighty forces of nature to human control, have made the Anakim our slaves. Here is an army of giants who never hunger and never tire, who never suffer and never complain; when ordered to stop working, they never raise bread riots. They always recognize their masters, and obey without question and without conscience. The availability and magnitude of these forces make the concentration of power both certain and dangerous. The masters of these forces are the Cæsars and Napoleons of modern society. Within certain limits, other things being equal, the larger the manufactory the cheaper the product, and the greater the percentage of profit on the investment. This law results in the massing of capital. These great enterprises demand able men to organize and conduct them. The employer is no longer a workman with his employees; his work is mental, not manual; it tasks and strengthens all his powers while that of his workmen tends to cramp their faculties. He has little personal acquaintance with his employees, and, with noble exceptions, has little personal interest in them. Thus these classes grow apart. Says Mr. Lecky: "Every change of conditions which widens the chasm and impairs the sympathy between rich and poor, cannot fail, however beneficial may be its effects, to bring with it grave dangers to the state. It is incontestable that the immense increase of manufacturing population has had this tendency." [21] And not only are these classes becoming further removed from each other, they are also becoming organized against each other. Capital is combining in powerful corporations and "trusts," and labor is combining in powerful trades-unions. And these opposing organizations make trials of strength, offer terms and conditions of surrender, like two hostile armies.

5. Again socialism fattens on discontent. A socialist paper says: "Create disgust with, and rebellion against, existing usages, for success lies through general dissatisfaction."

[21] William E. H. Lecky, *A History of England in the Eighteenth Century*, II (New York, 1878), 693–694.

It is easier to arouse the discontent of the workman now than it once was; among other reasons because the introduction of machinery and the division of labor have made a large proportion of work monotonous and void of all interest. Formerly in every trade there was a great variety of work. A blacksmith, for instance, was not master of his trade until he could make a thousand things, from a nail to an iron fence. There was relief from monotony, and scope for ingenuity and taste. But machinery is introduced, and with it important changes. It is discovered that the subdivision of labor both improves and cheapens the product. And this double advantage has stimulated the tendency in that direction until a single article that was once made by one workman now passes through perhaps threescore pairs of hands, each doing a certain part of the work on every piece. Manchester workmen, complaining of the monotony of their work, said to Mr. Cook: "It is the same thing day by day, sir; it's the same little thing; one little, little thing, over and over and over." Think of making pin-heads, ten hours a day, every working day in the week, for a year—twenty, forty, fifty years! In a nail mill, many workmen in the midst of a clatter enough to drown thought, do their day's work by pressing into the jaws of an ever-ravenous machine a small bar of iron, which they turn rapidly from side to side. Think of making that one movement for a life-time! Such dreary monotony is the most wearisome of all manual labor. It admits of little interest and no enthusiasm in one's work; and, worst of all, it tends to cramp the mind and to belittle the man. Once the man who made the nail could make the iron fence, also; now he cannot even make the nail, but only feed a machine that makes it. Political economists tell us that the minute division of labor tends to deteriorate the operative. This tendency may of course be more than counter-balanced by other and elevating influences, like those of education, the press, the ballot. Such influences have made the mechanics of to-day far more intelligent than were those of seventy-five or one hundred years ago, in spite of the deteriorating tendencies of the minute division of labor. But this increased intelligence enables the operator better to appreciate the belittling influence of his task, renders it the more irksome and makes him the more dissatisfied with the system under which he labors.

Furthermore, a sense of insecurity ministers to the discontent of working men. Invention is liable, any day, to render a given tool antiquated, and this or that technical skill useless. Every great labor-saving invention—though it eventually increases the demand for labor, helps forward civilization and adds to human comfort—temporarily throws great numbers out of employment. The operative, who for years confined himself to one thing, has, thereby, largely lost the power of adaptation. He cannot turn his hand to this or that; he is very likely too old to learn a new trade or acquire new technical skill; he has no alternative; and unless anchored by a family, probably turns tramp.

Competition leads to over-production, which results in closing mills and factories for long periods, thus for the time being swelling the floating population. One of the striking characteristics of modern cities is the instability of the poorer class of inhabitants, most of whom move every year or oftener, and many of them every three or four months. We are told that the condition of working men everywhere has vastly improved during the last half century, and this is probably true, but it has not prevented a rapid growth of socialism in Europe; and the fact that American workmen are better off than European, will not prevent its spread here. De Tocqueville observed and wondered that the masses find their position more intolerable the more it is improved. This is because the man improves faster than his condition; his wants increase more rapidly than his comforts. A savage, having nothing, is perfectly contented so long as he wants nothing. The first step toward civilizing him is to create a want. Men rise in the scale of civilization only as their wants rise; and, wherever a man may be on that scale, to awaken wants which cannot be satisfied is to provoke discontent as surely as if comforts were taken from him. Macaulay argues that the nineteenth century is the golden age of England, rather than the seventeenth, because then "noblemen were destitute of comforts, the want of which would be intolerable to a modern footman, and farmers and shop-keepers breakfasted on loaves the very sight of which would raise a riot in a modern workhouse," and especially because few knights had "libraries as good as may now perpetually be found in a servants' hall, or in the back parlor of a small shop-keeper." [22] The evidence of progress is found not so much in the fact that the footman *has* a library as that he *wants* it. There has been a wonderful "leveling up" of the common people, and their wants have risen accordingly. It is very true that within a century there has been a great multiplication of the comforts of life among the masses; but the question is *whether that increase has kept pace with the multiplication of wants.* The mechanic of to-day who has much, may be poorer than his grandfather, who had little. A rich man may be poor, and a poor man may be rich. Poverty is something relative, not absolute. I do not mean simply that a rich man is poor by the side of one richer. That man is poor who lacks the means of supplying what seem to him reasonable wants. The horizon of the working man, during this century, has been marvelously expanded; there has been a prodigious multiplication of his wants. The peasant of a few generations ago knew little of any lot save his own. He saw an aristocracy above him, which enjoyed peculiar privileges; but these were often justified in his eyes by superior intelligence and manners. The life of the rich and great was far removed from him and vague. He was not discontented for lack of luxuries of which he knew nothing. But modern manufactures and commerce and shop windows have made all luxuries familiar to all eyes. The working man of to-day in the United States has probably had a common school education, has traveled somewhat, attended expositions, visited libraries, art galleries and museums; through books he has become more or less acquainted with all countries and all classes of society; he reads the papers, he is vastly more intelligent than his grandfather was, he lives in a larger world and has many more wants. Indeed, his wants are as boundless as his means are limited. Education increases the capability

[22] Macaulay, *The History of England,* I (London, 1871), 408.

of enjoyment; and this capability is increasing among the many more rapidly than the means of gratification; hence a growing popular discontent.

There is much dissatisfaction among the masses of Europe. There would be more if there were greater popular intelligence. Place Americans in the circumstances under which the peasant of Continental Europe lives, and there would be a revolution in twenty-four hours. Hopeless poverty, therefore, in the United States, where there is greater intelligence, will be more restless, and more easily become desperate than in Europe. Many of our working men are beginning to feel that, under the existing industrial system, they are condemned to hopeless poverty. We have already seen that the average working man in Massachusetts and Illinois is unable to support his family. At that rate, how long will it take him to become the owner of a home? Of males engaged in the industries of Massachusetts in 1875, only one in one hundred owned a house. When a working man is unable to earn a home, or to lay by something for old age, when sickness or the closing of the factory for a few weeks, means debt, is it strange that he becomes discontented?

And how are such items as the following, which appeared in the papers of January, 1880, likely to strike discontented laborers? "The profits of the Wall Street Kings the past year were enormous. It is estimated that Vanderbilt made $30,000,000; Jay Gould, $15,000,000; Russell Sage, $10,000,000; Sidney Dillon, $10,000,000; James R. Keene, $8,000,000; and three or four others from one to two millions each; making a grand total for ten or twelve estates of about eighty millions of dollars." Is it strange if the working man thinks he is not getting his due share of the wonderful increase of national wealth?

Many wage-workers have come to feel that the capitalist is their natural enemy and that he is always ready, when opportunity offers, to sacrifice them and their families to his selfish gains. This does the greatest injustice to some employers, who, in times of depression, run their factories for months at a daily loss to themselves, rather than throw their workmen out of employment. But such capitalists are as rare as they are noble. More do not hesitate to enter in to combinations powerful enough to command the trade, and then stop work for weeks and months in order to inflate prices, already fair. In November, 1883, the Association of Nail-makers ordered a suspension in order to raise prices; and for five weeks 8,000 workmen were thrown out of employment, just as winter was coming on. Every mill in the West was in the "pool"; the suffering workmen, therefore, could not gain employment by going from one to another. They had learned to do but one thing, and could not turn their hand to anything else. There was nothing to do but nurse their discontent. Those November and December weeks were a good spring-time for sowing socialistic seed. The Liverpool Cotton Exchange in 1882 by manipulating prices, stopped 15,000,000 spindles, thus taking the bread out of the mouths of thousands of men, women, and children. The above simply illustrates a strong tendency toward combination and monopoly, which is one of the darkest clouds on our industrial and social horizon. Many industries are combining to force down production—that means that working men are thrown out of employment; and to force up prices—that means increased cost of living. There are great numbers of "syndicates" or "trusts," all formed in the interest of capitalists. Small dealers must enter the combination or be crushed. Once in, they must submit to the dictation of the "large" men. Thus power is being gathered more and more into the hands of conscienceless monopolies.

Adam Smith thought wheat was less liable than any other commodity to be monopolized by speculators, because "its owners can never be collected in one place." But this supposed impossibility is practically overcome by the railway and telegraph, and now Boards of Trade arbitrarily make and unmake the prices of food, and wheat is as easily "cornered" as anything else. A single firm in Chicago in 1880, gained control of the pork market, more than doubled the price, and cleared over seven million dollars on a single deal, the influence of which in advancing prices was felt in every part of the world. The full significance of such transactions is seen only when we consider, as has been shown by Drs. Drysdale and Farr, of England, that the death rate rises and falls with the prices of food. When the necessaries of life are "too easily" secured, combinations declare a war against plenty, production is stopped, and tens of thousands are forbidden to earn while prices rise. Thus, in this land of plenty, a few men may, at their pleasure, order a famine in thousands of homes.

This is modern and republican feudalism. These American barons and lords of labor have probably more power and less responsibility than many an olden feudal lord. They close the factory or the mine, and thousands of workmen are forced into unwilling idleness. The capitalist can arbitrarily raise the price of necessaries, can prevent men's working, but has no responsibility, meanwhile, as to their starving. Here is "taxation without representation" with a vengeance. We have developed a despotism vastly more oppressive and more exasperating than that against which the thirteen colonies rebelled.

Working men are apt to be improvident. It is often their own fault that enforced idleness so soon brings want. Though, at times, they know enough of want, as a class they know little of self-denial. They generally live up to the limit of their means. If wages are good, they have the best the market affords; when work and credit fail, they go hungry. Neither the capitalist nor the laborer has a monopoly of the fault for the difficulties existing between them. But our inquiry is after facts, not faults; and the fact of improvidence on the part of many working men only makes their discontent the deeper and more certain.

A communistic leader, who visited America thirty-five years ago, was asked what he thought of the condition of the working classes here. "It is very bad," he replied, "they are so discouragingly prosperous." But the growth of dissatisfaction and of socialism among our wage-workers, in recent years, has taken place notwithstanding generally good harvests and a great increase of aggregate wealth. Poor harvests were potent causes in bringing Louis XVI. to the guillotine, and precipitating the Reign of Terror. We must, of course, expect them to occur as heretofore, perhaps recur in successive years. The condition of the working man will then probably be bad enough to satisfy the most pessimistic agitator. Every such "winter of discontent" among laborers is made "glorious summer" for the growth of socialistic ideas.

We have glanced at the causes which are ministering to the growth of socialism among us: a wide-spread discontent on the part of our wage-working population, the development of classes and class antipathies, popular skepticism, a powerful individualism, and immigration. If these conditions should remain constant, socialism would continue to grow; but most of these causes are becoming more active. Within the life-time of some now living, population will be three times as dense in the United States as it is to-day. Wage-workers, now one-half of all our workers, will multiply more rapidly than the population. After our agricultural land is all occupied, as it will be a few years hence, our agricultural population which heretofore has not been socialistically inclined, will increase but little, while great manufacturing and mining towns will go on multiplying and to multiply. In the development of our manufacturing industries and our mining resources we have made, as yet, hardly more than a beginning. When these industries have been multiplied ten-fold, the evils which now attend them will be correspondingly multiplied, if present tendencies continue unchecked.

It must not be forgotten that, side by side with this deep discontent of intelligent and unsatisfied wants, has been developed, in modern times, a tremendous enginery of destruction, which offers itself to every man. Since the French Revolution nitro-glycerine, illuminating gas, petroleum, dynamite, the revolver, the repeating rifle and the Gatling gun have all come into use. Science has placed in man's hand superhuman powers. Society, also, is become more highly organized, much more complex, and is therefore much more susceptible of injury. There never was a time in the history of the world when an enemy of society could work such mighty mischief as today. The more highly developed a civilization is, the more vulnerable does it become. This is pre-eminently true of a material civilization. Learning, statesmanship, character, respect for law, love of justice, cannot be blown up with dynamite; palaces, factories, railways, Brooklyn bridges, Hoosac tunnels, and all the long inventory of our material wonders are destructible by material means. "The explosion of a little nitro-glycerine under a few water-mains would make a great city uninhabitable; the blowing-up of a few railroad bridges and tunnels would bring famine quicker than the wall of circumvallation that Titus drew around Jerusalem; the pumping of atmospheric air into the gas-mains, and the application of a match would tear up every street and level every house." [23] We are preparing conditions which make possible a Reign of Terror that would beggar the scenes of the French Revolution. I do not regard such a revolution as *probable,* but we have abundant reason to fear that such outbreaks as that which occurred in 1877 will recur with increased violence and greatly increased destruction of life and property.

Conditions at the West are peculiarly favorable to the growth of socialism. The much larger proportion of foreigners there, and the strong tendency of immigration thither, will have great influence. There is a stronger individuality in the West. The people are less conservative; there is less regard for established usage and opinion. The greater relative strength of Romanism there is significant; for apostate Catholics furnish the very soil to which socialism is indigenous. Mormonism also is doing a like preparatory work. It is gathering together great numbers of ill-balanced men, who are duped for a time by Mormon mummery; but many of them, becoming disgusted, leave the church and with it all faith in religion of any sort. Skeptical, soured, cranky, they are excellent socialistic material. Irreligion abounds much more than at the East; the proportion of Christian men is much smaller. "Into these Western communities the international societies and secret labor leagues and Jacobin clubs, and atheistic, infidel, rationalistic organizations of every name in the Old World, are continually emptying themselves. They are the natural reservoirs of whatever is uneasy, turbu-

[23] George, *Social Problems,* p. 14.

lent, antagonistic to either God or man among the populations across the sea. They are also the natural places of refuge for all in our own country who are soured by misfortune, misanthropic, seekers of radical reforms, renegades, moral pariahs. They are hence, in the nature of things, a sort of hotbed where every form of pestilent error is sure to be found and to come to quick fruitage. You can hardly find a group of ranchmen or miners from Colorado to the Pacific who will not have on their tongue's end the labor slang of Denis Kearney,[24] the infidel ribaldry of Robert Ingersoll,[25] the socialistic theories of Karl Marx." [26]

Heretofore socialism has made few proselytes among farmers. Less than one-half of all the land west of the Mississippi is arable. The agricultural element, therefore, will be a much smaller proportion of the whole population in the West than in the East. The industries of several of the great mountain states will be almost wholly mining and manufacturing; nearly the whole population, therefore, will be wage-workers—the class most easily discipled by socialistic agitators. The capitalist is a large figure in the West. He owns the mines, he owns vast reaches of grazing land, and the great herds of cattle.[27] He has also invested in many thousands of acres of farming lands. Railroads of immense length have been richly subsidized with lands which will steadily appreciate in value. These corporations bid fair to become much richer and more powerful than like monopolies in the East. The longest eastern roads

[24] [Denis Kearney (1847–1907), became president of the Workingmen's Party of California in 1877.]

[25] [Robert Green Ingersoll (1833–1899), lawyer, Republican politician after 1861, and America's outstanding agnostic, gained fame as one among the greatest of American orators.]

[26] Rev. E. P. Goodwin, D.D., Home Missionary Sermon, p. 16. [See Chapter V, above, n. 53.]

[27] At a meeting of cattle "kings" in St. Louis, there were many associations represented which own half a million head of stock or more. The Northern New Mexico Cattle Growers' Association owns 800,000 cattle, besides a large number of horses, which graze over 15,000,000 acres of land. The Texas Live Stock Association own 1,000,000 cattle, 1,000,000 sheep and 350,000 horses. A moderate estimate of their value would be $45,000,000.

would hardly be considered more than first-rate side-tracks out West; and some day the wealth and power of the western roads will be in proportion to their length.

There was no immense disparity of fortune among the early settlers of the East. They started pretty evenly in the race, and it has taken several generations to develop the wide extremes of modern society; but these differences exist at the outset in the West. Eastern capital has emptied itself into Western mines and herds and "bonanza" farms. The comparatively small population of the West has to-day more millionaires and more tramps than the whole country had a few years since. Many cattle and railway "kings," many gold and silver "kings," there rule their subjects. And in August, 1884, eighty tramps took possession of Castleton, Dakota, drove many families from their homes and committed numerous excesses. Western society is organized at the very beginning, on the class distinctions which are so favorable to the growth of socialism.

Modern civilization is called on to contend for its life with forces which it has evolved. Said President Seelye, a few years since, to the graduating class of Amherst College: "There is one question of our time toward which all other questions, whether of nature, of man, or of God, steadily tend. . . . No one will be likely to dispute the affirmation that the social question is, and is to be, the question of your time." That question must be met in the United States. We need not quiet misgiving with the thought that popular government is our safety from revolution. It is *because* of our free institutions that the great conflict of socialism with society as now organized is likely to occur in the United States. There is a strong disposition among men to charge most of the ills of their lot to bad government, and to seek a political remedy for those ills. They expect in the popularization of power to find relief. Constitutional government, a free press and free speech would probably quiet popular agitation in Russia for a generation. If Germany should become a republic, we should hear little of German socialism for a season. But all our salve of this sort is spent; there are no more political rights to bestow; the people are in full possession. Here then, where there is the fullest exercise of political rights, will the people first discover that the ballot is not a panacea. Here, where, as we believe, the ultimate evolution of government has taken place, will restless men first attempt to live without government.

There is nothing beyond republicanism but anarchism.

CHAPTER X

PERILS—WEALTH

THE wealth of the United States is phenomenal. It is now (1890) estimated at $61,459,000,000.[1] In 1880 it was valued at $43,642,000,000; more than enough to buy the Russian and Turkish Empires, the kingdoms of Sweden and Norway, Denmark and Italy, together with Australia, South Africa and all South America—lands, mines, cities, palaces, factories, ships, flocks, herds, jewels, moneys, thrones, scepters, diadems and all—the entire possessions of 177,000,000 people. The most remarkable point of this comparison is the fact that European wealth represents the accumulations of many centuries, while more than half of ours has been created in twenty years.

Between 1860 [2] and 1870 a million producers were destroyed by war, and not only were two great armies withdrawn from productive occupations, but they devoted marvelous energy and ingenuity to the work of destruction. But, notwithstanding all this, during those ten years we created wealth enough to cover all the losses of the war in both North and South, with $116,000,000 to spare.[3]

From 1870 to 1890 our wealth increased $31,391,000,000, al-

[1] *The World Almanac, 1890* (New York, 1890), pp. 116–117. These statistics were compiled from returns made by the financial officers of the several states and territories, and based on the assessed valuations.

[2] In the first edition, our wealth in 1860 was given as $16,160,000,000. This was the value of taxed property only. Taxed and untaxed property amounted to $31,202,000,000, and in 1870 to $30,068,000,000.

[3] That is, not counting as a loss the $1,250,000,000, which emancipation subtracted from the assets of the nation, we were $116,000,000 richer in 1870 than we were in 1860.

Wealth of the United States in 1890, $61,459,000,000.
Wealth of the United States in 1880, $43,642,000,000.
Wealth of the Russian and Turkish Empires, Sweden and Norway, Denmark, Italy, Australia, South Africa and all of South America in 1880, $43,000,000,000.

most twice the entire wealth of the Empire of Russia (in 1880), to be divided among 82,000,000 people. And this increase, it should be observed, was only a small part of the wealth created —the excess after supporting the best-fed people in the world. To the wealth of 1870 was added, during the next twenty years, an average of more than $200,000 every hour, night and day, except Sunday, or $5,000,000 every week-day for that period. Since 1880 our wealth has increased $17,817,000,000 or 40.8 per cent, while population has increased only about 25 per cent. Great Britain is, by far, the richest nation of the Old World, and our wealth exceeded hers in 1880 by $276,000,000; and during the past ten years our increase has been much more rapid than hers. The material progress of the United States from 1870 to 1890 is wholly without a parallel in the history of the world.

It is difficult to realize that the youngest of the nations is the richest, and that the richest of all nations has, as yet, only begun to develop its resources. The crops of 1888 were produced on less than one-sixth of our arable land, and much of our agriculture is rude; a much larger proportion of our mineral wealth is undeveloped; and the only limit which can be set to our possible manufactures is the world's need. Our domestic commerce, already $18,000,000,000 a year,[4] will double and quadruple with the growth of population. Here are forty-four nations, so to speak—and soon to be half a hundred—enjoying perfect freedom of intercourse, with but one language and one currency, with common interests and common institutions. In Europe, commerce must run a gauntlet of custom-houses, on a score of frontiers, and must stumble over thrice as many languages; while those nations, with conflicting interests and mutual jealousies and antipathies, exhaust much of their strength in watching, foiling, and crippling each other. Europe spends annually on the maintenance of fleets and armies nearly $900,000,000. And this is but little more than one-half the actual cost; for these 3,000,000 men and more are withdrawn

[4] J. L. Stevens, "Influence of European Industries on the United States," *International Review,* 11 (December 1881), 593.

from industrial pursuits in the flower of their youth. If the time of privates is worth seventy-five cents a day, and that of officers two dollars, the value of labor annually lost to Europe by her standing armies is $758,978,000. In 1889 we expended on our army and navy $65,000,000; and, reckoning the time of the private soldier here worth a dollar and a half a day, and that of the officer worth four dollars, the value of the labor lost by our army in 1889 was only $16,000,000. That is, in competing with Europe for wealth, our *location* is worth to us about $1,576,000,000 a year.[5] The editor of the London *Spectator* says: "Observers in the Old World cannot help admiring or envying the American Treasury, which does not know what to do with its wealth . . . . and which declares that its savings are so vast as to impede and endanger all commercial business. . . . Much credit is due to the American Constitution, if only because the people worship it after a century's experience; but this prosperity of the Treasury is not due to it, but to *a situation on this planet unparalleled* at once in its exemption from danger and in the natural wealth it places at the disposal of an industrious people."[6] In 1880 our wealth was 23.93 per cent of the wealth of all Europe; our earnings were 28.01 per cent of those of Europe; and our increase of wealth was 49.28 per cent of European increase. From 1870 to 1880 there was a decrease of wealth per caput, in Europe, of nearly 3 per cent, while here there was an increase of 39 per cent. If existing conditions continue, the time will undoubtedly come when the people of the United States will possess more wealth than all the nations of Europe. Our riches, together with the power, the problems and dangers which attend them, are to be multiplied many fold. The collective energy or working-power of a nation includes its human power, its horse power and its

[5] It is said our pensions cost us as much as a large standing army. This is true, but our pension appropriations in 1890 ($109,000,000), the largest ever made up to date, were not one-half as large as those made by Europe annually.

[6] "The Great Advantage of the United States," *The Spectator* (London, December 7, 1889), p. 800. Quoted in *Our Race: Its Origin and Destiny*, series I, no. 1 (New Haven, Connecticut, March 20, 1890), p. 124.

steam power. (The water power is not included.) Mr. Mulhall estimated in 1888 that our collective energy then reached 90,000 millions of "foot-tons daily." That is, it was sufficient to raise 90,000 million tons one foot in a day. Our working-power is thus found by Mr. Mulhall to be nearly equal to that of the United Kingdom and Germany combined, whose population aggregates 82,000,000 souls. He also estimated that in 1890 our working-power would reach "almost 100,000 millions of foot-tons daily."[7] This reduced to man-power would be equal to 333,000,000 men. Think of such a power at work for the enriching of our nation, and rapidly increasing. It is a promise of unspeakable wealth. And such wealth contains mighty possibilities, both for good and evil. Let us, in this connection, look at the latter.

1. As civilization increases, wealth has more meaning, and money a larger representative power. Civilization multiplies wants, which money affords the means of gratifying. With the growth of civilization, therefore, money will be an ever-increasing power, and the object of ever-increasing desire. Hence the danger of *Mammonism*, growing more and more intense and infatuated. The love of money is the besetting sin of commercial peoples, and runs in the very blood of Anglo-Saxons, who are the great wealth-creators of the world. Our soil is peculiarly favorable to the growth of this "root of all evil"; and for two reasons. First, wealth is more easily amassed here than anywhere else in the world, of which we have already seen sufficient proof; and, second, wealth means more, has more power, here than elsewhere. Every nation has its aristocracy. In other lands the aristocracy is one of birth; in ours it is one of wealth. It is useless for us to protest that we are democratic, and to plead the leveling character of our institutions. There is among us an aristocracy of recognized power, and that aristocracy is one of wealth. No heraldry offends our republican

[7] Michael G. Mulhall, "The Growth of American Industries and Wealth," paper read before the British Association at its 1888 meeting at Bath, and reprinted in J. Strong, *The United States and the Future of the Anglo-Saxon Race* (London, 1889), pp. 59, 69.

prejudices. Our ensigns armorial are the trade-mark. Our laws and customs recognize no noble titles; but men can forego the husk of a title who possess the fat ears of power. In England there is an eager ambition to rise in rank, an ambition as rarely gratified as it is commonly experienced. With us, aspiration meets with no such iron check as birth. A man has only to build higher the pedestal of his wealth. He may stand as high as he can build. His wealth cannot secure to him genuine respect, to be sure; but, for that matter, neither can birth. It will secure to him an obsequious deference. It may purchase political distinction. It *is* power. In the Old World, men commonly live and die in the condition in which they are born. The peasant may be discontented, may covet what is beyond his reach; but his desire draws no strength from expectation. Heretofore, in this country, almost any laborer, by industry and economy, might gain a competence, and even a measure of wealth; and, though now we are beginning to approximate the conditions of European labor, young men, generally, when they start in life, still expect to become rich; and, thinking not to serve their god for naught, they commonly become faithful votaries of Mammon. Thus the prizes of wealth in the United States, being at the same time greater and more easily won, and the lists being open to all comers, the rush is more general, and the race more eager than elsewhere.

"But they that will be rich, fall into temptation and a snare, and into many foolish and hurtful lusts, which drown men in destruction and perdition." [8] They who "will be rich," are tempted to resort to methods less laborious and more and more unscrupulous. Fierce competition is leading to frequent adulterations, and many forms of bribery. It is driving legitimate business to illegitimate methods. Merchants offer prizes to draw trade, and employ the lottery to enrich themselves and debauch the public. The growth of the spirit of speculation is ominous. The salaries of clerks, the business capital, the bank deposits and trust funds of all sorts which disappear "on 'change," indicate how widespread is the unhealthy haste to be rich. And

[8] I Tim. 6:9.

such have the methods of speculation become that "The Exchange" has degenerated into little better than a euphemism for "gambling hell." "While one bushel in seven of the wheat crop of the United States is received by the Produce Exchange of New York, its traders buy and sell two for every one that comes out of the ground. When the cotton plantations of the South yielded less than six million bales, the crop on the New York Cotton Exchange was more than thirty-two millions. Pennsylvania does well to run twenty-four millions of barrels of oil in a year; but New York City will do as much in two small rooms in one week, and the Petroleum Exchanges sold altogether last year two thousand million barrels." [9] Such facts indicate how small a portion of the transactions of the "Exchange" is legitimate business, and how large a proportion is simple gambling. Mammonism is corrupting popular morals in many ways. Sunday amusements of every kind—horse-racing, base ball, theaters, beer-gardens, steamboat and railroad excursions—are all provided *because there is money in them.* Licentious literature floods the land, poisoning the minds of the young and polluting their lives, *because there is money in it.* Gambling flourishes in spite of the law, and actually under its license, *because there is money in it.* And that great abomination of desolation, that triumph of Satan, that more than ten Egyptian plagues in one—the liquor traffic—grows and thrives at the expense of every human interest, *because there is money in it.* Ever since greed of gold sold the Christ and raffled for his garments, it has crucified every form of virtue between thieves. And, while Mammonism corrupts morals, it blocks reforms. Men who have favors to ask of the public are slow to follow their convictions into any unpopular reform movement. They can render only a surreptitious service. Their discipleship must needs be secret, "for fear of the" customers or clients or patients. It is Mammonism which makes most men *invertebrates.* When important Mormon legislation was pending, certain New York merchants telegraphed to members of Congress:

[9] Henry D. Lloyd, "Making Bread Dear," *North American Review,* 137 (August 1883), p. 118.

"New York sold $13,000,000 worth of goods to Utah last year. Hands off!" The tribe of Demetrius, the Ephesian silversmith, is everywhere: men quick to perceive when this their craft by which they have their wealth is in danger of being set at naught. "Nothing is more timorous than a million dollars—except two millions."

Mammonism is also corrupting the ballot-box. The last four presidential elections have shown that the two great political parties are nearly equal in strength. The vast majority of voters on both sides are party men, who vote the same way year after year. The result of the election is determined by the floating vote. Of this, a comparatively small portion is thoroughly intelligent and conscientious; the remainder is, for the most part, without convictions, without principle and thoroughly venal; hence the great temptation to bribery, to which both parties yield.[10] Moreover, the influence of great corporations, which so often controls legislation, is moneyed influence.

2. Again, by reason of our enormous wealth and its rapid increase, we are threatened with a gross materialism. The English epithet applied by Matthew Arnold to Chicago, "too beastly prosperous," has a subtile meaning, which perhaps was not intended by the distinguished visitor. Material growth may be so much more vigorous than the moral and intellectual as

[10] In the first edition, written in 1885, appeared the following sentence. "And if the two parties take distinct issue on economic questions—which seems likely—each believing that the success of the other would involve great financial disaster, corruption money will become an increasingly important political factor." Three years later the two parties did take issue on economic questions, as anticipated; and never before was bribery so extensive, so systematic and so unblushing. Said the *New York Times*, October 21, 1889, "This crime of bribery and corruption at the polls has been on the increase in recent years until it has become a portentous evil, menacing the very foundations of free institutions."

Hon. William M. Ivins, in an address before the Congregational Club of New York, November 19, 1888, said he was confident that over 85,000 men in New York City alone "received money for their alleged services or as bribers in the election during the recent campaign. . . . And this sum has no reference to the vast amounts placed in the hands of individuals with the *open* and *avowed* purpose of buying votes. . . . I have compared these figures with many practical politicians, and they all agree that they are conservative."

to have a distinctly brutalizing tendency. Life becomes sensuous; that is deemed real which can be seen and handled, weighed and transported; and that only has value which can be appraised in dollars and cents. Wealth was intended to minister to life, to enlarge it; when life becomes only a ministry to enlarge wealth, there is manifest perversion and degradation. We may say of it as Young said of life—"An end deplorable! A means divine!" Says Mr. Whipple: "—there is danger that the nation's worship of labors whose worth is measured by money will give a sordid character to its mightiest exertions of power, eliminate heroism from its motives, destroy all taste for lofty speculation, and all love for ideal beauty, and inflame individuals with a devouring self-seeking, corrupting the very core of the national life." [11] We have undoubtedly developed a larger proportion of men of whom the above is a faithful picture than any other Christian nation; men to whom Agassiz's remark, "I am offered five hundred dollars a night to lecture, but I decline all invitations, for I have no time to make money," is simply incomprehensible; it dazes them.

There is a "balance of power" to be preserved in the United States as well as in Europe. Our safety demands the preservation of a balance between our material power and our moral and intellectual power. The means of self-gratification should not outgrow the power of self-control. Steam-power would have been useless had we not found in iron, or something else, a greater power of resistance. And, should we discover a motor a hundred times more powerful than steam, it would prove not only useless but fearfully destructive, unless we could find a still greater resisting power. Increasing wealth will only prove the means of destruction, unless it is accompanied by an increasing power of control, a stronger sense of justice, and a more intelligent comprehension of its obligations.

There is a certain unfriendliness between the material and the spiritual. The vivid apprehension of the one makes the

[11] Edwin P. Whipple, *Character and Characteristic Men* (Boston, 1866), p. 142.

other seem unreal. When the life of the senses is intense, spiritual existence and truths are dim; and when St. Paul was exalted to a spiritual ecstasy, the senses were so closed that he could not tell whether he was "in the body or out of the body." A time of commercial stagnation is apt to be a time of spiritual quickening, while great material prosperity is likely to be accompanied by spiritual dearth. A poor nation is much more sensitive to the power of the gospel than a rich one. So Christ taught: "How hardly shall they that have riches enter into the kingdom of God!" "It is easier for a camel to go through the eye of a needle than for a rich man to enter into the kingdom of God!"[12] Words as true now as when they were first uttered, and having a fuller meaning in the nineteenth century than in the first.

3. Again, great and increasing wealth subjects us to all the perils of luxuriousness. Nations, in their beginnings, are poor; poverty is favorable to hardihood and industry; industry leads to thrift and wealth; wealth produces luxury, and luxury results in enervation, corruption, and destruction. This is the historic round which nations have run. "Nations have decayed, but it has never been with the imbecility of age."[13] "Avarice and luxury have been the ruin of every great state."[14] Her American possessions made Spain the richest and most powerful nation of Europe; but wealth induced luxury and idleness, whence came poverty and degradation. Rome was never stronger in all the seeming elements of power than at the moment of her fall. She had grown rich, and riches had corrupted her morals, rendered her effeminate, and made her an easy prey to the lusty barbarian of the North. The material splendor of Israel reached its climax in the glory of Solomon's reign, in which silver was made to be in Jerusalem as stones; but it was followed by the immediate dismemberment of the kingdom. Under all that magnificence, at which even Oriental monarchs wondered, was springing a discontent which led to

[12] Mark 10:23, 25.
[13] Charles Sumner.
[14] Livy.

speedy revolt. Bancroft has wisely said that, "Sedition is bred in the lap of luxury."

The influence of mechanical invention is to stimulate luxurious living. We are told by Edward Atkinson [15] that by the hand looms in the South ten hours' work will produce eight yards of cloth, while in the factory of New England ten hours' work will produce 800 yards. In 1888 the steam power of the United States was equal to the working-power of 161,333,000 men; [16] as if one-half of all the male workmen on the globe had engaged in our service. When we remember that this machinery is an enormous producer of the necessaries, comforts, and luxuries of life, but is not a consumer of the same, we see how immensely the average consumption per caput has increased. As luxuries are thus cheapened and brought within the reach of an ever-widening circle, there is an increasing tendency toward self-indulgence. Herodotus said: "It is a law of nature that faint-hearted men should be the fruit of luxurious countries; for we never find that the same soil produces delicacies and heroes." Is there not danger that our civilization will become tropical? The temperate zone has produced the great nations, because in it the conditions of life have been sufficiently hard to arouse energy and develop strength. Where men are pampered by nature, they sink to a low level; and where civilization is of the pampering sort the tendency is the same. By means of coal, which Mr. Emerson calls a "portable climate," together with increasing wealth and luxuries, we are multiplying tropical conditions here in the North.

The splendor of our riches will doubtless dazzle the world; but history declares, in the ruins of Babylon and Thebes, of Carthage and Rome, that wealth has no conserving power; that it tends rather to enervate and corrupt. Our wonderful material prosperity, which is the marvel of other nations, and the boast of our own, may hide a decaying core.

[15] [Edward Atkinson, see Chapter II, n. 6.]

[16] Mulhall, "Growth," in Strong, *The United States,* p. 70. [Mulhall and Strong used a ratio of 13.3 : 1 to convert adult male manpower into horsepower of steam.]

4. Again, another danger is the marked and increasing tendency toward a *congestion of wealth.* The enormous concentration of power in the hands of one man is unrepublican, and dangerous to popular institutions. The framers of our government aimed to secure the distribution of power. They were careful to make the several departments—executive, legislative, and judicial—operate as checks on each other. An executive, chosen by the people and responsible to them, may exercise but little authority; and after a short period he must return it to them. But a money-king may double, quadruple, centuple his wealth, if he can. He may exercise vastly more power than the governor of his state; but he is irresponsible. He is not a constitutional monarch, but a czar. He is not chosen by the people with reference to his fitness to administer so great a trust; he may lack utterly all moral qualifications for it. We have indeed, some rich men who are an honor to our civilization; but the power of many millions is almost certain to find its way into strong and unscrupulous hands. Our money-king must not, after two or four years, return his power to the people; he has a life tenure of office, provided only his grip upon his golden scepter be strong. Less than thirty years ago, Emerson wrote for our wonder: "Some English private fortunes reach, and some exceed, a million dollars a year." At least one American has had an income of $1,000,000 a month; and others follow hard after him. A writer in *The Forum* gives a list of seventy names of persons in the United States, representing an aggregate wealth of $2,700,000,000, or an average of $37,500,000 each. "It would be easy," he says, "for any specially well-informed person to make up a list of one hundred persons averaging $25,000,000 each, in addition to ten averaging $100,000,000 each. No such list of concentrated wealth could be given in any other country in the world." [17]

Superfluity on the one hand, and dire want on the other—the millionaire and the tramp—are the complement each of the other. The classes from which we have most to fear are the

[17] Thomas G. Shearman, "The Owners of the United States," *Forum*, 8 (November 1889), 260.

two extremes of society—the dangerously rich and the dangerously poor; and the former are much more to be feared than the latter. Said Dr. Howard Crosby: "The danger which threatens the uprooting of society, the demolition of civil institutions, the destruction of liberty, and the desolation of all, is that which comes from the rich and powerful classes in the community." [18] "The great estates of Rome, in the time of the Cæsars, and of France in the time of the Bourbons, rivaled those of the United States to-day; but both nations were on their way to the frenzy of revolution, not in spite of their wealth, but, in some true sense, because of it." [19] We have seen, in the preceding chapter, that mechanical invention tends to create operative and capitalist classes, and render them hereditary. It is the tendency of our civilization to destroy the easy gradation from poor to rich which now exists, and to divide society into only two classes—the rich and the comparatively poor. In a new country almost any one can do business successfully, and broad margins will save him from the results of blunders which would elsewhere be fatal. But, with growing population and increasing facilities of communication, competition becomes severe, and then a slight advantage makes the difference between success and failure. Accumulated capital is not a slight, but an immense advantage. "To him that hath, shall be given." There will, therefore, be an increasing tendency toward the centralization of great wealth in corporations, which will simply eat up the small manufacturers and the small dealers. As the two classes of rich and poor grow more distinct, they will become more estranged, and whether the rich, like Sydney Smith, come to regard poverty as "infamous," it is quite certain that many of the poor will look upon wealth as criminal.

We have traced some of the natural tendencies of great and increasing wealth. It should be observed that these tendencies

[18] Howard Crosby, "The Dangerous Classes," *North American Review,* 136 (April 1883), 346. [See Chapter VIII, n. 17.]

[19] Editorial, "The Nation's Highways," *Christian Union,* 30 (October 16, 1884), 364.

will grow stronger, because wealth is increasing much more rapidly than population. Remarkable as the growth of the latter is, it being four times the European rate of increase from 1870 to 1880, and three times that of England or Germany, the multiplication of wealth has been even more remarkable. In one generation, 1850–1880, our national wealth increased more than six fold, and, notwithstanding the growth of population, the wealth per caput increased nearly three fold. There is reason to believe that this rate of increase will be sustained for years to come. If it is, the danger from mammonism, materialism, luxuriousness, and the congestion of wealth will be a constantly increasing peril.

It remains to be shown that the dangers of wealth are greater at the West than at the East. There is more of mammonism there. With rare exceptions, the West is being filled with a *selected* population, and the principle of selection is the desire to better their worldly condition. Nineteen men of every twenty (and the twentieth is either an invalid or a home missionary) will tell you that they went there for the express purpose of making money. Where land is being rapidly taken, and real estate of all sorts is rapidly appreciating in value, men make every possible present endeavor with reference to the future. Under such conditions the race after wealth becomes peculiarly eager. The gambling spirit which always prevails in mining regions exerts a wide influence, even in agricultural states. Farmers often rent land, put their entire capital into a great acreage, and stake everything on a single crop. The sudden wealth often realized in the mines stimulates the general haste to be rich. And where riches are almost the sole object of endeavor, their possession gives greater power. In the Rocky Mountains a man may be to-day a caterer or bar-tender, fit for that and nothing more; to-morrow, without any good wit of his own, a millionaire; next day, because "Mammon wins his way where seraphs might despair," a lieutenant-governor or United States senator. The demoralizing atmosphere of the New West is seen in the fact that there are everywhere church-members who seem to have left their religion behind when they crossed the Missouri. Many men who lived reputable Christian lives in the East are there swept into the great maelstrom of worldliness.

As a comment on our gross materialism here in the United States, and especially in the far West, I will quote a short passage from the note book of the musician, Gottschalk.[20] Being ill for three days in a town in Nevada, and finding himself utterly deserted, he gives vent to his feelings in these words: "I defy your finding, in the whole of Europe, a village where an artist of reputation would find himself as isolated as I have been here. If, in place of playing the piano, of having composed two or three hundred pieces, of having given seven or eight thousand concerts, of having given to the poor one hundred and fifty thousand dollars, of having been knighted twice, I had sold successfully for ten years, quarters of salted hog, my poor, isolated chamber would have been invaded by adorers and admirers." [21]

There is more danger of luxuriousness at the West, a greater extravagance than among Eastern people of like means. Money comes faster and goes faster. There is little of that strict economy which is so often practiced at the East. A western town of ten thousand inhabitants will boast of "carrying all the style" of an eastern city of fifty thousand. New villages are likely to have more electric lights and telephones than some of the great cities of Europe. The millionaires of the West were not many of them born to wealth. They have made their riches within a few years; and such are the men to spend money freely. They become the social legislators, and help to create customs of free expenditure.

The striking centralization of capital which has already taken place at the West was sufficiently noticed in the preceding chapter. Enough has been said to show that the West is peculiarly exposed to the dangers with which wealth threatens the nation.

[20] [Louis Moreau Gottschalk (1829–1869), Paris-trained American pianist and composer, who achieved international fame through his concert tours in Europe and the Americas.]

[21] [Gottschalk, *Notes of a Pianist* (London, 1881), p. 390.]

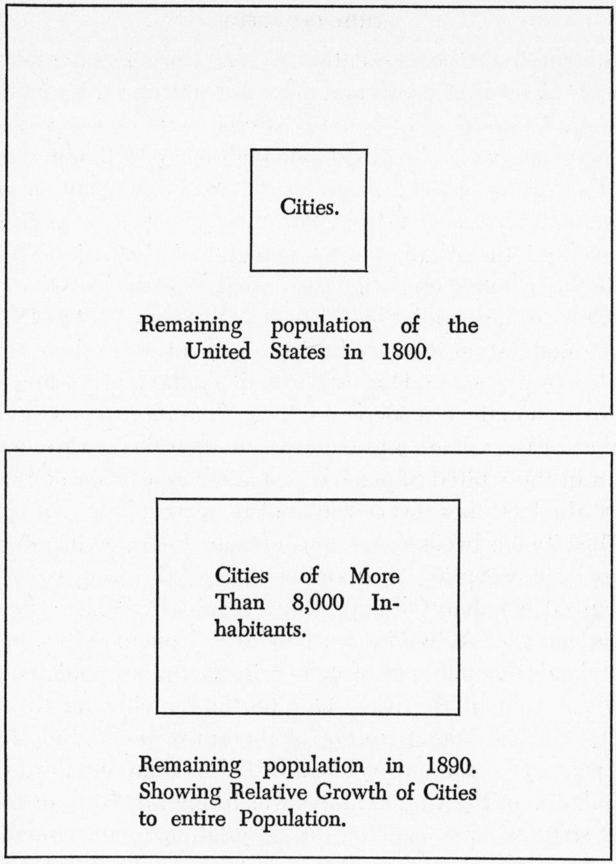

Cities.

Remaining population of the United States in 1800.

Cities of More Than 8,000 Inhabitants.

Remaining population in 1890. Showing Relative Growth of Cities to entire Population.

CHAPTER XI

PERILS—THE CITY

THE city is the nerve center of our civilization. It is also the storm center. The fact, therefore, that it is growing much more rapidly than the whole population is full of significance. In 1790 one-thirtieth of the population of the United States lived in cities of 8,000 inhabitants and over; in 1800, one twenty-fifth; in 1810, and also in 1820, one-twentieth; in 1830, one-sixteenth; in 1840, one-twelfth; in 1850, one-eighth; in 1860, one-sixth; in 1870, a little over one-fifth; and in 1880, 22.5 per cent, or nearly one-fourth.[1] From 1790 to 1880 the whole population increased twelve fold, the urban population eighty-six fold. From 1830 to 1880 the whole population increased a little less than four fold, the urban population thirteen fold. From 1870 to 1880 the whole population increased thirty per cent, the urban population forty per cent.[2] During the half century preceding 1880, population in the city increased more than four times as rapidly as that of the village and country. In 1800 there were only six cities in the United States which had a population of 8,000 or more. In 1880 there were 286, and in 1890, 437.[3]

The city has become a serious menace to our civilization, because in it, excepting Mormonism, each of the dangers we have discussed is enhanced, and all are focalized. It has a peculiar attraction for the immigrant. Our fifty principal cities in 1880 contained 39.3 per cent of our entire German population, and 45.8 per cent of the Irish. Our ten larger cities at that time contained only nine per cent of the entire population, but 23 per cent of the foreign. While a little less than one-third of the population of the United States was foreign by birth or parentage, sixty-two per cent of the population of Cincinnati was foreign, eighty-three per cent of Cleveland, sixty-three per cent of Boston,[4] eighty per cent of New York, and ninety-one

[1] *Compendium of the Tenth Census, 1880,* part I (Washington, D.C., 1883), pp. xxx and 8. The Eleventh Census has not yet given us the urban population in 1890.

[2] William M. Springer, in "City Growth and Party Politics," *Forum,* 10 (December 1890), 473–474, estimates from reports and semi-official data that the increase of rural population from 1880 to 1890 was only eight per cent, while that of the urban population was more than 57 per cent.

[3] The first official count. The final official count will doubtless make some change in this number.

[4] The *Census of Massachusetts, 1885* (Boston, 1887), showed 67 per cent.

per cent of Chicago.[5] A census of Massachusetts, taken in 1885, showed that in 65 towns and cities of the state 65.1 per cent of the population was foreign by birth or parentage.

Because our cities are so largely foreign, Romanism finds in them its chief strength.

For the same reason the saloon, together with the intemperance and the liquor power which it represents, is multiplied in the city. East of the Mississippi there was, in 1880, one saloon to every 438 of the population; in Boston, one to every 329; in Cleveland, one to every 192; in Chicago, one to every 179; in New York, one to every 171; in Cincinnati, one to every

[5] "Foreign by birth or parentage" includes those, only one of whose parents was foreign. Their number is comparatively small and even less important than they might seem, because in a large proportion of instances the native parent was of foreign parentage.

The Tenth Census gives the number of persons, foreign-born, in each of the fifty principal cities, but does not give the native-born population of foreign parentage. We have, however, tolerable satisfactory data for computing it. The parentage of the populations of twenty-eight states, seven territories and the District of Columbia was tallied according to a highly complicated form in order to secure the desired ratios. On this basis the Census Office made an elaborate estimate of those who were foreign by birth or parentage in the whole country and placed the number at 14,955,943. The whole number of the foreign-born was ascertained to be 6,679,943. The former number contains the latter 2.238 times; that is, the foreign-born population multiplied by 2.238 gives the population foreign by birth or parentage. It should be observed, however, that this ratio varies in different states, due doubtless to the preponderance of different races in different sections of the country. For instance, in Massachusetts those of foreign parentage were in 1880 almost exactly twice as many as those of foreign birth. Accordingly for any city in that state we multiply the number of foreign-born by two, which gives the total of the foreign-born and the native-born of foreign parentage, provided the ratio between the two is the same in the cities as in the whole state, which must be assumed as long as there is no evidence to the contrary. In Wisconsin, the Census showed that those of foreign parentage were 2.34 times the number of the foreign-born, while in Missouri the ratio was 2.63 to one.

Accordingly, in order to estimate the number of those foreign by birth or parentage in a given city in any one of the thirty-five states and territories in which the above tally was made, we multiply the number of the foreign born in that city by the number which the census showed to be the ratio between those of foreign parentage and those of foreign birth in the state in which the city is located. If the city is in a state in which the tally was not made, as for instance, Pennsylvania, Ohio or Il-

124. Of course the demoralizing and pauperizing power of the saloons and their debauching influence in politics increase with their numerical strength.

It is the city where wealth is massed; and here are the tangible evidences of it piled many stories high. Here the sway of Mammon is widest, and his worship the most constant and eager. Here are luxuries gathered—everything that dazzles the eye, or tempts the appetite; here is the most extravagant expenditure. Here, also, is the *congestion* of wealth the severest. Dives and Lazarus are brought face to face; here, in sharp contrast, are the *ennui* of surfeit and the desperation of starvation. The rich are richer, and the poor are poorer, in the city than elsewhere; and, as a rule, the greater the city, the greater are the riches of the rich and the poverty of the poor. Not only does the proportion of the poor increase with the growth of the city, but their condition becomes more wretched. The poor of a city of 8,000 inhabitants are well off compared with many in New York; and there are hardly such depths of woe, such utter and heart-wringing wretchedness in New York as in London. Read in *The Bitter Cry of Outcast London,* a prophecy of what will some day be seen in American cities, provided existing tendencies continue: "Few who will read these pages have any conception of what these pestilential human rookeries are, where tens of thousands are crowded together amidst horrors which call to mind what we have heard of the middle passage of the slave-ship. To get into them you have to penetrate courts reeking with poisonous and malodorous gases, aris-

---

linois, the best we can do is to multiply by the number which is average for the whole country, viz., 2.238.

We hear it objected that one does not see in our cities any such proportion of foreigners as is indicated by the above figures. It should be remembered that of the population foreign by birth or parentage, five-ninths were born in the United States; and at least one quarter of the foreign-born came to this country in childhood, so that six-ninths or two-thirds of this population though it remains largely foreign in ideas, becomes thoroughly Americanized in speech and appearance.

Accordingly if twenty-one per cent of the population of Boston *appear* foreign, we must not be surprised to learn that sixty-three per cent are foreign by birth or parentage.

ing from accumulations of sewage and refuse scattered in all directions, and often flowing beneath your feet; courts, many of them which the sun never penetrates, which are never visited by a breath of fresh air. You have to ascend rotten staircases, grope your way along dark and filthy passages swarming with vermin. Then, if you are not driven back by the intolerable stench, you may gain admittance to the dens in which these thousands of beings herd together. Eight feet square! That is about the average size of very many of these rooms. Walls and ceiling are black with the accretions of filth which have gathered upon them through long years of neglect. It is exuding through cracks in the boards; it is everywhere. . . . Every room in these rotten and reeking tenements houses a family, often two. In one cellar, a sanitary inspector reports finding a father, mother, three children, and four pigs. . . . Here are seven people living in one underground kitchen, and a little dead child lying in the same room. Elsewhere is a poor widow, her three children, and a child who had been dead thirteen days.[6] Her husband, who was a cabman, had shortly before committed suicide. . . . In another apartment, nine brothers and sisters, from twenty-nine years of age downward, live, eat, and sleep together. Here is a mother who turns her children into the street in the early evening, because she lets her room for immoral purposes until long after midnight, when the poor little wretches creep back again, if they have not found some miserable shelter elsewhere. Where there are beds, they are simply heaps of dirty rags, shavings, or straw; but for the most part these miserable beings find rest only upon the filthy boards. . . . There are men and women who lie and die, day by day, in their wretched single room, sharing all the family trouble, enduring the hunger and the cold, and waiting, without hope, without a single ray of comfort, until God curtains their staring eyes with the merciful film of death." Says the writer: "So far from making the most of our facts for the purpose of appealing to emotion, we have been compelled to tone down everything, and wholly to omit what most needs to be known, or the ears

[6] The investigations here reported were made in the *summer*.

and eyes of our readers would have been insufferably outraged. Indeed, no respectable printer would print, and certainly no decent family would admit, even the driest statement of the horrors and infamies discovered in one brief visitation from house to house."[7] Such are the conditions under which many tens of thousands live in London. So much space is given to this picture, only because London is a future New York, or Brooklyn, or Chicago. It gives a very dim impression of what may exist in a great city side by side with enormous wealth. Is it strange that such conditions arouse a blind and bitter hatred of our social system?

Socialism centers in the city, and the materials of its growth are multiplied with the growth of the city. Here is heaped the social dynamite; here roughs, gamblers, thieves, robbers, lawless and desperate men of all sorts, congregate; men who are ready on any pretext to raise riots for the purpose of destruction and plunder; here gather foreigners and wage-workers who are especially susceptible to socialist arguments; here skepticism and irreligion abound; here inequality is the greatest and most obvious, and the contrast between opulence and penury the most striking; here is suffering the sorest. As the greatest wickedness in the world is to be found not among the cannibals of some far-off coast, but in Christian lands where the light of truth is diffused and rejected, so the utmost depth of wretchedness exists not among savages who have few wants, but in great cities, where, in the presence of plenty and of every luxury men starve. Let a man become the owner of a home, and he is much less susceptible to socialistic propagandism. But real estate is so high in the city that it is almost impossible for a wage-worker to become a householder. In 1888 the Health Department of New York made a census which revealed the fact that there were then in the city 32,390 tenement houses,[8] occupied by 237,972 families, and 1,093,701 souls. In-

[7] Anon., *The Bitter Cry of Outcast London* (Boston, 1883), pp. 2–4, 10.

[8] In New York under the law of 1887, a tenement house is one occupied by three or more families, living separately. The above census did not include the better class of apartment houses.

vestigation in 1890 showed that the tenement houses had increased in two years about 5,000. If there were an average of 33.76 to each house, as in 1888, the tenement house population in 1890 was nearly 1,260,000. The law in New York requires a juror to be owner of real or personal property valued at not less than two hundred and fifty dollars; and this, the Commissioner says, relieves seventy thousand of the registered voters of New York City from jury duty. Let us remember that those seventy thousand voters represent a population of two hundred and eighty thousand, or fifty-six thousand families, not one of which has property to the value of two hundred and fifty dollars. "During the past three years, 220,976 persons in New York have asked for outside aid in one form or another."[9] Said a New York Supreme Judge, a few years ago: "There is a large class—I was about to say a majority—of the population of New York and Brooklyn, who just live, and to whom the rearing of two or more children means inevitably a boy for the penitentiary, and a girl for the brothel."[10] "When an English Judge tells us, as Mr. Justice Wills did the other day, that there were any number of parents who would kill their children for a few pounds' insurance money, we can form some idea of the horrors of the existence into which many of the children of this highly favored land are ushered at their birth."[11] Under such conditions smolder the volcanic fires of a deep discontent.

We have seen how the dangerous elements of our civilization are each multiplied and all concentered in the city. Do we find there the conservative forces of society equally numerous and strong? Here are the tainted spots in the body-politic; where is the salt? In 1890 there was in the United States one Protestant church organization to every 438 of the population. Including all Protestant churches, together with missions, there was in Boston one church to every 1778 of the population, and in St. Louis, one to 2662; not including missions, there was in

[9] Mrs. Josephine Shaw Lowell, "The Bitter Cry of the Poor in New York," *Christian Union,* 31 (March 26, 1885), 6.

[10] Henry George, *Social Problems* (New York, 1886), p. 98.

[11] William Booth, *In Darkest England* (New York and London, 1890), p. 65.

Cincinnati one Protestant church to every 2195; in Buffalo, one to 2650; in Chicago, one to 3601. The average city church is larger than the average country church, but allowing for this fact we may say that the city, where the forces of evil are massed, and where the need of Christian influence is peculiarly great, is from one-half to one-quarter as well supplied with churches as the nation at large. And church accommodations in the city are growing more inadequate every year. Including all Protestant churches, Chicago had in 1836 one church to every 1042 of the population; in 1851, one to every 1577; in 1860, one to 1820; in 1870, one to 2433; in 1880, one to 3062; and in 1890, one to 3601. Brooklyn had in 1840 one Evangelical church to 1575 souls; in 1850, one to 1760; in 1860, one to 2035; in 1870, one to 2085; in 1880, one to 2673; in 1890, one to 2997. In New York City there was in 1840 one Evangelical church to every 2071 of the population; in 1850, one to 2442; in 1860, one to 2777; in 1870, one to 2480; in 1880, one to 3048; in 1890, according to the government census, one to 3544, and according to the police census, one to 4006. That is, if we accept the latter enumeration, New York had in round numbers, one Evangelical church in 1840 to 2000 people; in 1880, one to 3000; and in 1890, one to 4000. These three cities seem to be exceptional only in degree. So far as I have made investigations, there is a general tendency, with variations, in the growth of urban population to outrun church provision. It is true that church buildings are larger now than they used to be, but after recognizing this fact, it is evident that church provision is becoming more and more inadequate to the needs of the city.

In Chicago, "There is a certain district of which a careful examination has been made; and in that district, out of a population of 50,000, there are 20,000 under twenty years of age, and there are Sunday-school accommodations for less than 2,000; that is, over 18,000 of the children and youth are compelled to go without the gospel of Jesus Christ, because the Christian churches are asleep. Mr. Gates says: 'What wonder that the police arrested last year 7,200 boys and girls for various petty crimes? The devil cares for them. There are 261 saloons and dago shops, three theaters and other vile places, and the Christian church offers Sunday-school accommodation to only 2,000!' "[12] The writer has found similar destitution in the large cities of Ohio. And the statistics given above indicate that in the large cities generally, it is common to find extensive districts nearly or quite destitute of the gospel. In the Fourth and Seventh wards of New York City there are 70,000 people, and seven Protestant churches and chapels, or one place of worship to every 10,000 of the population. In the Tenth ward there is a population of 47,000 and two churches and chapels.[13] South of Fourteenth Street there was in 1880 a population of 541,726, for whom there were 109 Protestant churches and missions, or about one to every 5000 souls. In 1890, according to the police census, there was in the same quarter a population of 596,878, an increase of 50,000 people, while of churches and missions there was an increase of *one*. Indeed, the Christian force is not so large now as it was ten or even twenty years ago, because churches have moved out and been replaced by missions. It was stated by Dr. Schauffler in 1888 that during the preceding twenty years nearly 200,000 people had moved in below Fourteenth Street, and seventeen Protestant churches had moved out. One Jewish synagogue and two Roman Catholic churches had been added.[14] So that counting churches of every kind, there were fourteen less than there were twenty years before, notwithstanding the great increase of population.

If moral and religious influences are peculiarly weak at the point where our social explosives are gathered, what of city government? Are its strength and purity so exceptional as

[12] Dr. H. A. Schauffler's address at Saratoga, June 1884. [In *Home Missionary*, 57 (October 1884), 233. Henry Albert Schauffler (1837–1905), Congregational clergyman, served as missionary in Constantinople, Prague, and Brünn, and, in 1884, became the Congregational Home Missionary Society's superintendent for work among Polish and Bohemian immigrants in the United States.]

[13] Dr. A. F. Schauffler in Chickering Hall Conference, 1888. [Adolphus Frederick Schauffler (1843–1919), brother of Henry Albert, was a Congregational minister in New York City, and served as superintendent and president of the New York City Mission and Tract Society.]

[14] A. F. Schauffler, Chickering Hall Conference.

to insure the effective control of these dangerous elements? In the light of notorious facts, the question sounds satirical. It is commonly acknowledged that the government of large cities in the United States is a failure. "In all the great American cities there is to-day as clearly defined a ruling class as in the most aristocratic countries in the world. Its members carry wards in their pockets, make up the slates for nominating conventions, distribute offices as they bargain together, and—though they toil not, neither do they spin—wear the best of raiment and spend money lavishly. They are men of power, whose favor the ambitious must court, and whose vengeance he must avoid. Who are these men? The wise, the good, the learned—men who have earned the confidence of their fellow-citizens by the purity of their lives, the splendor of their talents, their probity in public trusts, their deep study of the problems of government? No; they are gamblers, saloon-keepers, pugilists, or worse, who have made a trade of controlling votes and of buying and selling offices and official acts."[15] It has come to this, that holding a municipal office in a large city almost impeaches a man's character. Known integrity and competency hopelessly incapacitate a man for any office in the gift of a city rabble. In a certain western city, the administration of the mayor had convinced good citizens that he gave constant aid and comfort to gamblers, thieves, saloon-keepers and all the worst elements of society. He became a candidate for a second term. The prominent men and press of both parties and the ministry of all denominations united in a Citizens' League to defeat him; but he was triumphantly returned to office by the "lewd fellows of the baser sort." And again, after a desperate

[15] Henry George, *Progress and Poverty* (New York, 1879), p. 480. The twenty-eight leaders of Tammany, which organization governs New York City, are thus classified by *The Evening Post:* Twenty-eight professional politicians; one convicted murderer; one tried for murder and acquitted; one indicted for felonious assault; one indicted for bribery; four professional gamblers; five gambling house or "dive" keepers; four liquor-dealers; five former liquor-dealers; three sons of liquor-dealers; three former pugilists; four former "toughs;" six members of the Tweed gang; and seventeen office holders.

struggle on the part of the better elements to defeat him, he was re-elected to a third term of office.

Popular government in the city is degenerating into government by a "boss." During his visit to this country, Herbert Spencer said: "You retain the forms of freedom; but so far as I can gather, there has been a considerable loss of the substance. It is true that those who rule you do not do it by means of retainers armed with swords; but they do it through regiments of men armed with voting papers, who obey the word of command as loyally as did the dependents of the old feudal nobles, and who thus enable their leaders to override the general will, and make the community submit to their exactions as effectually as their prototypes of old. Manifestly those who framed your Constitution never dreamed that twenty thousand citizens would go to the polls led by a 'boss.' "

As a rule, our largest cities are the worst governed. It is natural, therefore, to infer that, as our cities grow larger and more dangerous, the government will become more corrupt, and control will pass more completely into the hands of those who themselves most need to be controlled. If we would appreciate the significance of these facts and tendencies, we must bear in mind that the disproportionate growth of the city is undoubtedly to continue, and the number of great cities to be largely increased. The extraordinary growth of urban population during this century has not been at all peculiar to the United States. It is a characteristic of nineteenth century civilization. And this growth of the city is taking place not only in England and Germany, where the increase of population is rapid, but also in France, where population is practically stationary, and even in Ireland where it is declining. This strong tendency toward the city is the result chiefly of agricultural machinery, of manufactures and railway communication, and their influence will, of course, continue. If the growth of the city in the United States has been so rapid during this century, while many millions of acres were being settled, what may be expected when the settlement of the West has been completed? The rise in the value of land, when once the agricultural lands have all been occupied and population has become dense, will stimulate yet more the growth of the city; for the man of small means will be unable to command a farm, and the town will become his only alternative. When the public lands are all taken, immigration, though it will be considerably restricted thereby, will continue, and will crowd the cities more and more. This country will undoubtedly have a population of several hundred millions, for the simple reason that it is capable of sustaining that number. And it looks as if the larger proportion of it would be urban. There can be no indefinite increase of our agricultural population. Its growth must needs be slow after the farms are all taken, and it is necessarily limited; but the cities may go on doubling and doubling again. Even if the growth of population should be very greatly and unexpectedly retarded, there are many now living who will see 150,000,000 inhabitants in the United States, and more than a quarter of that number living in cities of 8,000 and upward. And the city of the future will be more crowded than that of to-day, because the elevator makes it possible to build, as it were, one city above another. Thus is our civilization multiplying and focalizing the elements of anarchy and destruction. Nearly forty years ago De Tocqueville wrote: "I look upon the size of certain American cities, and especially upon the nature of their population, as a real danger which threatens the security of the democratic republics of the New World." That danger grows more real and imminent every year.

And this peril, like the others which have been discussed, peculiarly threatens the West. The time will doubtless come when a majority of the great cities of the country will be west of the Mississippi. This will result naturally from the greater eventual population of the West; but, in addition to this fact, what has been pointed out must not be forgotten, that agriculture will occupy a much smaller place *relatively* in the industries of the West than in those of the East, because a much smaller proportion of the land is arable. The vast region of the Rocky Mountains will be inhabited chiefly by a mining and manufacturing population, and such populations live in cities.

1. In gathering up the results of the foregoing discussion of these several perils, it should be remarked that to preserve republican institutions requires a *higher average* intelligence and virtue among large populations than among small. The government of 5,000,000 people was a simple thing compared with the government of 50,000,000; and the government of 50,000,000 is a simple thing compared with that of 500,000,000. There are many men who can conduct a small business successfully, who are utterly incapable of managing large interests. In the latter there are multiplied relations whose harmony must be preserved. A mistake is farther reaching. It has, as it were, a longer leverage. This is equally true of the business of government. The man of only average ability and intelligence discharges creditably the duties of mayor in his little town; but he would fail utterly at the head of the state or the nation. If the people are to govern, they must grow more intelligent as the population and the complications of government increase. And a higher morality is even more essential. As civilization increases, as society becomes more complex, as labor-saving machinery is multiplied and the division of labor becomes more minute, the individual becomes more fractional and dependent. Every savage possesses all the knowledge of his tribe. Throw him upon his own resources, and he is self-sufficient. A civilized man in like circumstances would perish. The savage is independent. Civilize him, and he becomes dependent; the more civilized, the more dependent. And, as men become more dependent on each other, they should be able to rely more implicitly on each other. More complicated and multiplied relations require a more delicate conscience and a stronger sense of justice. And any failure in character or conduct under such conditions is farther reaching and more disastrous in its results.

Is our progress in morals and intelligence at all comparable to the growth of population? The nation's illiteracy has not been discussed, because it is not one of the perils which peculiarly threaten the West; but any one who would calculate our political horoscope must allow it great influence in connection with the baleful stars which are in the ascendant. But the danger which arises from the corruption of popular morals is much greater. The republics of Greece and Rome, and, if I mistake not, all the republics that have ever lived and died, were more intelligent at the end than at the beginning; but growing intelligence could not compensate decaying morals. What, then, is our moral progress? Are popular morals as sound as they were twenty years ago? There is, perhaps, no better index of general morality than Sabbath observance; and everybody knows there has been a great increase of Sabbath desecration in twenty years. We have seen that we are now using as a beverage 29 per cent more of alcohol per caput than we were fifty years ago. Says Dr. S. W. Dike: "It is safe to say that divorce has been doubled, in proportion to marriages or population, in most of the Northern States within thirty years. Present figures indicate a still greater increase." [16] And President Woolsey, speaking of the United States, said in 1883: "On the whole, there can be little, if any, question that the ratio of divorces to marriages or to population exceeds that of any country in the Christian world." [17] While the population increased thirty per cent from 1870 to 1880, the number of criminals in the United States increased 82.33 per cent. It looks very much as if existing tendencies were in the direction of the deadline of vice. Excepting Mormonism, all the perils which have been discussed seem to be increasing more rapidly than the population. *Are popular morals likely to improve under their increasing influence?*

2. The fundamental idea of popular government is the distribution of power. It has been the struggle of liberty for ages to wrest power from the hands of one or the few, and lodge it in the hands of the many. We have seen, in the foregoing discussion, that centralized power is rapidly growing. The "boss" makes his bargain, and sells his ten thousand or fifty thousand

[16] Samuel W. Dike, "Some Aspects of the Divorce Question," *Princeton Review* (March 1884), p. 170.

[17] Theodore D. Woolsey, "Divorce," *North American Review,* 136 (April 1883), 314.

voters as if they were so many cattle. Centralized wealth is centralized power; and the capitalist and corporation find many ways to control votes. The liquor power controls thousands of votes in every considerable city. The president of the Mormon Church casts, say, sixty thousand votes. The Jesuits, it is said, are all under the command of one man in Washington. The Roman Catholic vote is more or less perfectly controlled by the priests. That means that the Pope can dictate some hundreds of thousands of votes in the United States. Is there anything un-republican in all this? And we must remember that, if present tendencies continue, these figures will be greatly multiplied in the future. And not only is this immense power lodged in the hand of one man, which in itself is perilous, but it is wielded without the slightest reference to any policy or principle of government, solely in the interests of a church or a business, or for personal ends.

The result of a national election may depend on a single state; the vote of that state may depend on a single city; the vote of that city may depend on a "boss," or a capitalist, or a corporation; or the election may be decided, and the policy of the government may be reversed, by the socialist, or liquor, or Roman Catholic or immigrant vote.

It matters not by what name we call the man who wields this centralized power—whether king, czar, pope, president, capitalist, or boss. Just so far as it is absolute and irresponsible, it is dangerous.

3. These several dangerous elements are singularly netted together, and serve to strengthen each other. It is not necessary to prove that any *one* of them is likely to destroy our national life, in order to show that it is imperiled. A man may die of wounds no one of which is fatal. No sober-minded man can look fairly at the facts, and doubt that *together* these perils constitute an array which will seriously endanger our free institutions, if the tendencies which have been pointed out continue; and especially is this true in view of the fact that these perils peculiarly confront the West, where our defense is weakest.

These dangerous elements are now working, and will continue to work, incalculable harm and loss—moral, intellectual, social, pecuniary. But the supreme peril, which will certainly come unless there is found for existing tendencies some effectual check, and must probably be faced by many now living, will arise, when, the conditions having been fully prepared, some great industrial or other crisis precipitates an open struggle between the destructive and the conservative elements of society. As civilization advances, and society becomes more highly organized, commercial transactions will be more complex and immense. As a result, all business relations and industries will be more sensitive. Commercial distress in any great business center will the more surely create wide-spread disaster. Under such conditions, industrial paralysis is likely to occur from time to time, more general and more prostrating than any heretofore known. When such a commercial crisis has closed factories by the ten thousand, and wage-workers have been thrown out of employment by the million; when the public lands, which hitherto at such times have afforded relief, are all exhausted; when our urban population has been multiplied several fold, and our Cincinnatis have become Chicagos, our Chicagos New Yorks, and our New Yorks Londons; when class antipathies are deepened; when socialistic organizations, armed and drilled, are in every city, and the ignorant and vicious power of crowded populations has fully found itself; when the corruption of city governments is grown apace; when crops fail, or some gigantic "corner" doubles the price of bread; with starvation in the home; with idle workmen gathered, sullen and desperate, in the saloons; with unprotected wealth at hand; with the tremendous forces of chemistry within easy reach; then, with *the opportunity, the means, the fit agents, the motive, the temptation to destroy, all brought into evil conjunction,* THEN will come the real test of our institutions, then will appear whether we are capable of self-government.

CHAPTER XII

THE INFLUENCE OF EARLY SETTLERS

OLIVER WENDELL HOLMES, on being asked when the training of a child should begin, replied: "A hundred years before he is born." Not only *should* it begin then, it *does;* for inheritance, together with that which necessarily accompanies it, is the great conservative influence which perpetuates national characteristics, and preserves the identity of races. In the case of nations, education, though it may modify the results of inheritance, is, itself, for the most part, determined by inheritance. What is the difference between North and South America? It is the difference between the Anglo-Saxon race and the Spanish race. What is the difference between Massachusetts and Virginia? It is the difference between the Pilgrim and the Cavalier. How unlike are Boston, New York, Philadelphia, New Orleans, Montreal, and Quebec? Religiously, morally, intellectually, socially, commercially, in enterprise and spirit, they differ to-day pretty much as their founders differed generations ago. It is true of the city and nation as of the herb, that its seed is in itself, after its kind.

Communities and commonwealths, like men, have their childhood, which is the formative period. *It is the first permanent settlers who impress themselves and their character on the future.* Powerful influences may, in later years, produce important modifications; but it is early influence which is farthest reaching, and is generally decisive. It is easier to form than to reform; easier to mold molten iron than to file the cold cast.

Look at a few illustrations of the above truths. On the Western Reserve are two adjoining townships, which were settled by men of radically different character. The southern township was founded by a far-seeing and devoted home missionary. He had become convinced that he could do more to establish Christian institutions on the Reserve "by one conspicuous example of a well organized and well Christianized township, with all the best arrangements and appliances of New England civilization, than by many years of desultory effort in the way of missionary labor." The settlers were carefully selected. None but professing Christians were to become landholders. As soon as a few families had moved into the township, public worship was commenced, and has ever since been maintained without interruption. A church was organized under the roof of the first log cabin. At the center of the township, where eight roads meet, was located the church building, fitly representing the central place occupied by the service of God in the life of the colony. Soon followed the school house and the public library. And there, in the midst of the unconquered forest, only eight years after the first white settlement, the people, mindful of higher education, and true to their New England antecedents, planted an academy. At a very early period several benevolent societies were organized, and here was opened the first school for the deaf and dumb in the State of Ohio.

The northern township was first settled by an infidel, who seems to have given to the community not only his name, but, in large measure, his character also. He naturally attracted men of the same sort. It is said he expressed the desire that there might never be a Christian church in the township; and, though this desire was not gratified, the general character of the town has been irreligious. One of the best colleges in the West was founded within five miles, but I am unable to learn that any young man from this township has ever taken a college course.

A few [1] have entered professional life, none of whom has gained a wide reputation. On the other hand, the southern township is widely known to-day for its moral and religious character, its wealth [2] and liberality, and for the exceptionally large number of young men and women it sends to colleges and seminaries. It has furnished many members of the state legislature and senate. It has been fruitful of ministers and educators, some of whom have gained a national reputation. From this little village of a few hundred inhabitants have gone forth men to college professorships, East and West, to the Supreme Bench of the state, and to the United States Congress. The general character of these two townships was fixed at the beginning of the century. Their founders placed a stamp upon them which abides.

The town of Boscawen, New Hampshire, was settled in 1734, by a colony of Massachusetts people. Scarcely were they settled, when they took steps to secure "some suitable man and a Christian learned" to preach the gospel. The original stock was good, and the formative influences were Christian. We now find that its collegiate and professional record contains more than 130 names, among which there are those of two missionaries, six journalists, twenty-one lawyers, thirty-five physicians, and forty-two ministers. Among the eminent men whom this town has produced are General John A. Dix [3] and William Pitt Fessenden.[4]

[1] I can gain definite knowledge of only seven, though it is quite likely there have been more.

[2] Though the northern township had the advantage of a better soil, the assessed valuation of real and personal property in the southern now (1885) exceeds that of the other by fifty-six per cent. Godliness is profitable to the life that now is.

[3] [John Adams Dix (1798–1879), served successively as U.S. Senator from New York, Secretary of the Treasury, major general in the U.S. Army, Ambassador to France, and governor of New York.]

[4] [William Pitt Fessenden (1806–1869), served in the Congress as Representative and Senator from Maine, was appointed Secretary of the Treasury in 1864 and, returning to the Senate in 1865, became chairman of the Joint Committee on Reconstruction.]

When Northampton, Massachusetts, was settled, in 1654, it was "way out west" on the frontier. Among the early settlers in the then wilderness, who shaped the character and history of the town, were the Allens, Bartletts, Bridgmans, Clapps, Dwights, Elliotts, Hawleys, Kings, Lymans, Mathers, Parsons, Stoddards, Strongs, Tappans, and Wrights. The town early became distinguished for its marked religious character and its educational advantages. For a century and a quarter the entire population, save the very old and the very young, the sick and their attendants, were found in the church every Sabbath. In 1735, during the pastorate of Jonathan Edwards, over 600, out of a population of 1,100, were members of the church. For seven generations the impress given by the early settlers has remained. Their influence upon the community, and that of the community upon the state and the nation, may be, in some measure, estimated from the following record.[5] Among the natives and residents of the town are about 354 college graduates, besides fifty-six graduates of other institutions, one hundred and fourteen ministers, eighty-four ministers' wives, ten missionaries, twenty-five judges, about one hundred and two lawyers, ninety-five physicians; one hundred and one educators, including seven college presidents and thirty professors, twenty-four editors, six historians, and twenty-four authors, among whom are George Bancroft,[6] John Lothrop Motley,[7] Professor W. D. Whitney,[8] and J. G. Holland;[9] thirty-eight officers of state, among them two governors, two secretaries of the Com-

[5] Solomon Clark, *Antiquities, Historicals and Graduates of Northampton* (Northampton, 1882).

[6] [George Bancroft (1800–1891), author of a ten-volume *History of the United States* (1834–1874), served as Secretary of the Navy, and as Ambassador to Britain (1846) and Germany (1867–1874).]

[7] [John Lothrop Motley (1814–1877), author of *The Rise of the Dutch Republic* (1851) and *The History of the United Netherlands* (1866–1867), served as Ambassador to Austria and to England.]

[8] [William Dwight Whitney (1827–1894), Yale professor and American Sanskrit scholar, contributed also to linguistics, lexicography, and the study of modern languages.]

[9] [Josiah Gilbert Holland (1819–1881), editor and author of numerous popular prose and poetry works, was associated with the *Springfield Republican* (1850–1869) and *Scribner's Monthly*.]

monwealth, seven senators, and eighteen representatives; twenty-one army officers, including six colonels and two generals; twenty-eight officers of the United States, among them a Secretary of the Navy, two Foreign Ministers, a Treasurer of the United States, five senators, eight members of Congress, and one President.

If a community produces or fails to produce good citizens and able men, the records of the founders will rarely fail to afford an explanation, for the influence of the early settlers continues operative until their descendants are displaced by some other stock. It is true the glory is departing from many a New England village, because men, alien in blood, in religion, and in civilization, are taking possession of homes in which were once reared the descendants of the Pilgrims. But the fact that the character of New England is undergoing important changes is no proof that the impress now being given to the new communities of the West will not be permanent. There is no likelihood that the foreign immigration now pouring in upon us is ever to be supplanted by another stock. Instead, it will be reinforced until there is an equalization of population, between the Old World and the New, then it will cease. Beyond a peradventure, the character, and hence the destiny, of the great West, for centuries to come, is now being determined.

"I hear the tread of pioneers,
Of nations yet to be;
The first low wash of waves, where soon
Shall roll a human sea.

"The rudiments of empire here
Are plastic yet, and warm;
The chaos of a mighty world
Is rounding into form."

What the final form of that western world is likely to be, we may infer from the forces which are at work shaping it. How do they compare with the influences which molded New England institutions? The Pilgrim Fathers sought these shores not simply as refugees, but also as missionaries. "A great hope and inward zeal they had of laying some good foundation (or, at least, to make some way thereunto) for propagating and advancing the Gospel of the Kingdom of Christ in those remote parts of the world." They came not for gold; but for conscience' sake and soul's sake. The early settlers of New England were sufficiently homogeneous to enable them to labor harmoniously and successfully to make religion, learning, liberty and law, the four corner-stones of their civilization. New England ideas gave form to the national government, and shaped the institutions of the Middle States; but does any one suppose they are dominant to-day in the great territories of the West? Is there no danger that an alien and materialistic civilization will spring up in the Rocky Mountains and beyond?

The population of the frontier is thoroughly heterogeneous. In a town in Montana of about 7,000 inhabitants, a religious census discovered, in addition to the usual Protestant sects, evangelical and otherwise, 3,000 Catholics, several members of the Greek Church, three Mohammedans and 360 Buddhists. In a single congregation there were representatives of fifteen states of the Union, scattered from the Atlantic to the Pacific, and the following nationalities: German, French, Italian, English, Scotch, Irish, Welsh, Norwegian, Swedish, Greek and Russian, besides a native of Alaska. The West is being settled by well-nigh every variety of race, representing every type of religion and irreligion—peoples different in antecedents, language, customs, habits, ideas and character. The one thing in which a frontier population agrees is the universal and unbending purpose to make money.

We have already seen that the West is peculiarly exposed to the dangers of Mammonism, materialism, luxuriousness and the centralization of wealth; that conditions are exceptionally favorable to the spread of socialism; that the relative power of the saloon is two and a half times greater in the far West than in the East; that Mormonism is still vigorous; that Romanism as compared with the population, is about three times as strong in the territories as in the whole United States; and that into the West is pouring a large percentage of our foreign immigration. These forces of evil, which are severely trying the established institutions of the East, are brought to bear with increased power upon the plastic and formative society of the West. It is like subjecting a child to evil influences, for resistance to which the full strength of mature years is none too great.

We have seen (Chap. IV.) that nearly all of the perils which have been discussed are greatly enhanced by the presence of the foreign element. It is of the utmost significance that this element constitutes so large a proportion of the settlers who are now shaping the future of the great commonwealths of the West. Those of foreign birth or extraction[10] were, in 1880, 38.2 per cent of the population of Washington Territory. Of Montana, they constituted 48.8 per cent of the population; of Wyoming, 50.5 per cent; of Utah, 51.9 per cent; of Idaho, 53.2 per cent; of Arizona, 55.2 per cent; of Dakota, 66.5 per cent; of the State of Nebraska, 43.5 per cent; of California, 59.9 per cent; of Nevada, 63.3 per cent; and of Minnesota, 71.6 per cent. Not including Alaska, New Mexico, or the Indian Territory, 53.9 per cent of the population of the territories was, in 1880, of foreign birth or extraction. The population of New Mexico, though almost wholly native, is essentially foreign—foreign in race, language, education (or rather the lack of it), in religious ideas, habits and character. It is much more difficult to assimilate than any of the European races. The same is true of the population of the Indian Territory. Counting these peoples, then, as foreign, 66 per cent of the population of the territories is of foreign birth or extraction; and these territories include nearly 44 per cent of all the land between the Mississippi and Alaska. If we add California, Colorado, Minnesota, Nebraska, Nevada and Oregon, these states, together with the territories, constitute nearly two-thirds of all the West, and 58.9 per cent of their inhabitants are of foreign extraction or birth.

We have seen that dangerous influences are being brought to bear upon the new settlements of the West with peculiar power. Are the neutralizing and saving influences of the Chris-

[10] By foreign extraction is meant natives, one or both of whose parents were foreign-born. See *Compendium of the Tenth Census, 1880,* part II (Washington, D.C., 1883), pp. 1408, 1409.

tian religion equally strong? According to Dr. Dorchester, the evangelical church membership of the United States in 1880, was one-fifth of the entire population; [11] but in Oregon, the same year, only one in eleven of the population was in some evangelical church; in Dakota, one in twelve; in Washington, one in sixteen; in California and Colorado, one in twenty; in Idaho, one in thirty-three; in Montana, one in thirty-six; in Nevada, one in forty-six; in Wyoming, one in eighty-one; in Utah, one in 224; in New Mexico, one in 657; in Arizona, one in 685.

If, as Milton says, "Childhood shows the man as morning shows the day," what will be the manhood of the West, unless the churches of the East are speedily aroused to some appreciation of their opportunity and their obligation?

Important changes are taking place in the East and South, but they do not possess the almost boundless significance which attaches to beginnings. East of the Mississippi, state constitutions and laws were formed long since; society is no longer chaotic, it has crystallized; religion has its recognized institutions which are thoroughly established. A vast work remains to be done, both in the North and South—a work which sustains important relations to our national welfare; but it is the West, not the South or the North, which holds the key to the nation's future. The center of population, of manufactures, of wealth, and of political power is not moving south but west. The Southern States will never have a majority of our population; the West will. To-day, the constitutions and laws of many of the future states of our western empire are unformed.[12] Those great territories, as Edmund Burke once said of the nation, are yet "in the gristle;" society is still chaotic; religious, educational and political institutions are embryonic; but their character is being rapidly fashioned by the swift, impetuous forces of intense western life. "Know thy opportunity."

[11] [Daniel Dorchester, *The Problem of Religious Progress* (New York, 1881), p. 545.]

[12] Since this sentence was written, five years ago, six of the western territories have adopted constitutions and been admitted as states.

CHAPTER XIII

THE EXHAUSTION OF THE PUBLIC LANDS

THOMAS CARLYLE once said to an American: "Ye may boast o' yer dimocracy, or any ither 'cracy, or any kind o' poleetical roobish; but the reason why yer laboring folk are so happy is thot ye have a *vost deal o' land for a verra few people.*" Carlyle was not the man to take an unprejudiced view of republican institutions; but he was not mistaken in finding great significance in the fact that heretofore our land has been vastly greater than its population. The rapid accumulation of our wealth, our comparative immunity from the consequences of unscientific legislation, our financial elasticity, our high wages, the general welfare and contentment of the people hitherto have all been due, in very large measure, to an abundance of cheap land. When the supply is exhausted, we shall enter upon a new era, and shall more rapidly approximate European conditions of life. The gravity of the change was clearly foreseen by Lord Macaulay, and expressed in his well-known letter to Hon. H. S. Randall, in 1857—a letter which General Garfield said startled him "like an alarm bell in the night." "Your fate," says Macaulay, "I believe to be certain, though it is deferred by a physical cause. As long as you have a boundless extent of fertile and unoccupied land, your laboring population will be far more at ease than the laboring population of the Old World. . . . But the time will come when New England will be as thickly peopled as Old England. Wages will be as low, and will fluctuate as much with you as with us. You will have your Manchesters and Birminghams. And in those Manchesters and Birminghams, hundreds of thousands of artisans will assuredly be some time out of work. Then your institutions will be fairly brought to the test. . . . Through such seasons the United States will have to pass in the course of the next century, if not of this. I wish you a good deliverance. But my reason and my wishes are at war, and I cannot help foreboding the worst."

What is the extent of these public lands whose occupation means so much? The public domain west of the Mississippi, not including Alaska, is estimated to have been, in 1880, 880,787,746 acres.[1] This includes land necessary to fill railroad grants, estimated at 110,000,000 acres, also private land-claims estimated at 80,000,000 acres, together with military and Indian reservations estimated at 157,356,952 acres. Supposing all of the military and Indian reservations to revert to the public domain save 57,000,000 acres, there remained of the public lands west of the Mississippi, in 1880, yet to be disposed of, about 633,787,746 acres. This seems an almost inexhaustible supply, but we must remember the magnitude of the demand. The following table shows how much land the Government has disposed of each year since 1880.

	Acres		*Acres*
In 1881	10,893,390	In 1885	20,995,515
" 1882	14,309,166	" 1886	22,124,563
" 1883	19,430,032	" 1887	25,858,038
" 1884	27,531,170	" 1888	30,116,684

Here is a total in eight years, of 171,258,565 acres, a million more than are contained in the state of Texas, or more than twice the area of Great Britain and Ireland, leaving in the hands of the government in 1889, about 462,529,181 acres. If the rate since 1880 should be sustained, all of the public lands west of the Mississippi would be exhausted in twenty years. It

[1] George W. Spaulding, *A Treatise on the Public Land System of the United States* (San Francisco, 1884), pp. 6, 7.

must not be forgotten that these figures include the great mountain ranges, and all the barren lands. Only a comparatively small portion is arable. The farming lands of the West therefore, will all be taken before the close of this century. And under private ownership they will naturally appreciate in value with the increase of population. Senator Wade, of Ohio, predicted, in the United States Senate, some twenty-five years ago, that, by 1900, every acre of good agricultural land in the Union would be worth at least fifty dollars. This is very much of an overestimate, but it is nevertheless certain that our wide domain will soon cease to palliate popular discontent, because it will soon be beyond the reach of the poor.

But the settlement of the public lands has a further and even deeper significance. The first permanent settlers, as we have seen in the preceding chapter, impress their character on the community and commonwealth for generations and centuries; and this abiding stamp is to be given to the great West in the course of the *next fifteen or twenty years.* True, the land is not settled as rapidly as it is disposed of by the government. Many acres have passed into the hands of wealthy syndicates or individual capitalists, and are held by them for a rise in value; but this can delay actual settlement for a short time only, and does not modify the general statement that the great West is to be settled by this generation. Robert Giffen, President of the London Statistical Society, in an address on "World Crowding," after following several lines of reasoning to the same conclusion, says: "Whatever way we may look at the matter, then, it seems certain that, in twenty-five years' time, and probably before that date, the limitation of area in the United States will be felt. There will be no longer vast tracts of virgin land for the settler. The whole available area will be peopled agriculturally, as the Eastern States are now peopled." [2] Suppose the entire region west of the Mississippi—not excepting bald mountains and alkaline deserts—were divided into town-

[2] Robert Giffin, "World Crowding," in Titus Munson Coan, ed., *Social Problems,* Topics of the Time, vol. I, no. 1 (New York, 1883), pp. 36–37.

ships six miles square. From 1870 to 1880 the trans-Mississippi population increased a little more than sixty-one per cent.[3] The Census of 1890 shows in this region a population of 16,419,459—an increase in ten years of 45.8 per cent. Even if the ratio of increase during the next ten years should fall to thirty-three per cent, which is unlikely, there would be in 1900 a population of nearly 22,000,000—sufficient, if it were evenly distributed, to place 384 souls in every township west of the great river. The natural distribution of such a population would manifestly result in the settlement of about all the habitable regions. Consider the location of the unoccupied land. It is not a vast island, like Australia, separated by thousands of miles from its sources of population. It lies close to one of the greatest peoples on the earth; and not on our north or south, but on our *west,* which is important, because great migrations move along lines of latitude. Moreover, this great territory is gridironed with transcontinental railways. Every circumstance favors its rapid occupation.

We must note, also, the order of settlement. In the Middle States the farms were first taken, then the town sprung up to supply their wants, and at length the railway connected it with the world; but in the West the order is reversed—first the railroad, then the town, then the farms. Settlement is, consequently, much more rapid, and the city stamps the country, instead of the country's stamping the city. It is the cities and towns which will frame state constitutions, make laws, create public opinion, establish social usages, and fix standards of morals in the West. The character of the West will, therefore, be substantially determined some time before the land is all occupied.

In 1880, fifty-three per cent of our national domain (not including Alaska) contained only six per cent of our population. That is, one-half of our territory was, for the most part, uninhabited. The character of this vast region, equal in area to

[3] During the same period the average per cent of increase of population in all the states of the Union was 29—in the territories, 77. Idaho increased 117 per cent, Wyoming, 127, Washington, 213, Arizona, 318, Dakota, 853.

Great Britain, France, Spain, Italy, Austria, Germany, Norway and Sweden, together with a dozen of the smaller European states, is being determined during the last twenty years of the century. Suppose all of Western Europe were practically uninhabited, that to-day the pioneer were pitching his tent by the Thames and Seine, and building his log cabin on the banks of the Tiber. He takes with him not the rude implements of centuries ago, but the locomotive, the telegraph, the steam-press, and all the swift appliances of modern civilization. Suppose the countries named above were all to be settled in twenty years; that, instead of the slow evolutions of many centuries, their political, social, religious, and educational institutions were to be determined by one generation; that from this one generation were to spring a civilization, like Minerva from the head of Jupiter, full-grown and fully equipped. What a period in the world's history it would be, unparalleled and tremendous! Yet such a Europe is being created by this generation west of the Mississippi. And within the bosom of these few years is folded not only the future of the mighty West, but the nation's destiny: for, as we have seen, the West is to dominate the East.

CHAPTER XIV

THE ANGLO-SAXON AND THE WORLD'S FUTURE[1]

EVERY race which has deeply impressed itself on the human family has been the representative of some great idea—one or more—which has given direction to the nation's life and form to its civilization. Among the Egyptians this seminal idea was life, among the Persians it was light, among the Hebrews it was purity, among the Greeks it was beauty, among the Romans it was law. The Anglo-Saxon is the representative of two great ideas, which are closely related. One of them is that of civil liberty. Nearly all of the civil liberty of the world is enjoyed by Anglo-Saxons: the English, the British colonists, and the people of the United States. To some, like the Swiss, it is permitted by the sufferance of their neighbors; others, like the French, have experimented with it; but, in modern times, the peoples whose love of liberty has won it, and whose genius for self-government has preserved it, have been Anglo-Saxons. The noblest races have always been lovers of liberty. The love ran strong in early German blood, and has profoundly influenced the institutions of all the branches of the great German family; but it was left for the Anglo-Saxon branch fully to recognize the right of the individual to himself, and formally to declare it the foundation stone of government.

[1] It is only just to say that the substance of this chapter was given to the public as a lecture some three years before the appearance of Prof. John Fiske's "Manifest Destiny," in *Harper's Magazine,* 70 (March 1885), 578–590, which contains some of the same ideas.

The other great idea of which the Anglo-Saxon is the exponent is that of a pure *spiritual* Christianity. It was no accident that the great reformation of the sixteenth century originated among a Teutonic, rather than a Latin people. It was the fire of liberty burning in the Saxon heart that flamed up against the absolutism of the Pope. Speaking roughly, the peoples of Europe which are Celtic are Roman Catholic, and those which are Teutonic are Protestant; and where the Teutonic race was purest, there Protestantism spread with the greatest rapidity. But, with beautiful exceptions, Protestantism on the continent has degenerated into mere formalism. By confirmation at a certain age, the state churches are filled with members who generally know nothing of a personal spiritual experience. In obedience to a military order, a regiment of German soldiers files into church and partakes of the sacrament, just as it would shoulder arms or obey any other word of command. It is said that, in Berlin and Leipsic, only a little over one per cent of the Protestant population are found in church. Protestantism on the continent seems to be about as poor in spiritual life and power as Romanism. That means that most of the spiritual Christianity in the world is found among Anglo-Saxons and their converts; for this is the great missionary race. If we take all of the German missionary societies together, we find that, in the number of workers and amount of contributions, they do not equal the smallest of the three great English missionary societies. The year that the Congregationalists in the United States gave one dollar and thirty-seven cents per caput to foreign missions, the members of the great German State Church gave only three-quarters of a cent per caput to the same cause.[2] Evidently it is chiefly to the English and American peoples that we must look for the evangelization of the world.

It is not necessary to argue to those for whom I write that the two great needs of mankind, that all men may be lifted up into the light of the highest Christian civilization, are, first, a pure,

[2] Theodore Christlieb, *Protestant Foreign Missions* (Boston, 1880), pp. 34, 37.

spiritual Christianity, and second, civil liberty. Without controversy, these are the forces which, in the past, have contributed most to the elevation of the human race, and they must continue to be, in the future, the most efficient ministers to its progress. It follows, then, that the Anglo-Saxon, as the great representative of these two ideas, the depositary of these two greatest blessings, sustains peculiar relations to the world's future, is divinely commissioned to be, in a peculiar sense, his brother's keeper. Add to this the fact of his rapidly increasing strength in modern times, and we have well-nigh a demonstration of his destiny. In 1700 this race numbered less than 6,000,000 souls. In 1800, Anglo-Saxons (I use the term somewhat broadly to include all English-speaking peoples) had increased to about 20,500,000, and now, in 1890, they number more than 120,000,000, having multiplied almost six-fold in ninety years. At the end of the reign of Charles II. the English colonists in America numbered 200,000. During these two hundred years, our population has increased two hundred and fifty-fold. And the expansion of this race has been no less remarkable than its multiplication. In one century the United States has increased its territory ten-fold, while the enormous acquisition of foreign territory by Great Britain—and chiefly within the last hundred years—is wholly unparalleled in history. This mighty Anglo-Saxon race, though comprising only one-thirteenth part of mankind, now rules more than one-third of the earth's surface, and more than one-fourth of its people. And if this race, while growing from 6,000,000 to 120,000,000, thus gained possession of a third portion of the earth, is it to be supposed that when it numbers 1,000,000,000, it will lose the disposition, or lack the power to extend its sway?

This race is multiplying not only more rapidly than any other European race, but more rapidly than *all* the races of continental Europe taken together. There is no exact knowledge of the population of Europe early in the century. We know, however, that the increase on the continent during the ten years from 1870 to 1880 was 6.89 per cent. If this rate of increase is sustained for a century, the population on the continent in 1980 will be 534,000,000; while the one Anglo-Saxon race, if it should multiply for a hundred years as fast as from 1870 to 1880, would in 1980 number 1,111,000,000 souls, an incredible increase, of course.

What then will be the probable numbers of this race a hundred years hence? It is hazardous to venture a prophecy, but we may weigh probabilities. In studying this subject several things must be borne in mind. Heretofore, the great causes which have operated to check the growth of population in the world have been war, famine, and pestilence; but, among civilized peoples, these causes are becoming constantly less operative. Paradoxical as it seems, the invention of more destructive weapons of war renders war less destructive; commerce and wealth have removed the fear of famine, and pestilence is being brought more and more under control by medical skill and sanitary science. Moreover, Anglo-Saxons, with the exception of the people of Great Britain, who now compose less than one-third of this race, are much less exposed to these checks upon growth than the races of Europe. Again, Europe is crowded, and is constantly becoming more so, which will tend to reduce continually the ratio of increase; while over two-thirds of the Anglo-Saxons occupy lands which invite almost unlimited expansion—the United States, Canada, Australia, and South Africa. Again, emigration from Europe, which will probably increase, is very largely into Anglo-Saxon countries; and, though these foreign elements exert a modifying influence on the Anglo-Saxon stock, their descendants are certain to be Anglo-Saxonized. From 1870 to 1880, Germany lost 987,000 inhabitants by emigration, most of whom came to the United States. In one generation, their children will be counted Anglo-Saxons. This race has been undergoing an unparalleled expansion during the eighteenth and nineteenth centuries, and the conditions for its continued growth are singularly favorable.

We are now prepared to ask what light statistics cast on the future. In Great Britain, from 1840 to 1850, the ratio of increase of the population was 2.49 per cent; during the next ten years it was 5.44 per cent; the next ten years, it was 8.60; from

1870 to 1880, it was 10.57; and from 1880 to 1889 it was 10.08 per cent. That is, for fifty years the ratio of increase has been rapidly rising.

It is not unlikely to continue rising for some time to come; but, remembering that the population is dense, in making our estimate for the next hundred years, we will suppose the ratio of increase to be only one-half as large as that from 1870 to 1880, which would make the population in 1980, 57,000,000. All the great colonies of Britain, except Canada, which has a great future, show a very high ratio of increase in population; that of Australia, from 1870 to 1880, was 56.50 per cent; that of South Africa was 73.28. It is quite reasonable to suppose that the colonies, taken together, will double their population once in twenty-five years for the next century. In the United States, population has, on the average, doubled once in twenty-five years since 1685. Adopting this ratio, then, for the English colonies, their 11,000,000 in 1880 will be 176,000,000 in 1980, and about 234,000,000 in 1990. Turning now to our own country, we find in the following table the ratio of increase of population for each decade of years since 1800:

From	1800	to	1810	36.38	per	cent.
"	1810	"	1820	34.80	"	"
"	1820	"	1830	33.11	"	"
"	1830	"	1840	32.66	"	"
"	1840	"	1850	35.87	"	"
"	1850	"	1860	35.58	"	"
"	1860	"	1870	22.59	"	"
"	1870	"	1880	30.06	"	"
"	1880	"	1890	24.57	"	"

Here we see a falling ratio of increase of about one per cent every ten years from 1800 to 1840—a period when immigration was inconsiderable. During the next twenty years the ratio was decidedly higher, because of a large immigration. It fell off during the war, and again arose from 1870 to 1880, while it seems to have fallen from 1880 to 1890.[3]

[3] It should be remembered, however, that great populations do not show sudden changes in the rate of increase without such causes as war, anarchy, pestilence, famine or great migrations. No such cause has been operative with us during the past ten years, except a great immigration,

If the rate of increase for the next century is as great with immigration as it was from 1800 to 1840 without immigration, we shall have a falling ratio of increase of about one per cent every ten years. Beginning, then, with an increase of twenty-four per cent from 1890 to 1900, our population in 1990 would be 373,000,000, making the total Anglo-Saxon population of the world, at that time, 667,000,000, as compared with 570,000,000 inhabitants of continental Europe. When we consider how much more favorable are the conditions for the increase of population in Anglo-Saxon countries than in continental Europe, and remember that we have reckoned the growth of European population at its rate of increase from 1870 to 1880, while we have reckoned Anglo-Saxon growth at much less than its rate of increase during the same ten years, we may be reasonably confident that a hundred years hence this one race will outnumber all the peoples of continental Europe. And it is possible that, by the close of the next century, the Anglo-Saxons will outnumber all the other civilized races of the world. Does it not look as if God were not only preparing in our Anglo-Saxon civilization the die with which to stamp the peoples of the earth, but as if he were also massing behind that die the mighty power with which to press it? My confidence that this race is eventually to give its civilization to mankind is not based on mere numbers—China forbid! I look forward to what the world has never yet seen united in the same race; viz., the greatest numbers, *and* the highest civilization.

---

which would of course raise the rate of increase. It is, therefore, hardly credible that our ratio of increase fell five and a half per cent during that period. Still less likely is it that, conditions remaining substantially the same from 1870 to 1890, the rate of increase could have risen so rapidly during the first half of the period, and then have fallen so rapidly during the last half. The explanation is to be found in the Census of 1870, which General Francis A. Walker, the superintendent, says was "grossly defective." As the returns of that census were undoubtedly too small there was no such rise in the rate of increase from 1870 to 1880 and, therefore, no such fall in that rate from 1880 to 1890 as the above figures indicate. The superintendent of the late census says "there is but little question that the population in 1870 was at least 40,000,000," which would make the rate of increase from 1870 to 1880 not far from 25 per cent or about the same as from 1880 to 1890.

There can be no reasonable doubt that North America is to be the great home of the Anglo-Saxon, the principal seat of his power, the center of his life and influence. Not only does it constitute seven-elevenths of his possessions, but here his empire is unsevered, while the remaining four-elevenths are fragmentary and scattered over the earth. Australia will have a great population; but its disadvantages, as compared with North America, are too manifest to need mention. Our continent has room and resources and climate, it lies in the pathway of the nations, it belongs to the zone of power, and already, among Anglo-Saxons, do we lead in population and wealth. Of England, Franklin once wrote: "That pretty island which, compared to America, is but a stepping-stone in a brook, scarce enough of it above water to keep one's shoes dry." England can hardly hope to maintain her relative importance among Anglo-Saxon peoples when her "pretty island" is the home of only one-twentieth part of that race. With the wider distribution of wealth, and increasing facilities of intercourse, intelligence and influence are less centralized, and peoples become more homogeneous; and the more nearly homogeneous peoples are, the more do *numbers tell.*

America is to have the great preponderance of numbers and of wealth, and by the logic of events will follow the scepter of controlling influence. This will be but the consummation of a movement as old as civilization—a result to which men have looked forward for centuries. John Adams records that nothing was "more ancient in his memory than the observation that arts, sciences and empire had traveled westward; and in conversation it was always added that their next leap would be over the Atlantic into America." He recalled a couplet that had been inscribed or rather drilled, into a rock on the shore of Monument Bay in our old colony of Plymouth:

> " 'The Eastern nations sink, their glory ends,
> And empire rises where the sun descends.' " [4]

[4] *The Works of John Adams,* IX (Boston, 1854), 599–600. [From "Letter to Benjamin Rush," May 23, 1807.]

The brilliant Galiani, who foresaw a future in which Europe should be ruled by America, wrote, during the Revolutionary War: "I will wager in favor of America, for the reason merely physical, that for 5,000 years genius has turned opposite to the diurnal motion, and traveled from the East to the West."[5] Count d'Aranda, after signing the Treaty of Paris of 1773, as representative of Spain, wrote his king: "This Federal Republic is born a pigmy. . . . . a day will come when it will be a giant, even a colossus formidable in these countries."

Adam Smith, in his *Wealth of Nations,* predicts the transfer of empire from Europe to America. The traveler, Burnaby, found, in the middle of the last century, that an idea had "entered into the minds of the generality of mankind, that empire is traveling westward; and every one is looking forward with eager and impatient expectation to that destined moment when America is to give the law to the rest of the world." Charles Sumner wrote of the "coming time when the whole continent, with all its various states, shall be a Plural Unit, with one Constitution, one Liberty and one Destiny," and when "the national example will be more puissant than army or navy for the conquest of the world."[6] It surely needs no prophet's eye to see that the civilization of the *United States* is to be the civilization of America, and that the future of the continent is ours. In 1880, the United States had already become the home of more than one-half of the Anglo-Saxon race; and, if the computations already given, are correct, a much larger proportion will be here a hundred years hence. It has been shown that we have room for at least a thousand millions. According to the latest figures, there is in France (1886), a population of 187 to the square mile; in Germany (1885), 221.8; in England and Wales (1889), 498; in Belgium (1888), 530; in the United States (1890)—not including Alaska—21. If our population

[5] *Correspondance Inédite de l'Abbé Ferdinand Galiani,* II, (Paris, 1818), 275.

[6] See "Prophetic Views about America," *Atlantic Monthly,* 20 (September 1867), 275–306. [Strong relied on this article for his citations of John Adams, Galiani, the Count d'Aranda, Adam Smith, Burnaby, and Charles Sumner.]

were as dense as that of France, we should have, this side of Alaska, 555,000,000; if as dense as that of Germany, 658,000,000; if as dense as that of England and Wales, 1,452,000,000; if as dense as that of Belgium 1,574,000,000, or more than the present estimated population of the globe.

And we are to have not only the larger portion of the Anglo-Saxon race, but we may reasonably expect to develop the highest type of Anglo-Saxon civilization. If human progress follows a law of development, if

> "Time's noblest offspring is the last,"

our civilization should be the noblest; for we are

> "The heirs of all the ages in the foremost files of time,"

and not only do we occupy the latitude of power, but *our land is the last to be occupied in that latitude.* There is no other virgin soil in the North Temperate Zone. If the consummation of human progress is not to be looked for here, if there is yet to flower a higher civilization, where is the soil that is to produce it? Whipple says: "There has never been a great migration that did not result in a new form of national genius."[7] Our national genius is Anglo-Saxon, but not English, its distinctive type is the result of a finer nervous organization, which is certainly being developed in this country. "The history of the world's progress from savagery to barbarism, from barbarism to civilization, and, in civilization, from the lower degrees toward the higher, is the history of increase in average longevity,[8] corresponding to, and accompanied by, increase of nervousness. Mankind has grown to be at once more delicate and more enduring, more sensitive to weariness and yet more patient of toil, impressible, but capable of bearing powerful irri-

[7] "The New World and the New Man," *Atlantic Monthly,* 2 (October 1858), 516.

[8] "It is ascertained that the average measure of human life, in this country, has been steadily increasing during this century, and is *now considerably longer than in any other country.*" Daniel Dorchester, *The Problem of Religious Progress* (New York, 1881), p. 288. [The italics are Strong's.]

tation; we are woven of finer fiber, which, though apparently frail, yet outlasts the coarser, as rich and costly garments oftentimes wear better than those of rougher workmanship." [9] The roots of civilization are the nerves; and other things being equal, the finest nervous organization will produce the highest civilization. Heretofore, war has been almost the chief occupation of strong races. The mission of the Anglo-Saxon has been largely that of the soldier; but the world is making progress, we are leaving behind the barbarism of war; as civilization advances, it will learn less of war, and concern itself more with the arts of peace, and for these the massive battle-ax must be wrought into tools of finer temper. The physical changes accompanied by mental, which are taking place in the people of the United States are apparently to adapt men to the demands of a higher civilization. But the objection is here interposed that the "physical degeneracy of America" is inconsistent with the supposition of our advancing to a higher civilization. Professor Huxley, when at Buffalo he addressed the American Association for the Advancement of Science, said he had heard of the degeneration of the original American stock, but during his visit to the states he had failed to perceive it. We are not, however, in this matter, dependent on the opinion of even the best observers. During the War of the Confederacy, the Medical Department of the Provost Marshal General's Bureau gathered statistics from the examination of over half a million of men, native and foreign, young and old, sick and sound, drawn from every rank and condition of life, and, hence, fairly representing the whole people. Dr. Baxter's Official Report shows that our native whites were over an inch taller than the English, and nearly two-thirds of an inch taller than the Scotch, who, in height, were superior to all other foreigners. At the age of completed growth, the Irish, who were the stoutest of the foreigners, surpassed the native whites, in girth of chest, less than a quarter of an inch. Statistics as to weight are meager, but Dr. Baxter remarks that it is perhaps not too much to say that the war statistics show "that the mean weight of the white native of the United States

[9] George M. Beard, *American Nervousness* (New York, 1881), p. 287.

is not disproportionate to his stature." Americans were found to be superior to Englishmen not only in height, but also in chest measurement and weight. "Dealers in ready-made clothing in the United States assert that they have been obliged to adopt a larger scale of sizes, in width as well as length, to meet the demands of the average American man, than were required ten years ago." [10] Such facts afford more than a hint that the higher civilization of the future will not lack an adequate physical basis in the people of the United States.

Mr. Darwin is not only disposed to see, in the superior vigor of our people, an illustration of his favorite theory of natural selection, but even intimates that the world's history thus far has been simply preparatory for our future, and tributary to it. He says: "There is apparently much truth in the belief that the wonderful progress of the United States, as well as the character of the people, are the results of natural selection; for the more energetic, restless, and courageous men from all parts of Europe have emigrated during the last ten or twelve generations to that great country, and have there succeeded best. Looking at the distant future, I do not think that the Rev. Mr. Zincke takes an exaggerated view when he says: 'All other series of events—as that which resulted in the culture of mind in Greece, and that which resulted in the Empire of Rome—only appear to have purpose and value when viewed in connection with, or rather as subsidiary to, the great stream of Anglo-Saxon emigration to the West.' " [11]

There is abundant reason to believe that the Anglo-Saxon race is to be, is, indeed, already becoming, more effective here than in the mother country. The marked superiority of this race is due, in large measure, to its highly mixed origin. Says Rawlinson: "It is a general rule, now almost universally admitted by ethnologists, that the mixed races of mankind are superior to the pure ones"; and adds: "Even the Jews, who are so often cited as an example of a race at once pure and strong,

[10] David A. Wells, *Recent Economic Changes* (New York, 1889), pp. 348–349.

[11] Charles Darwin, *The Descent of Man* (New York, 1888), p. 142.

may, with more reason, be adduced on the opposite side of the argument." [12] The ancient Egyptians, the Greeks, and the Romans, were all mixed races. Among modern races, the most conspicuous example is afforded by the Anglo-Saxons. Mr. Green's studies show that Mr. Tennyson's poetic line,

> "Saxon and Norman and Dane are we,"

must be supplemented with Celt and Gaul, Welshman and Irishman, Frisian and Flamand, French Huguenot and German Palatine. What took place a thousand years ago and more in England again transpires to-day in the United States. "History repeats itself"; but, as the wheels of history are the chariot wheels of the Almighty, there is, with every revolution, an onward movement toward the goal of His eternal purposes. There is here a new commingling of races; and, while the largest injections of foreign blood are substantially the same elements that constituted the original Anglo-Saxon admixture, so that we may infer the general type will be preserved, there are strains of other bloods being added, which, if Mr. Emerson's remark is true, that "the best nations are those most widely related," may be expected to improve the stock, and aid it to a higher destiny. If the dangers of immigration, which have been pointed out, can be successfully met for the next few years, until it has passed its climax, it may be expected to add value to the amalgam which will constitute the new Anglo-Saxon race of the New World. Concerning our future, Herbert Spencer says: "One great result is, I think, tolerably clear. From biological truths it is to be inferred that the eventual mixture of the allied varieties of the Aryan race, forming the population, will produce a more powerful type of man than has hitherto existed, and a type of man more plastic, more adaptable, more capable of undergoing the modifications needful for complete social life. I think, whatever difficulties they may have to surmount, and whatever tribulations they may have to pass through, the Americans may reasonably look forward to a time

[12] George Rawlinson, "Duties of Higher Toward Lower Races," *Princeton Review* (November 1878), pp. 837, 840.

when they will have produced a civilization grander than any the world has known."

It may be easily shown, and is of no small significance, that the two great ideas of which the Anglo-Saxon is the exponent are having a fuller development in the United States than in Great Britain. There the union of Church and State tends strongly to paralyze some of the members of the body of Christ. Here there is no such influence to destroy spiritual life and power. Here, also, has been evolved the form of government consistent with the largest possible civil liberty. Furthermore, it is significant that the marked characteristics of this race are being here emphasized most. Among the most striking features of the Anglo-Saxon is his money-making power—a power of increasing importance in the widening commerce of the world's future. We have seen, in a preceding chapter, that, although England is by far the richest nation of Europe, we have already outstripped her in the race after wealth, and we have only begun the development of our vast resources.

Again, another marked characteristic of the Anglo-Saxon is what may be called an instinct or genius for colonizing. His unequaled energy, his indomitable perseverance, and his personal independence, made him a pioneer. He excels all others in pushing his way into new countries. It was those in whom this tendency was strongest that came to America, and this inherited tendency has been further developed by the westward sweep of successive generations across the continent. So noticeable has this characteristic become that English visitors remark it. Charles Dickens once said that the typical American would hesitate to enter heaven unless assured that he could go farther west.

Again, nothing more manifestly distinguishes the Anglo-Saxon than his intense and persistent energy, and he is developing in the United States an energy which, in eager activity and effectiveness, is peculiarly American.

This is due partly to the fact that Americans are much better fed than Europeans, and partly to the undeveloped resources of a new country, but more largely to our climate, which acts as a constant stimulus. Ten years after the landing of the Pilgrims, the Rev. Francis Higginson, a good observer, wrote: "A sup of New England air is better than a whole flagon of English ale." Thus early had the stimulating effect of our climate been noted. Moreover, our social institutions are stimulating. In Europe the various ranks of society are, like the strata of the earth, fixed and fossilized. There can be no great change without a terrible upheaval, a social earthquake. Here society is like the waters of the sea, mobile; as General Garfield said, and so signally illustrated in his own experience, that which is at the bottom to-day may one day flash on the crest of the highest wave. Every one is free to become whatever he can make of himself; free to transform himself from a rail-splitter or a tanner or a canal-boy, into the nation's President. Our aristocracy, unlike that of Europe, is open to all comers. Wealth, position, influence, are prizes offered for energy; and every farmer's boy, every apprentice and clerk, every friendless and penniless immigrant, is free to enter the list. Thus many causes co-operate to produce here the most forceful and tremendous energy in the world.

What is the significance of such facts? These tendencies infold the future; they are the mighty alphabet with which God writes his prophecies. May we not, by a careful laying together of the letters, spell out something of his meaning? It seems to me that God, with infinite wisdom and skill, is training the Anglo-Saxon race for an hour sure to come in the world's future. Heretofore there has always been in the history of the world a comparatively unoccupied land westward, into which the crowded countries of the East have poured their surplus populations. But the widening waves of migration, which millenniums ago rolled east and west from the valley of the Euphrates, meet to-day on our Pacific coast. There are no more new worlds. The unoccupied arable lands of the earth are limited, and will soon be taken. The time is coming when the pressure of population on the means of subsistence will be felt here as it is now felt in Europe and Asia. Then will the world enter upon a new stage of its history—*the final compe-*

tition of races, for which the Anglo-Saxon is being schooled. Long before the thousand millions are here, the mighty *centrifugal* tendency, inherent in this stock and strengthened in the United States, will assert itself. Then this race of unequaled energy, with all the majesty of numbers and the might of wealth behind it—the representative, let us hope, of the largest liberty, the purest Christianity, the highest civilization—having developed peculiarly aggressive traits calculated to impress its institutions upon mankind, will spread itself over the earth. If I read not amiss, this powerful race will move down upon Mexico, down upon Central and South America, out upon the islands of the sea, over upon Africa and beyond. And can any one doubt that the result of this competition of races will be the "survival of the fittest"? "Any people," says Dr. Bushnell, "that is physiologically advanced in culture, though it be only in a degree beyond another which is mingled with it on strictly equal terms, is sure to live down and finally live out its inferior. Nothing can save the inferior race but a ready and pliant assimilation. Whether the feebler and more abject races are going to be regenerated and raised up, is already very much of a question. What if it should be God's plan to people the world with better and finer material?

"Certain it is, whatever expectations we may indulge, that there is a tremendous overbearing surge of power in the Christian nations, which, if the others are not speedily raised to some vastly higher capacity, will inevitably submerge and bury them forever. These great populations of Christendom—what are they doing, but throwing out their colonies on every side, and populating themselves, if I may so speak, into the possession of all countries and climes?" [13] To this result no war of extermination is needful; the contest is not one of arms, but of vitality and of civilization. "At the present day," says Mr. Darwin, "civilized nations are everywhere supplanting barbarous nations, excepting where the climate opposes a deadly barrier; and they succeed mainly, though not exclusively,

[13] Horace Bushnell, *Christian Nurture* (New York, 1861), pp. 207, 213.

through their arts, which are the products of the intellect."[14] Thus the Finns were supplanted by the Aryan races in Europe and Asia, the Tartars by the Russians, and thus the aborigines of North America, Australia and New Zealand are now disappearing before the all-conquering Anglo-Saxons. It seems as if these inferior tribes were only precursors of a superior race, voices in the wilderness crying: "Prepare ye the way of the Lord!" The savage is a hunter; by the incoming of civilization the game is driven away and disappears before the hunter becomes a herder or an agriculturist. The savage is ignorant of many diseases of civilization which, when he is exposed to them, attack him before he learns how to treat them. Civilization also has its vices, of which the uninitiated savage is innocent. He proves an apt learner of vice, but dull enough in the school of morals.

Every civilization has its destructive and preservative elements. The Anglo-Saxon race would speedily decay but for the salt of Christianity. Bring savages into contact with our civilization, and its destructive forces become operative at once, while years are necessary to render effective the saving influences of Christian instruction. Moreover, the pioneer wave of our civilization carries with it more scum than salt. Where there is one missionary, there are hundreds of miners or traders or adventurers ready to debauch the native.

Whether the extinction of inferior races before the advancing Anglo-Saxon seems to the reader sad or otherwise, it certainly appears probable. I know of nothing except climatic conditions to prevent this race from populating Africa as it has peopled North America. And those portions of Africa which are unfavorable to Anglo-Saxon life are less extensive than was once supposed. The Dutch Boers, after two centuries of life there, are as hardy as any race on earth. The Anglo-Saxon has established himself in climates totally diverse—Canada, South

[14] Charles Darwin, *The Descent of Man* (New York, 1871), p. 154. [Strong here quoted from the first edition. The reference in note 11 is taken from the revised second edition.]

Africa, and India—and, through several generations, has preserved his essential race characteristics. He is not, of course, superior to climatic influences; but even in warm climates, he is likely to retain his aggressive vigor long enough to supplant races already enfeebled. Thus, in what Dr. Bushnell calls "the out-populating power of the Christian stock," may be found God's final and complete solution of the dark problem of heathenism among many inferior peoples.

Some of the stronger races, doubtless, may be able to preserve their integrity; but, in order to compete with the Anglo-Saxon, they will probably be forced to adopt his methods and instruments, his civilization and his religion. Significant movements are now in progress among them. While the Christian religion was never more vital, or its hold upon the Anglo-Saxon mind stronger, there is taking place among the nations a widespread intellectual revolt against traditional beliefs. "In every corner of the world," says Mr. Froude, "there is the same phenomenon of the decay of established religions. . . . Among the Mohammedans, Jews, Buddhists, Brahmins, traditionary creeds are losing their hold. An intellectual revolution is sweeping over the world, breaking down established opinions, dissolving foundations on which historical faiths have been built up."[15] The contact of Christian with heathen nations is awakening the latter to new life. Old superstitions are loosening their grasp. The dead crust of fossil faiths is being shattered by the movements of life underneath. In Catholic countries, Catholicism is losing its influence over educated minds, and in some cases the masses have already lost all faith in it. Thus, while on this continent God is training the Anglo-Saxon race for its mission, a complemental work has been in progress in the great world beyond. God has two hands. Not only is he preparing in our civilization the die with which to stamp the nations, but, by what Southey called the "timing of Providence," he is preparing mankind to receive our impress.

Is there room for reasonable doubt that this race, unless

[15] James Anthony Froude, "Romanism and the Irish Race in the United States," *North American Review,* 129 (December 1879), 535–536.

devitalized by alcohol and tobacco, is destined to dispossess many weaker races, assimilate others, and mold the remainder, until, in a very true and important sense, it has Anglo-Saxonized mankind? Already "the English language, saturated with Christian ideas, gathering up into itself the best thought of all the ages, is the great agent of Christian civilization throughout the world; at this moment affecting the destinies and molding the character of half the human race." [16] Jacob Grimm, the German philologist, said of this language: "It seems chosen, like its people, to rule in future times in a still greater degree in all the corners of the earth." He predicted, indeed, that the language of Shakespeare would eventually become the language of mankind. Is not Tennyson's noble prophecy to find its fulfillment in Anglo-Saxondom's extending its dominion and influence—

"Till the war-drum throbs no longer, and the battle-flags are furl'd
In the Parliament of man, the Federation of the world." [17]

In my own mind, there is no doubt that the Anglo-Saxon is to exercise the commanding influence in the world's future; but the exact nature of that influence is, as yet, undetermined. How far his civilization will be materialistic and atheistic, and how long it will take thoroughly to Christianize and sweeten it, how rapidly he will hasten the coming of the kingdom wherein dwelleth righteousness, or how many ages he may retard it, is still uncertain; but *is now being swiftly determined.* Let us weld together in a chain the various links of our logic which we have endeavored to forge. Is it manifest that the Anglo-Saxon holds in his hands the destinies of mankind for ages to come? Is it evident that the United States is to be the home of this race, the principal seat of his power, the great center of his influence? Is it true (see Chap. III.) that the great West is to dominate the nation's future? Has it been shown

[16] Rev. Nathaniel George Clark. [Clark (1825–1896), a linguist, taught at the University of Vermont and at Union College. In 1865 he was elected Secretary of the American Board of Commissioners for Foreign Missions.]

[17] "Locksley Hall."

(Chapters XII. and XIII.) that this generation is to determine the character, and hence the destiny of the West? Then may God open the eyes of this generation! When Napoleon drew up his troops before the Mamelukes, under the shadow of the Pyramids, pointing to the latter, he said to his soldiers: "Remember that from yonder heights forty centuries look down on you." Men of this generation, from the pyramid top of opportunity on which God has set us, *we look down on forty centuries!* We stretch our hand into the future with power to mold the destinies of unborn millions.

"We are living, we are dwelling,
In a grand and awful time,
In an age on ages telling—
To be living is sublime!"

Notwithstanding the great perils which threaten it, I cannot think our civilization will perish; but I believe it is fully in the hands of the Christians of the United States, during the next ten or fifteen years, to hasten or retard the coming of Christ's kingdom in the world by hundreds, and perhaps thousands, of years. We of this generation and nation occupy the Gibraltar of the ages which commands the world's future.

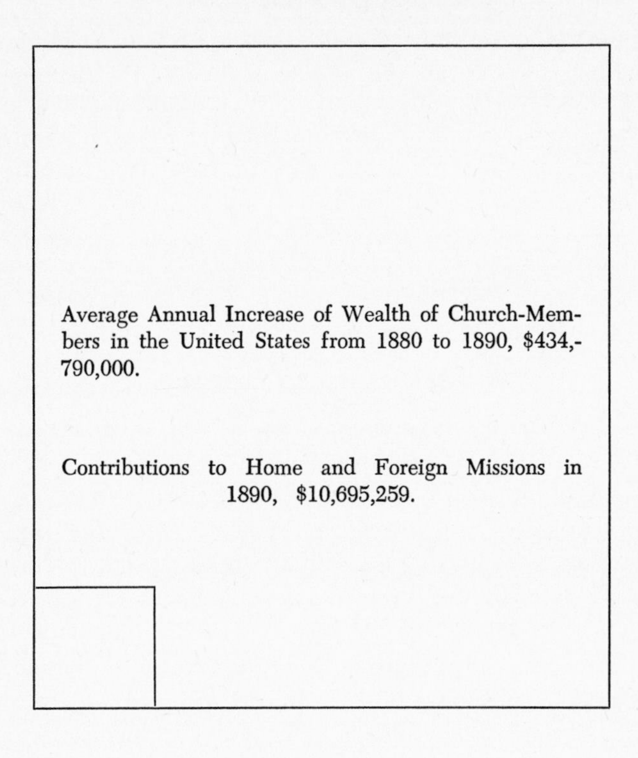

CHAPTER XV

MONEY AND THE KINGDOM

PROPERTY is one of the cardinal facts of our civilization. It is the great object of endeavor, the great spring of power, the great occasion of discontent, and one of the great sources of danger. For Christians to apprehend their true relations to money, and the relations of money to the kingdom of Christ and its progress in the world, is to find the key to many of the great problems now pressing for solution.

Money is power in the concrete. It commands learning, skill, experience, wisdom, talent, influence, numbers. It represents the school, the college, the church, the printing-press, and all evangelizing machinery. It confers on the wise man a sort of omnipresence. By means of it, the same man may, at the same moment, be founding an academy among the Mormons, teaching the New Mexicans, building a home missionary church in Dakota, translating the Scriptures in Africa, preaching the gospel in China, and uttering the precepts of ten thousand Bibles in India. It is the modern miracle worker; it has a wonderful multiplying and transforming power. Sarah Hosmer, of Lowell, though a poor woman, supported a student in the Nestorian Seminary, who became a preacher of Christ. Five times she gave fifty dollars, earning the money in a factory, and sent out five native pastors to Christian work. When more than sixty years old, she longed to furnish Nestoria with one more preacher of Christ; and, living in an attic, she took in sewing until she had accomplished her cherished purpose. In the hands of this consecrated woman, money transformed the factory girl and the seamstress into a missionary of the Cross, and then multiplied her six-fold. God forbid that I should attribute to money power which belongs only to faith, love, and the Holy Spirit. In the problem of Christian work, money is like the cipher, worthless alone, but multiplying many fold the value and effectiveness of other factors.

In the preceding chapter has been set forth the wonderful opportunity enjoyed by this generation in the United States. It lays on us a commensurate obligation. We have also seen (Chap. X.) that our wealth is stupendous. If our responsibility is without a precedent, the plenitude of our power is likewise without a parallel. Is not the lesson which God would have us learn so plain that he who runs may read it? Has not God given us this matchless power that it may be applied to doing this matchless work?

The kingdoms of this world will not have become the kingdoms of our Lord until the money power has been Christianized. "Talent has been Christianized already on a large scale.

The political power of states and kingdoms has been long assumed to be, and now at least really is, as far as it becomes their accepted office to maintain personal security and liberty. Architecture, arts, constitutions, schools, and learning have been largely Christianized. But the money power, which is one of the most operative and grandest of all, is only beginning to be; though with promising tokens of a finally complete reduction to Christ and the uses of His Kingdom. . . . That day, when it comes, is the morning, so to speak, of the new creation."[1] Is it not time for that day to dawn? If we would Christianize our Anglo-Saxon civilization, which is to spread itself over the earth, has not the hour come for the Church to teach and live the doctrines of God's Word touching possessions? Their general acceptance on the part of the church would involve a reformation scarcely less important in its results than the great Reformation of the sixteenth century. What is needed is not simply an increased giving, an enlarged estimate of the "Lord's share," but a *radically different conception* of our relations to our possessions. Most Christian men need to discover that they are not proprietors, apportioning their own, but simply trustees or managers of God's property. All Christians would admit that there is a sense in which their all belongs to God, but deem it a very poetical sense, wholly unpractical and practically unreal. The great majority treat their possessions exactly as they would treat property, use their substance exactly as if it were their own.

Christians generally hold that God has a thoroughly real claim on some portion of their income, possibly a tenth, more likely no definite proportion; but some small part, they acknowledge, belongs to him, and they hold themselves in duty bound to use it for him. This low and unchristian view has sprung apparently from a misconception of the Old Testament doctrine of tithes. God did not, for the surrender of a part, renounce all claim to the remainder. The Jew was taught, in language most explicit and oft-repeated, that he

[1] Horace Bushnell, *Sermons on Living Subjects* (New York, 1872), pp. 264–265.

and all he had belonged absolutely to God. "Behold, the heaven and the heaven of heavens is the Lord's, thy God, and the earth also, with all that therein is" (Deut. x, 14). "The earth is the Lord's, and the fullness thereof; the world, and they that dwell therein" (Ps. xxiv, 1). "The silver is mine and the gold is mine, saith the Lord" (Hag. ii, 8). "Behold, all souls are mine; as the soul of the father, so also the soul of the son is mine" (Ezek. xviii, 4). When the priest was consecrated, the blood of the ram was put upon the right ear, the thumb of the right hand, and the great toe of the right foot, to indicate that he should come and go, use his hands and powers of mind, in short, his entire self, in the service of God. These parts of the body were selected as representative of the whole man. The tithe was likewise representative. "For, if the first fruit be holy, the lump is also holy" (Rom. xi, 16). Tithes were devoted to certain uses, specified by God, in recognition of the fact that all belonged to him.

THE PRINCIPLE STATED

God's claim to the whole rests on exactly the same ground as his claim to a part. As the Creator, he must have an absolute ownership in all his creatures; and, if an absolute claim could be strengthened, it would be by the fact that he who gave us life sustains it, and with his own life redeemed it. "Ye are not your own; for ye are bought with a price" (I Cor. vi, 19, 20). Manifestly, if God has absolute ownership in us, we can have absolute ownership in nothing whatever. If we cannot lay claim to our own selves, how much less to that which we find in our hands. When we say that no man is the absolute owner of property to the value of one penny, we do not take the socialistic position that private property is theft. Because of our individual trusts, for which we are held personally responsible, we have individual rights touching property, and may have claims one against another; but, between God and the soul, the distinction of *thine* and *mine* is a snare. Does one-tenth belong to God? Then ten-tenths are his. He did not one-tenth create us and we nine-tenths create ourselves. He did not one-tenth redeem us and we nine-tenths redeem ourselves. If his claim to a part is good, his claim to the whole is equally good. His ownership in us is no joint affair. We are not in partnership with him. All that we are and have is utterly his, and his only.

When the Scriptures and reason speak of God's ownership in us they use the word in no accommodated sense. It means all that it can mean in a court of law. It means that God has a right to the service of his own. It means that, since our possessions are his property, they should be used in his service—not a fraction of them, but the whole. When the lord returned from the far country, to reckon with his servants to whom he had entrusted his goods, he demanded not simply a small portion of the increase, but held his servants accountable for both principal and interest—"mine own with usury." Every dollar that belongs to God must serve him. And it is not enough that we make a *good* use of our means. We are under exactly the same obligations to make the *best* use of our money that we are to make a *good* use of it; and to make any use of it other than the best is a maladministration of trust. Here, then, is the principle always applicable, that *of our entire possessions, every dollar, every cent, is to be employed in the way that will best honor God.*

THE PRINCIPLE APPLIED

The statement of this principle at once suggests difficulties in its application. Let us glance at some of them.

1. An attempt to regulate personal expenditures by this principle affords opportunity for fanaticism on the one hand and for self-deception on the other; but an honest and intelligent application of it will avoid both.

Surely, it is right to supply our necessities. But what are necessities? Advancing civilization multiplies them. Friction matches were a luxury once, they are a necessity now. And may we allow ourselves nothing for the comforts and luxuries of life? Where shall we draw the line between justifiable and unjustifiable expenditure?

The Christian has given himself to God, or, rather, has recognized and accepted the divine ownership in him. He is under obligations to apply every power, whether of mind, body, or possessions, to God's service. He is bound to make that service as effective as possible. Certain expenditures upon himself are necessary to his highest growth and greatest usefulness, and are, therefore, not only permissible, but obligatory. All the money which will yield a larger return of usefulness in the world, of greater good to the Kingdom, by being spent on ourselves or families than by being applied otherwise, is used for the glory of God, and is better spent than it would have been if given to missions. And whatever money is spent on self that would have yielded larger returns of usefulness, if applied otherwise, is misapplied; and, if it has been done intelligently, it is a case of embezzlement.

A narrow view at this point is likely to lead us into fanaticism. We must look at life in its wide relations, and remember that character is its supreme end. Character is the one thing in the universe, so far as we know, which is of absolute worth, and therefore beyond all price. The glory of the Infinite is all of it the glory of character. Every expenditure which serves to broaden and beautify and upbuild character is worthy. The one question ever to be kept in mind is whether it is the wisest application of means to the desired end. Will this particular application of power in money produce the largest results in character!

But what of the beautiful? How far may we gratify our love of it? A delicate and difficult question to answer, especially to the satisfaction of those living in the midst of a luxurious civilization. Our guiding principle holds here as everywhere, only its application is difficult. It is difficult to determine how useful the beautiful may be. Doubtless, at times, as Victor Hugo has said, "The beautiful is as useful as the useful; perhaps more so." The ministry of art widens with the increasing refinement of the nervous organization. There are those to whom the beautiful is, in an important sense, a necessity. God loves the beautiful. Each flower would yield its seed and perpetuate its kind as surely if each blossom were not a smile of its Creator. The stars would swing on in their silent, solemn march as true to gravitation, if they did not glow like mighty rubies and emeralds and sapphires. The clouds would be as faithful carriers of the bounty of the sea, if God did not paint their morning and evening glory from the rainbow as his palette. Yes; God loves the beautiful, and intended we should love it; but he does not have to economize his power; his resources are not limited. When he spreads the splendors of the rising East, it is not at the cost of bread enough to feed ten thousand starving souls. Art has an educational value in our homes and schools and parks and galleries; but how far may one who recognizes his Christian stewardship conscientiously go in the encouragement of art and the gratification of taste? *If every man did his duty,* gave according to ability, there would be abundant provision for all Christian and philanthropic work, and substance left for the patronage of art. But not one man in a hundred is doing his duty; hence those who appreciate the necessities of Christian work must fill the breach, are not at liberty to make expenditures which would otherwise be wholly justifiable. Many expenditures are right abstractly considered. That is, would be right in an ideal condition of society. But the condition of the world is not ideal; we are surrounded by circumstances which must be recognized exactly as they are. Sin is abnormal, the world is out of joint; and such facts lay on us obligations which would not otherwise exist, make sacrifices necessary which would not otherwise be binding, forbid the gratification of tastes which are natural, and might otherwise be indulged. Thrice true is this of us who live in this great national crisis and world emergency. It is well to play the violin, but not when Rome is burning.

Here is a large family of which the husband and father is a contemptible lounger (if loafers had any appreciation of the eternal fitness of things, they would die); he does simply nothing for the support of the family. Exceptional cares are, therefore, laid on the wife and mother. She must expend all her time and strength to secure the bare necessaries of life for her children; and with the utmost sacrifice on her part they go hungry and cold. If her wretched husband did his duty, she could command time and means to beautify the home and make the dress of herself and children attractive; but, under the circumstances, it would be worse than foolish for her to spend her scant earnings on vases and flowers, laces and velvets. God has laid upon Christian nations the work of evangelizing the heathen world. He has laid on us the duty of Christianizing our own heathen, and under such conditions that the obligation presses with an overwhelming urgency. If this duty were accepted by all Christians, the burden would rest lightly upon each; but great multitudes in the church are shirking all responsibility. So far as the work of missions is concerned, these members of the household of faith are loungers. The unfaithful many throw unnatural burdens on the faithful few. Under these circumstances he who would be faithful must accept sacrifices which would not otherwise be his duty. That is, the principle always and everywhere applicable, that we are under obligations to make the wisest use of every penny, binds him to a use of his means which, if every Christian did his duty, would not be necessary. Notwithstanding all the sacrifices made by some, there are vast multitudes, which the established channels of beneficence have placed within our reach, who are starving for the Bread of Life. As long as this is true, must not high uses of money yield to the highest? It is not enough to be sure that we are making a good use of means; for, as the Germans say, the good is a great enemy of the best. The expenditure of a large sum on a work of art may be a good use of the money, but can any one not purblind with selfishness fail to see that, when a thousand dollars actually represents the salvation of a certain number of souls, there are higher uses for the money?

The purchase of luxuries is often justified by the following fallacy: "I am giving work and hence bread to the poor; and it is much wiser thus to let them earn it than to encourage them in idleness by bestowing the price of the lace in charity." Thus many justify extravagance and make their luxuries flatter their pride into the complacent conviction that they are unselfish. An economy in truth—forcing the same act to minister at once to self-indulgence and self-righteousness! Does it make no difference to the world how its labor is expended, whether on something useful or useless, for high uses or low? Your one elegant dress has given many days' work to many persons. But is there no selfishness in the fact that their labor was consumed on yourself alone when it might have clothed a score or more who are now shivering in rags? "Do not cheat yourself into thinking that all the finery you can wear is so much put into the hungry mouths of those beneath you: it is not so; it is what you yourselves, whether you will or no, must sometime instinctively feel it to be—it is what those who stand shivering in the streets, forming a line to watch you as you step out of your carriages, *know* it to be; those fine dresses do not mean that so much has been put into their mouths, but that so much has been taken out of their mouths. The real politico-economical signification of every one of those beautiful toilettes is just this: that you have had a certain number of people put for a certain number of days wholly under your authority by the sternest of slavemasters, —hunger and cold; and you have said to them, 'I will feed you, indeed, and clothe you, and give you fuel for so many days: but during those days you shall work for me only; your little brothers need clothes, but you shall make none for them; your sick friend needs clothes, but you shall make none for her; you yourself will soon need another, and a warmer dress, but you shall make none for yourself. You shall make nothing but lace and roses for me; for this fortnight to come, you shall work at the patterns and petals, and then I will crush and consume them away in an hour.' . . . As long as there are cold and nakedness in the land around you, so long there can be no question at all but that splendor of dress is a crime. In due time when we have nothing better to set people to work at, it may be right to let them make lace and cut jewels; but, as long as there are any who have no blankets for their beds, and no rags for their bodies, so long it is blanket-making and tailoring we must set people to work at—not lace." [2] These principles which Mr. Ruskin applies to splendor of dress are equally applicable to all luxuries, and are an answer to all those self-deceivers who excuse their selfish expenditures on the ground that they give work to persons needing it. "Many hold that an enormous expenditure of wealth is highly commendable, because it 'makes trade.' They forget that waste is not wealth-making; war, fire, the sinking of a ship also 'make trade,' because by destroying existing capital they increase demand. The wealth thus wasted would, more wisely used, give work to many more people in creating more wealth." [3]

Again, the advocates or excusers of self-indulgence pose as the vindicators of God's love. They tell us that he gave all good things for the uses of his children, and that he rejoices in their delight. Yes; God is even more benevolent than such suppose. So greatly does he desire our joy that he is not content to see us satisfied with the low delights of self-gratification, but would fain have us know the blessedness of self-sacrifice for others. The writer has no sympathy with asceticism. There is no virtue in deformity; good taste is not unchristian; beauty often costs no more than ugliness. Away with the idea of penance. It belies God, and caricatures the Christian religion. It differs from the self-sacrifice which Christ taught and exemplified as widely as the suicide of Cato differed from the heroic death of Arnold von Winkelried.[4] Christ did not die for the sake of

[2] John Ruskin, *The True and the Beautiful* (New York, 1859), pp. 421–422.

[3] Richard Rogers Bowker, *Of Work and Wealth,* Economic Tract No. X (New York, 1883), p. 46.

[4] [Arnold von Winkelried, Swiss folk hero who, according to tradition, brought about a Swiss victory in the battle of Sempach, July 9, 1386, by drawing spears upon him and thus allowing his fellow warriors to break the Austrian line.]

dying, but to save a world; and he does not inculcate self-denial for the sake of self-denial, but for the sake of others.

Many practice self-denial, if not for its own sake, only for the sake of saving, and with little or no reference to giving. Let a Japanese heathen show us a more excellent way. I take the following account from *The Missionary Herald,* (Sept., 1885). In a certain place, and generation by generation, the owner and relatives of a certain house prospered greatly. Year by year, those persons, on the second day of the New Year, assembled and worshiped the god *Kannin Daimiyo-jin-san.* The meaning of the name in English is "the great, bright god of self-restraint." After engaging in worship, the head of the house opened the *Kannin-bako* (self-restraint box), and distributed to the needy money enough to enable them to live in comfort for a time. The money in the box was the annual accumulation of his offering to his god.

Outsiders, learning of the prosperity, worship, and large giving to the needy, which characterized this family, were astonished, and presented themselves to inquire into the matter. The master of the house, in reply, gave the following account of the practice of his household:

"From ancient times, my family has believed in and worshiped 'the great, bright god of self-restraint.' We have also made a box, and called it, 'the self-restraint box,' for the reception of the first-fruits and other percentages, all of which are offered to our god.

"As to percentages, this is our mode of proceeding: If I would buy a dollar garment, I manage by self-restraint and economy to get it for eighty cents, and the remaining twenty cents I drop into 'the self-restraint box'; or if I would give a five-dollar feast to my friends, I exercise self-restraint and economy, and give it for four, dropping the remaining dollar into the box; or, if I determine to build a house that shall cost one hundred dollars, I exercise self-restraint and economy, and build it for eighty, putting the remaining twenty dollars into the box as an offering to *Kannin Daimiyo-jin-san.* . . . In proportion to my annual outlays, the sum in this box is large or small. This year my outlays have been large; hence by the practice of the virtues named, the amount in 'the self-restraint box' is great. Yet, notwithstanding this, we are living in comfort, peace and happiness." [5] Among us, outlays and benefactions are apt to be in inverse, instead of direct, ratio. I am strongly inclined to think that Christians could gain easy forgiveness for a little idolatry of "the great, bright god of self-restraint." And if the "self-restraint box" were marked Home Missions, and the savings resulting from our self-denial were dropped into it, the "million dollars a year" called for by Dr. Goodell,[6] in 1881, would be given ten times over.

The general acceptance, by the Church, of the Christian principle that every penny is to be used in the way that will best honor God, would cause every channel of benevolence to overflow its banks, and occasion a blessed freshet of salvation throughout the world. "But," says some one, "that principle demands daily self-denial." Undoubtedly; and that fact is the Master's seal set to its truth. "If any man will come after me, let him deny himself, and take up his cross DAILY, and follow me" (Luke ix, 23).

2. And there are no exceptions to this law of sacrifice; it binds all alike. Christian people will agree that missionaries are called to make great sacrifices for Christ; but why does the obligation rest on them any more than on all? Does the missionary belong absolutely to God? No less do we. Do the love and sacrifice of Christ lay him under boundless obligation? Christ died for every man. Why is not the rich man in America under as great obligation to practice self-sacrifice for the salvation of the heathen as the missionary in Central Africa, provided his sacrifice can be made fruitful of their good? And that is exactly the provision which is made by missionary boards to-day. They establish channels of inter-communication which bring us into contact with all heathendom, and make Africa, which, centuries ago, fell among thieves, and has ever since been robbed and sore wounded, our neighbor. To live in luxury, and then leave a legacy for missions, does not fulfill the

[5] [Strong erred in his attribution of the foregoing account to *The Missionary Herald*. There is no such report in the September 1885 issue.]

[6] [See Chapter II, above, n. 3.]

law of sacrifice. Every steward is responsible for the disposition of his trust made by will. The obligation still rests upon him to bestow his possessions where, after his death, they will do most for God. Legacies to benevolent societies ought to be greatly multiplied, and would be, if the principle of Christian stewardship were accepted; but such a legacy cannot compound for an unconsecrated life. If the priest or Levite, who passed by on the other side, wrote a codicil to his will, providing for wounded wayfarers, I fear it was hardly counted unto him for righteousness, was hardly a proof that he loved his neighbor as himself. Christ said: "Go ye into all the world, and preach the gospel;" and he did not say it to the twelve, but to the whole body of believers. If we cannot go in person, we are under obligations to go by proxy. The rich man has more power to send than the missionary has to go; he can, perhaps, send a dozen. And why is he not called to make as great sacrifices in *sending* as the missionary in *going*? [7] The obligations of all men rest on the same grounds. The law of sacrifice is universal.

[7] Glance at some of the sacrifices of missionaries who go to the frontier. Writing to the *Congregational Union* for aid to build a parsonage, one says:

"Am sleeping in a shack three miles from town, and taking my meals at the hotel. Not a house or building of any kind to be had to live in. My family are in Ohio, awaiting arrangements for a home. Can you help us?"

Another writes: "During the first two years' service here, was obliged to live in Seattle, seven miles away, going to and fro on foot. For one year since, have occupied such a building as I could erect in thirty days, with my own hands."

Another: "My wife and myself, with our daughter of six years, have been doing our best to live (if it can be called living) in an attic of a store. It is all unfinished inside. By putting up a board partition we have two rooms. To reach our rooms we have to go around to the rear of the store, and make our way among boxes, barrels, tin cans, etc., to the foot of the outside stairway that leads to our attic. We are doing our best to keep warm; but with mercury twenty degrees below zero we do not find it easy. Then for these accommodations, which are the best and all we can get, we have to pay $10 a month. Our salary is only $500. Cannot the Union loan us $250, to help us build?"

Another, writing for a loan, says, "My family of seven lived all summer, in a house twelve by sixteen, having only two rooms."

Many are heroically enduring hardship for the Kingdom, at the front, whose sacrifices would be less if ours were greater, whose sufferings could be relieved if our luxuries were curtailed.

"If ANY man will come after me;" that means Dives and Lazarus alike; the terms are all-inclusive. And not only must all men sacrifice, but *the measure of sacrifice is the same for all.* God does not ask of any two the same *gift,* because to no two are his gifts the same; but he does require of every man the same *sacrifice.* "Whosoever he be of you that forsaketh not ALL THAT HE HATH, he cannot be my disciple" (Luke xiv, 33). To give the little all is as hard as to give the abounding all. In both cases the sacrifice is the same; for it is measured less by what is given than by what remains. Only when the sacrifice is all-inclusive is it perfect and entire. It is the sacrifice, not the gift, which is the essential thing in God's eye. What he demands of every soul is a complete sacrifice—the absolute surrender of self, of all powers and all possessions; not the *abandoning* of the latter any more than of the former, but their entire surrender to God to be used honestly for him. In George Herbert's noble words:

> "Next to Sincerity, remember still,
> Thou must resolve upon *Integrity.*
> God will have *all* thou hast; thy mind, thy will,
> Thy thoughts, thy words, thy works."

Whatever their occupation, Christians have but one business in the world; viz., the extending of Christ's kingdom; and merchant, mechanic, and banker are under exactly the same obligations to be wholly consecrated to that work as is the missionary.

3. One who believes that every dollar belongs to God, and is to be used for him, will not imagine that he has discharged all obligation by "giving a tenth to the Lord." One who talks about the "Lord's tenth," probably thinks about "his own" nine-tenths. The question is not what proportion belongs to God, but having given all to him, what proportion will best honor him by being applied to the uses of myself and family, and what proportion will best honor him by being applied to benevolent uses. Because necessities differ this proportion will differ. One man has a small income and a large family; another has a large

income and no family at all. Manifestly the proportion which will best honor God by being applied to benevolence is much larger in the one case than in the other. God, therefore, requires a different proportion to be thus applied in the two cases. If men's needs varied directly as their incomes, it might, perhaps, be practicable and reasonable to fix on some definite proportion as due from all to Christian and benevolent work. But, while men's wants are quite apt to grow with their income, their needs do not.[8] A man whose income is five hundred dollars may have the same needs as his neighbor whose income is fifty thousand.

There are multitudes in the land who, after having given one-tenth of their increase, might fare sumptuously every day, gratify every whim, and live with the most lavish expenditure. Would that fulfill the law of Christ, "If any man will come after me let him deny himself, and take up his cross daily and follow me"?

There is always a tendency to substitute form for spirit, rules for principles. It is so much easier to conform the conduct to a rule than to make a principle inform the whole life. Moses prescribed rules; Christ inculcated principles—rules for children, principles for men.

The law of tithes was given when the race was in its childhood, and the relations of money to the kingdom of God were radically different from what they are now. The Israelite was not held responsible for the conversion of the world. Money had no such spiritual equivalents then as now; it did not represent the salvation of the heathen. The Jew was required simply to make provisions for his own worship; and its limited demands might appropriately be met by levying upon a certain proportion of his increase. Palestine was his world and his kindred the race; but, under the Christian dispensation, the world is our country, and the race our kindred. The needs of the world to-day are boundless; hence, every man's obliga-

[8] When John Wesley's income was £30, he lived on £28, and gave two; and when his income rose to £60, and afterwards to £120, he still lived on £28, and gave all the remainder.

tion to supply that need is the full measure of his ability; not one-tenth, or any other fraction of it. *And no one exercises that full measure until he has sacrificed.*

By all means let there be system. It is as valuable in giving as in anything else. Proportionate giving to benevolence is both reasonable and scriptural—"as God hath prospered." It is well to fix on some proportion of income, *less* than which we will not give, and then bring expenses within the limit thus laid down. But when this proportion has been given—be it a tenth, or fifth, or half—it does not follow necessarily that duty has been fully done. There can be found in rules no substitute for an honest purpose and a consecrated heart.

4. The principle that every dollar is to be used in the way that will best honor God is as applicable to capital as to increase or income, and in many cases requires that a portion of capital be applied directly to benevolent uses. "But," says one, "I must not give of my capital, because that would impair my ability to give in the future. I must not kill the goose that lays the golden egg." The objection is of weight, especially in ordinary times; but these are times wholly extraordinary; this is the world's emergency. It may be quite true that giving one dollar now out of your capital would prevent your giving five dollars fifteen years hence. But it should be remembered that, for home missionary work, one dollar now is worth ten dollars fifteen years later. This saying has become proverbial among the Home Missionaries of the West.

Money, like corn, has a two-fold power—that of ministering to want and that of reproduction. If there were a famine in the land, no matter how sore it might be, it would be folly to grind up all the seed-corn for food. But, on the other hand, suppose, in the midst of the famine, after feeding their families and doling out a handful in charity, the farmers put all the increase back into the ground, and do it year after year, while the world is starving. That would be something worse than foolish. It would be criminal. Yet that is what multitudes of men are doing. Instead of applying the power in money to the end for which it was entrusted to them, they use it almost wholly to accumulate more power. A miller might as well spend his life building his dam high and higher, and never turn the water to his wheel. Bishop Butler said to his secretary: "I should be ashamed of myself, if I could leave ten thousand pounds behind me." Many professed Christians die disgracefully and "wickedly rich." The shame and sin, however, lie not in the fact that the power was gathered, but that it was unwielded.

It is the duty of some men to make a great deal of money. God has given to them the money-making talent; and it is as wrong to bury that talent as to bury a talent for preaching. It is every man's duty to wield the widest possible power for righteousness: and the power in money must be gained before it can be used. But let a man beware! This power in money is something awful. It is more dangerous than dynamite. The victims of "saint-seducing gold" are numberless. If a Christian grows rich, it should be with fear and trembling, lest the "deceitfulness of riches" undo him; for Christ spoke of the salvation of a rich man as something miraculous (Luke xviii, 24–27).

Let no man deceive himself by saying: "I will give when I have amassed wealth. I desire money that I may do good with it; but I will not give now, that I may give the more largely in the future." That is the pit in which many have perished. If a man is growing large in wealth, nothing but constant and generous giving can save him from growing small in soul. In determining the amount of his gifts and the question whether he should impair his capital, or to what extent, a man should never lose sight of a distinct and intelligent aim to do the greatest possible good in a life-time. Each must decide for himself what is the wisest, the highest, use of money; and we need often to remind ourselves of the constant tendency of human nature to selfishness and self-deception.

THE PRINCIPLE NOT ACCEPTED

The principle which has been stated and briefly applied, and which is as abundantly sustained by reason as it is clearly taught in the Scriptures, is not accepted by the Christian Church. There are many noble gifts and noble givers; but they only help us to demonstrate that great multitudes in the church have not yet learned the first principles of Christian giving. There were, in 1890, 13,411,000[9] members of Evangelical Protestant churches in the United States. The accompanying table gives their contributions to home missions[10] for the fiscal year closing in 1890.

Of course a great deal of money was given to various benevolences of which there could be no record, but $6,717,000 represents approximately what was given through the regular denominational channels for home missions, which is an average of fifty-six cents per member. If, however, we include the several hundred thousand church members whose denominations report no home missionary contributions, and bear in mind that a considerable portion of the above sum was given by church-goers who were not church-members and that another large portion was made up of legacies—the gifts of the dead—we may fairly say that the home missionary contributions of the evangelical church-membership in 1890 did not average more than fifty cents per caput.[11] But many thousands give a

[9] *New York Independent* (July 31, 1890.) [The figure quoted by Strong is not given in the July 31 issue.] The religious statistics of the Eleventh Census are not yet available, but as those of the *Independent* and of the Census were compiled by the authority, Rev. H. K. Carroll, D.D., the former, which are used in this division, are presumably reliable.

[10] In "home missions" are included in this instance the ordinary domestic missions, mission church building, work among the Mormons, New Mexicans, colored people, Indians and Chinese in the United States and the work of the missionary department of the denominational publishing societies. Of course city missions are "home missions," but the city missionary work of local churches is not included because it is impossible to get anything more than fragmentary statistics concerning it.

The accompanying table includes only 11,889,427 of the evangelical church membership in the United States in 1890. But the remainder is made up of colored people (600,000) and foreigners who give very little to missions, and of small denominations which, so far as I can learn, have no regular denominational channels through which they give to home missionary objects. If the gift of these denominations to missions could be ascertained, they would not very materially change our total.

[11] This is a decided advance on ten years before, when home and foreign missions together received only about fifty cents for each church-member.

CONTRIBUTIONS TO HOME MISSIONS IN 1890

	Membership	*Contribution*	*Average per caput*
Congregational	491,985	$1,365,507.55	$2.77
Presbyterian—North	753,749	1,137,205.80	1.50
Protestant Episcopal	470,076	657,018.31	1.39
Moravian	11,358	15,594.15	1.37
Evangelical Association	145,703	183,330.38	1.25
United Presbyterian	101,858	111,644.40	1.09
Primitive Methodist	5,502	5,453.01	.99
Baptist—North	780,000	633,267.74	.81
Reformed (Dutch)	88,812	66,128.66	.78
Wesleyan Methodist	18,000	12,000.00 *	.66
Reformed Presbyterian	6,800	3,786.78	.55
Seventh-Day Baptist	9,000	4,857.29	.53
Presbyterian—South	161,742	74,003.96	.45
Methodist Epis.—North	2,236,463	891,850.00	.39
Disciple	750,000	216,279.44	.28
Reformed (German)	194,044	45,000.00 *	.23
Lutheran	1,188,876	268,358.62	.22
Baptist—South	1,100,000	244,334.26	.22
Methodist Epis.—South	1,161,666	245,836.37	.21
United Brethren	199,709	38,653.29	.19
Cumberland Presbyterian	160,185	27,216.39	.16
Free-Will Baptist	86,297	13,073.88	.15
Methodist Protestant	147,604	11,842.00	.08
Free Methodist	19,998	1,525.70	.07
Baptist—Colored	1,200,000	40,432.47	.03
African Meth. Epis.	400,000	9,000.00 *	.02
American Bible Soc.		173,640.00 *	
American S.S. Union		86,326.94	
American Tract Soc.		93,673.90	
Massachusetts Bible Soc.		24,316.74	
Am. Seamen's Friend Soc.		15,500.00 *	
Western Tract Soc.		9,000.00 *	
	11,889,427	$6,717,558.03	.56

* Estimated.

dollar each, which means that as many thousands more give nothing. There are some thousands who give ten dollars; and for every thousand of this class there are nineteen thousand who do not give anything. Dr. Cuyler says he once had a seamstress in his church who used to give a hundred dollars a year to missions. Not a few out of larger means, give as much; and, for every one of them, there are one hundred and ninety-nine who give nothing. Some give five thousand dollars; and for each of them there are ten thousand church-members who do not give one cent to redeem this land for which He, with whom they profess to be in sympathy, gave His life. There are hundreds of churches that do not give anything to home or foreign missions; and of those that do many members give nothing. A church in Hartford gave eleven hundred dollars to home missions. One lady said to another: "Didn't we do well this morning?" "No; not as a church," was the reply; "for one lady gave six hundred dollars and one gentleman gave three hundred." If church collections were analyzed, it would appear that, as a rule, by far the greater part is given by a very few persons, and they not the most able. The great majority of church-members give only a trifle or nothing at all for the work of missions.

During the year 1889–1890 contributions in the United States for foreign missions were $3,977,701.[12] A total of $10,695,259 for home and foreign missions sounds like a large sum. But great and small are relative terms. Compared with the need of the world and the ability of the church it is pitiable indeed. Look at that ability. The Christian religion, by rendering men temperate, industrious, and moral, makes them prosperous. There are but few of the very poor in our churches. The great question has come to be: "How can we reach the masses?" Church-membership is made up chiefly of the well-to-do and the rich.[13] On the other hand, a majority of the membership is

[12] *Almanac for 1891 issued by the American Board of Commissioners for Foreign Missions* (Boston), p. 35.

[13] *The Century* says that, of the fifty leading business men of Columbus, Ohio, and Springfield, Mass. (if we are not mistaken in the unnamed cities), four-fifths are attendants upon the churches and supporters of them, while three-fifths are communicants.

composed of women, who control less money than men. It is, therefore, fair to say that the church-member is at least as well off as the average citizen. In 1890, one in every 4.7 of the population was a member of some evangelical church, that is, 21.92 per cent of all the people. We may reasonably infer, then, that this percentage of the wealth of the United States, or $13,076,-300,000 was in the hands of evangelical church-members at that time; and this takes no account of the immense capital in brains and muscles. Of this great wealth *one thirty-second part of one per cent* or one dollar out of 3,287, was given in 1890 to foreign missions for the salvation of seven or eight hundred million heathen. We do not know what the income of our church-members is, but if in 1890 they had spent every cent of wages, salary and other income on themselves and had given to home and foreign missions only *one one-hundredth part* of their real and personal property (which would have been unspeakably mean and unchristian) their contribution would have been $130,763,000 instead of $10,695,259. For the one item of uncut jewels, largely consisting of diamonds, the people of the United States in 1888 paid $10,000,000; and in 1880, church-members paid out nearly six times as much for sugar and molasses as for the world's salvation, seven times as much for boots and shoes, sixteen times as much for cotton and woolen goods, eleven times as much for meat, and eighteen times as much for bread. From 1880 to 1890 the average annual increase of the wealth of church-members was $434,790,000. And this, remember, was over and above all expense of living and all benevolences! That is, the average annual increase of wealth in the hands of professed Christians was forty times greater than their offering to missions, home and foreign. How that offering looks, when compared with their wealth and its annual increase, may be seen on the opposite page.

If the members of our Sunday-schools in America, gave, each, one cent a Sabbath to missions, it would aggregate about one-half as much as is now secured, with endless writing and pleading and praying, from our entire church-membership. If each of these professed Christians gave five cents—the price of one cigar—once a week, it would amount in a year to

$35,000,000. If each gave one cent every day to that which he professes is the object of his life—the building of the Kingdom—it would amount to $49,202,000.

Immense sums are invested freely if there is only a chance of large dividends. The *Times of India* says that "nearly $25,-000,000 have been invested in search for gold in India, and that not $2,500 worth of the precious metal has been obtained after three years of labor." Christians have opportunities to invest, and with perfect security, where they will realize thirty, sixty, a hundred-fold—that is three thousand, six thousand, ten thousand per cent—yet how few and small the investments!

Seventy business men of New York subscribed $1,400,000, or $20,000 each, toward the Metropolitan Opera House in that city, which was completed a few years ago; and this without receiving or expecting pecuniary return. Where are the seventy men who will give one-half that amount to home missions? Is the love of Italian opera a more powerful motive than love of country, love of souls, and love of Christ?

It is estimated [14] that in 1889 the liquor bill of the nation was $1,000,000,000. As comparatively few women and children use intoxicating drinks, and many men do not, it is safe to say that this bill was paid by one quarter or one-fifth of the population. That is, in 1890, about 13,000,000 people paid $1,000,000,000 for liquors, and a like number of professed Christians gave $10,695,000 for missions. Any one that did not know better might naturally infer that the one class loves beer and whiskey better than the other loves souls.

A while ago a brutal prize-fighter got a purse of $12,000 for pounding an opponent into pulp. Money can be had in abundance for illegitimate uses, but a thousand interests, dear to the Master as the apple of his eye, must languish for the lack of funds. We have seen that there is no lack of wealth; there is money enough in the hands of church-members to sow every acre of the earth with the seed of truth; but the average Christian deems himself a despot over his purse. God has

[14] *The Cyclopedia of Temperance and Prohibition* (New York, 1891), p. 137.

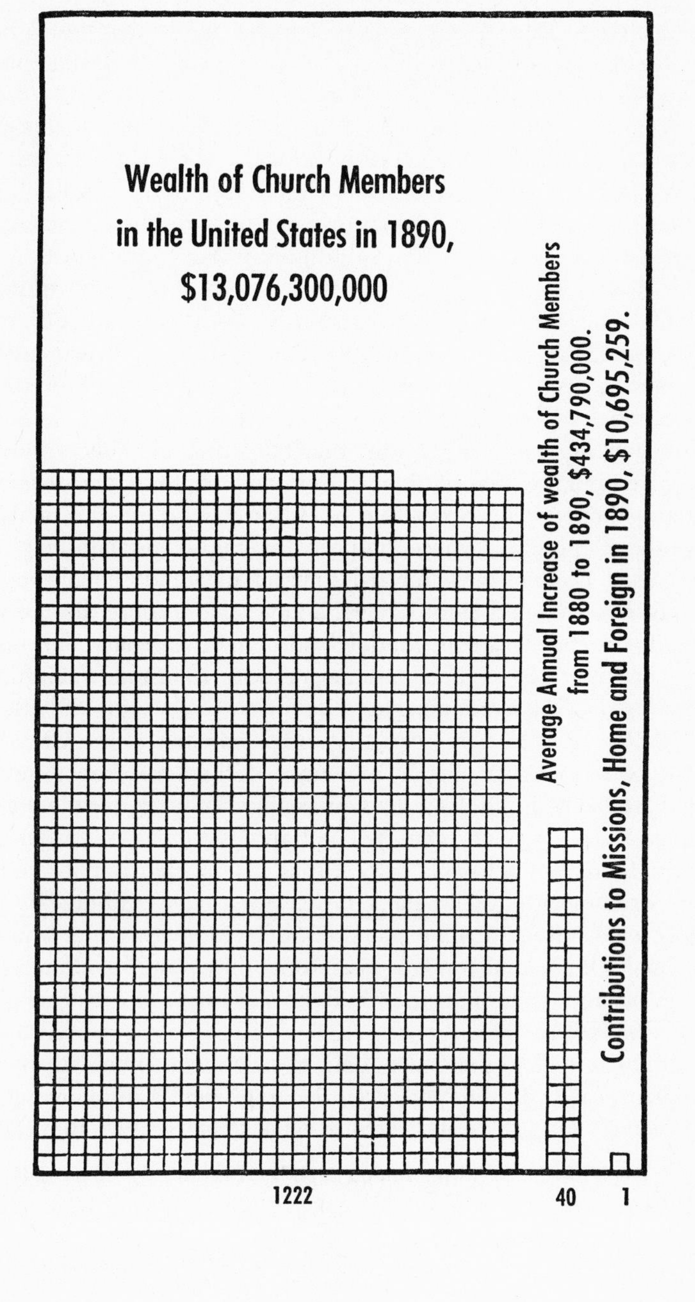
Wealth of Church Members
in the United States in 1890,
$13,076,300,000
Average Annual Increase of wealth of Church Members
from 1880 to 1890, $434,790,000.
Contributions to Missions, Home and Foreign in 1890, $10,695,259.
1222
40
1

intrusted to his children power enough to give the gospel to every creature by the close of this century; but it is being misapplied. Indeed, the world would have been evangelized long ago, if Christians had perceived the relations of money to the Kingdom, and had accepted their stewardship. There has been too much of the spirit of an Ohio church treasurer (a professed Christian), who, when his pastor brought his annual contribution to the American Board, said to him: "You ought not to do it. I don't think it's right. You ought to stop giving to missions and preach for us on a smaller salary"; adding, in conclusion, "*We* are heathen." A proposition which few enlightened men would be disposed to controvert, though it is a hard rub on the heathen.

When the heathen come to the light, they are much more Christian in their conceptions of duty and privilege, and shame us by their giving. Six native Christians, living on the banks of the Euphrates, whose property averaged, perhaps, eight hundred dollars, gave toward their chapel and school-room three hundred and eight dollars, an average of more than fifty dollars each. "This contribution," adds the missionary, "means for one of those poor mountaineers *more than one thousand days' work.*" "It is an amazing circumstance that, in 1881, the 1,200 church-members belonging to the missions of the United Presbyterian Board, in Egypt—most of them very poor men and women—raised £4,546, or more than $17 each, for the support of churches and schools. The Baptists, among the Karens, have done equally well." [15] Yes; that is amazing; but it is far more amazing that Christians in rich America should give only fifty cents each to home missions. If we gave as much per caput to home and foreign missions as they gave for churches and schools, our offering would be $241,000,000, instead of $10,695,000.

Is it not evident that most of our church-members have failed to learn the first principles of Christian giving? And many who give most largely do not seem to have grasped fully the idea

[15] Joseph Cook, *Occident,* Boston Monday Lectures (Boston, 1884), p. 125.

of stewardship, and to hold themselves under obligations to use every dollar in the way that will most honor God. A wealthy clergyman(!), who was a munificent giver, saw, in Paris, a pin that struck his fancy, and gave $800 for it. If, in the wide world that was the highest use he could find for the money, it was his duty to spend it as he did. Many give largely, and spend as lavishly on themselves; nor is it strange, in view of the instructions often given. A pastor, whose fame is in all the churches, and justly, writes: "I say not, indeed, that it is wrong for a man to take such a position in society as his riches warrant him to assume, or that there is sin in spending money on our residences, or in surrounding ourselves with the treasures of human wisdom in books, or the triumphs of human art in pictures and statuary; but I do say that our gifts to the cause of God ought to be at least abreast of our expenditure for these other things." And a worthy secretary of one of our most honored benevolent societies said: "He shall see the travail of his soul and be satisfied—When? *Not till beneficence keeps pace with luxury.*" Will that satisfy Him who commended her that cast into the treasury all her living, who requires of his followers daily cross-bearing, and admits no one to discipleship who has not forsaken "all that he hath"? Is the Master satisfied when a rich man to gratify "a nice and curious palate," spends ten thousand a year on his table, provided only beneficence keeps pace with his luxury, and he gives as much more to missions? Or, is it untrue that God requires every one to make the wisest and the best use of *all* his money?

Many churches are never taught that the consecration of all our property to God is no more optional than the practice of justice or chastity or any other duty. Most Christians leave their giving to mere impulse; they give something or nothing, much or little, as they feel like it. They might as well attempt to live a Christian life and be honest or not as they felt like it. The churches are not adequately instructed as to this duty. They hear too often of the "Lord's share." The reformation must begin with the pulpit. While I would not seem censorious of my brethren, it must nevertheless be said that too many ministers have not laid hold of this truth, or, at least, it has not *laid hold of them.*

No, there is no lack of wealth in the churches, even in hard times. When the rod of conviction and consecration smites the flinty rock of selfishness, it will break asunder and send forth abundant streams of benefaction, which shall make glad the waste places and prove the water of life to the perishing multitudes.

ACCEPTANCE OF THE PRINCIPLE URGED

Having defined the true principle of Christian giving, and glanced at some of the questions of casuistry which spring from its application, and having shown that the Church does not act on it, it remains to present briefly some of the considerations which urge its acceptance.

1. Duty. It is common to urge benevolence by appealing to the hope of larger returns, which are assured by many promises of the Word. And such motives were needed in the childhood of the race; but with all our light they should not be needed now. Did not Christ place giving on a higher plane? He said, "It is more blessed to give than to receive," not because of the return; but because giving is more God-like. Men urge benevolence as an investment. It is true that the steward whom God finds faithful, he is very apt to honor with a larger trust; but this should not be the motive of giving. We should "do good, and lend, hoping for nothing again." It is true that honesty is the best policy; but if this be the motive of honest dealing, there is no real honesty. So when men give because they expect a larger return, there is no real giving. In the region of right and wrong we may not ask what is politic; we stand under the scepter of the absolute *Ought,* which does not reason or advise or plead, but simply says, *Thou shalt.* Whether or not we have learned that only that which we give is truly and forever ours, the duty to give remains the same. The fact that God requires the entire consecration of all our substance, ought, alone, to be sufficient to move us; but there are other considerations.

2. The spiritual life and power of the churches demand the acceptance of the true doctrine touching possessions. We talk about "our crosses." There is no such expression in the Bible. The word does not occur there in the plural. It has been belittled; it has come to mean trial, disagreeable duty, anything which crosses our inclination; but its meaning in the Scriptures is never so meager as that. There it always means crucifixion; like the word gallows, in modern speech, it means death. To take one's cross means, in the Bible, to start for the place of execution. "If any man will come after me, let him *take up his cross and follow me.*" Follow him where? To Golgotha. He in whose experience there is no Calvary where he himself has been crucified with Christ, knows little of Christian discipleship. Christ demands actual self-abnegation; but where the Christian name is honored, and its profession confers obvious advantages, self-deception is common and Christian experience is liable to be shallow. As quaint old Rutherford said: "Men get Christ for the half of nothing—such maketh loose work." Too many church-members know little or nothing of self-surrender; hence the lack of spiritual life and power. At such times the Church suffers for the want of some decisive test, the application of which will show men to themselves, and separate, with a good degree of accuracy, those who have been crucified with Christ from those who know not what it is to "take up the cross."

In a commercial age, and especially in a luxurious civilization, the form of worldliness to which the Church is most likely to be tempted is the love of money. As the means of almost every possible self-gratification it becomes the *representative of self;* hence the true principle of Christian giving, the actual surrender of all substance to God, is exactly the test for the application of which the Church is suffering to-day. If this test were applied now to every church-member as Christ applied it to the young ruler (and the need is the same, for the human heart is the same, and heaven and the conditions of entrance are the same), would not the record in many a case be, "and he went away sorrowful, for he had great possessions"?

What right has any one, who has light on this subject, to believe he has given himself to God, if he has not given his possessions? If he has kept back the less, what reason is there to think he has given the greater? As Jeremy Taylor says: "He never loved God who will quit anything of his religion to save his money." [16]

Is not much that the Master said concerning possessions a dead letter in the church to-day? "Lay not up *for yourselves* treasures upon earth." Is not that exactly what many in the church are doing, and many more striving with eager energy to do? "The deceitfulness of riches." How many are afraid of being deceived by them? How many refuse to run the risk? "How hardly shall they that have riches enter into the Kingdom of Heaven." How many are unwilling to become rich or richer? Multitudes now complain that they have so little who, on the great day of accounts, will mourn that they had so much. The Word declares covetousness to be idolatry; but how many church-members were ever disciplined for this idolatry? There is, however, a sign of the millennium down in Maine, where, a few years ago, a church disciplined five members because they would give nothing. The spiritual life and power of the Church can vitalize and save the world only when there is a spirit of consecration sufficiently deep and inclusive to accept the true principle of Christian giving.

3. Again, our safety from the perils which have been discussed demands the acceptance of this principle.

It is not urged as a panacea; specific remedies, which there is no space to discuss, must be applied; reform must be pressed; we need patriotic and wise legislation, and to this end fewer politicians and more statesmen; but statesmanship cannot save the country. Christ's refusal to be made a king, and his rejection of Satan's offer of the world's scepter, ought to teach those who seek to save the world that moral means are necessary to moral ends. Christ saw that the world could not be saved by legislation, that only by his being "lifted up" could all men be

[16] Jeremy Taylor, *The Rule and Exercises of Holy Living* (London, 1885), p. 184. [The quotation is from ch. 4, section 3.]

drawn unto him. He saw that he could not save the world without sacrificing for it; no more can we. The saving power of the Church is its sacrificing power.

The gospel is the radical cure of the world's great evils, and its promulgation, like its spirit, requires sacrifice. Money is the sinews of spiritual warfare as well as carnal, and a sufficient amount of it would enable us to meet these perils with the gospel.

Christianize the immigrant and he will be easily Americanized. Christianity is the solvent of all race antipathies. Give the Romanist a pure gospel and he will cease to be a Romanist. It has already been shown that Christian education will solve the Mormon problem. The temperance reform, like all others which depend on popular agitation, must have money, and is being retarded by the lack of it. Concerning the remedy for socialism, accept the opinion of an economist who has made it a subject of special study. Says Prof. Ely: "It is an undoubted fact that modern socialism of the worst type is spreading to an alarming extent among our laboring classes, both foreign and native. I think the danger is of such a character as should arouse the Christian people of this country to most earnest efforts for the evangelization of the poorer classes, particularly in large cities. What is needed is Christianity, and the Christian Church can do far more than political economists toward a reconciliation of social classes. The Church's remedy for social discontent and dynamite bombs is Christianity as taught in the New Testament. Now in all this you will find nothing new. It is only significant in this regard: others have come to these conclusions from the study of the Bible; from a totally different starting point, from the study of political economy, I have come to the same goal." [17]

But the acceptance of the Christian doctrine concerning property would have a direct, as well as indirect, influence on

[17] From a letter by Prof. R. T. Ely to Rev. H. A. Schauffler, D.D. I regret that lack of space forbids my quoting the entire letter, which may be found in *Home Missionary*, 58 (October 1884), 227–229. [Ely's letter is dated May 26, 1884, and is addressed to Samuel H. Virgin.]

socialism. Let us therefore dwell a moment on the subject. In the popular ferment, a hundred years ago, which culminated in the French Revolution, the demand was for equal rights and the watchword was *Liberty*. There is a popular ferment throughout Europe to-day which is more universal and extends to the United States. The popular demand now is equality of condition, and the watchword is *Property*—a cry the meaning of which the dullest and most earthly can understand. This movement, which is steadily gathering force, results from the two most striking facts of the nineteenth century: first, the general diffusion of knowledge through the press, which has wonderfully multiplied wants up and down the entire social scale; and, second, the creation of immense wealth by means of the steam engine. But this wealth, which is necessary to the satisfaction of these wants, has been massed. In a word, the difficulty is *knowledge multiplied and popularized, and wealth multiplied and centralized.*

The right distribution of property, which is the kernel of the social question, is the great problem of our civilization; and it may well be doubted whether the true solution will be found until the Church accepts, both in doctrine and practice, the teachings of God's Word touching possessions. For the Church is responsible for public opinion on all moral questions, and no great question of rights can be settled for the world until Christian men come into right relations with it.

The inexorable law of our present industrial system is that the cost of subsistence determines the rate of wages. This makes no provision for the higher wants of increasing intelligence, and therefore insures an increasing popular discontent. It would seem that the solution of the great difficulties between capital and labor must be found in some form of co-operation by which the workman will be admitted to a just share in the profits of his labor. Professor Cairns, who is considered one of the greatest economists England has produced, believes that co-operative production affords the laboring classes "the sole means of escape from a harsh and hopeless destiny" (*Leading Principles,* p. 338). Referring to several thousand co-operative societies in England, having some millions of capital, Thomas Hughes [18] says: "I still look to this movement as the best hope for England and other lands." The eminent statistician, Carroll D. Wright,[19] Commissioner of the Department of Labor, Washington, referring to the duty of the rich manufacturer to regard himself as "an instrument of God for the upbuilding of the race," and the promotion of the highest welfare of those in his employ, says: "This may sound like sentiment. I am willing to call it sentiment; but I know it means the best material prosperity, and that every employer who has been guided by such sentiments has been rewarded twofold: first, in witnessing the wonderful improvement of his people, and, second, in seeing his dividends increase, and the wages of his operatives increase with his dividends. The factory system of the future will be run on this basis. The instances of such are multiplying rapidly now." [20] Manifestly, the acceptance on the part of Christian capitalists of the scriptural doctrine of possessions would greatly facilitate the introduction of co-operation or any other plan which promised justice to the workman.

The Christian man who is not willing to make the largest profits which an honest regard for the laws of trade permits is a rare man. But the laws of trade permit much that the laws of God do not permit. Many transactions are commercially honest which are not righteous. If, now, a man accepts the truth that his possessions are a trust to be administered for God's glory, he will not consent to increase them by any unrighteous means. And since justice and righteousness, like honesty, will prove to be the best *policy,* the acceptance on the part of Christian men of a thoroughly righteous plan of co-operation between capital and labor would eventually compel its general acceptance. Let Christian men gain a correct conception of their relations to their possessions, let them ac-

[18] [See Chapter IV, n. 9.]

[19] [Carroll Davidson Wright (1840–1909), statistician, economist, lawyer, served as first Chief of the Massachusetts Bureau of Labor Statistics and as U.S. Commissioner of Labor.]

[20] For a history of profit-sharing see Nicholas Paine Gilman, *Profit-Sharing Between Employer and Employee* (Boston, 1889).

cept the duty of Christian stewardship, and it would command their getting as well as their spending. There would be no motive to drive a sharp bargain. It would purify trade. It would mediate between capital and labor. It would destroy the foundation on which the rising structure of socialism rests. It would cut one of the principal roots of popular unbelief; for extended inquiry in Cincinnati elicited the almost unanimous response that the reason workingmen neglect the churches is that there are on the church rolls the names of employers who wrong their employees.

The acceptance of the true principle of Christian giving is urged upon us by the fact that money is power, which is needed everywhere for elevating and saving men. It is further urged upon us by the fact that only such a view of possessions will save us from the great and imminent perils of wealth. God might have sent his angels to sing his gospel through the world, or he might have written it on the sky, and made the clouds his messengers; but we need to bear the responsibility of publishing that gospel. He might make the safe of every benevolent society a gold mine as unfailing as the widow's cruse of oil; but we need to give that gold. The tendency of human nature, intensified by our commercial activity, is to make the life a whirlpool—a great maelstrom which draws everything into itself. What is needed to-day is a grand reversal of the movement, a transformation of the life into a fountain. And in an exceptional degree is this the need of Anglo-Saxons. Their strong love of liberty, and their acquisitiveness, afford a powerful temptation to offer some substitute for self-abnegation. We would call no man master; we must take Christ as master. We would possess all things; we must surrender all things.

One of the grave problems before us is how to make great material prosperity conduce to individual advancement. The severest poverty is unfavorable to morality. Up to a certain point increase of property serves to elevate man morally and intellectually, while it improves him physically. But, as nations grow rich, they are prone to become self-indulgent, effeminate, immoral. The physical nature becomes less robust, the intellectual nature less vigorous, the moral less pure. The pampered civilizations of old had to be reinvigorated, from time to time, with fresh infusions of barbaric blood—a remedy no longer available. If we cannot find in Christianity a remedy or preventive, our Christian civilization and the world itself is a failure; and our rapidly increasing wealth, like the "cankered heaps of strange-achieved gold," will curse us unto destruction.

But the recognition of God's ownership in all our substance is a perfect antidote for the debilitating and corrupting influence of wealth. It prevents self-indulgence, and the apprehension of religious truth implied in such recognition affords the strongest possible motives to sacrifice and active effort of which men are capable. A hundred years ago poverty compelled men to endure hardness, and so served to make the nation great. Now that we are exposed to the pampering influence of riches, Christian principle must inspire the spirit of self-denial for Christ's sake, and the world's sake, and so make the nation greater.

Where that spirit obtains, Mammonism and materialism, as well as luxuriousness, lose their power, and wealth, instead of being centralized, is distributed. So that Christian stewardship, so far as it is accepted, affords perfect protection against all the perils of wealth.

Our cities, which are gathering together the most dangerous elements of our civilization, will, in due time, unless Christianized, prove the destruction of our free institutions. During the last hundred years, the instruments of destruction have been wonderfully multiplied. Offensive weapons have become immeasurably more effective. Not so the means of defense. Your life is in the hand of every man you meet. Society is safe to-day only so far as every man becomes a law unto himself. The lawless classes are growing much more rapidly than the whole population; and nothing but the gospel can transform lawless men and women into good citizens.

The number of missionaries in our cities ought to be increased ten- or twenty-fold; and their work is expensive. It is usually the densest populations which are most neglected, and in such quarters mission chapels cannot be built without large expenditures. If our cities are to be evangelized, laymen must greatly enlarge their ideas of the demands of the work, and of their pecuniary responsibility for it.

The perils which have been discussed (Chaps. IV.–XI.) have, all of them with the single exception of Mormonism, continued to grow more rapidly during the past five years than the whole population. It is also true that the membership of the evangelical churches has increased more rapidly than the population. The Church of Christ has aroused herself in some measure, but, so far as I can judge, the dangerous and destructive elements of society are still making greater progress than the conservative.

Has not the time fully come when the Church must make a new departure of some sort? And is it not evident that one of the first needs is a true view of the relations of money to the Kingdom, and such a spirit of consecration as will lay it and all else on the altar?

4. We have seen, in the preceding chapters, that a mighty emergency is upon us. Our country's future, and much of the world's future, depend on the way in which Christian men meet the crisis. Do you say: "I trust in God, and therefore have no fear; I believe what some one has said, 'If God intends to save the world, he cannot afford to make an exception of America.' This country is his chosen instrument of blessing to mankind; and God's plans never fail"? The difference between a true and a false faith is that one inspires action while the other paralyzes it. God saved the nation during the War of the Rebellion; but it was not by a false faith, which, with folded arms, rehearsed its confidence in the divine decrees. It was by a faith which inspired sacrifice. At the time of Paul's shipwreck, it was revealed to him that they were all to be saved; but, nevertheless, there were conditions with which they must comply, or be lost. Their salvation was *certain,* but not *necessary;* it was conditioned. I believe our country will be saved. Its salvation may be certain in the counsels of God; but it is not necessary.

I believe it to be conditioned on the Church's rising to a higher spirit of sacrifice.

When the drum beat the nation to battle, a generation ago, no sacrifice was too great; wives gave their husbands, parents gave their sons. A Christian mother had sent seven sons into the Union army. Near the close of the war, the eighth, and only remaining son, paid a visit to his mother, and, speaking of the war, said: "Mother, what would you do if one of the boys should fall in the struggle?" Turning her deep eyes upon him, she said: "God has given me nine noble sons; one he has taken to himself, seven are in the army, and I want you to understand, my son, that I *only hold you as a reserve* for your country's defense; and the first breach that you hear of as being made in our number, go quickly, and fill it; and may God take care of you, and I will take care of your children." Is it easier to give one's flesh and blood than to give silver and gold? We are engaged in what Lord Bacon called the "heroic work of making a nation;" for which heroic sacrifices are demanded.

And our plea is not America for America's sake; but America for the world's sake. For, if this generation is faithful to its trust, America is to become God's right arm in his battle with the world's ignorance and oppression and sin. If I were a Christian African or Arab, I should look into the immediate future of the United States with intense and thrilling interest; for as Professor Hoppin of Yale has said: "America Christianized means the *world* Christianized." And, "If America fail," says Professor Park, "the *world* will fail." During this crisis, Christian work is unspeakably more important in the United States than anywhere else in the world. "The nations whose conversion is the most pressing necessity of the world to-day," says Professor Phelps, "are the Occidental nations. Those whose *speedy* conversion is most vital to the conversion of the rest are the nations of the Occident. The pioneer stock of mind must be the Occidental stock. The pioneer races must be the Western races. And of all the Western races, who that can read skillfully the providence of God, or can read it at all, can hesitate in affirming that the signs of divine decree point to this land of ours as the one which is fast gathering to itself the races which must take the lead in the final conflicts of Christianity for possession of the world? Ours is the elect nation for the age to come. We are the chosen people. We cannot afford to wait. The plans of God will not wait. Those plans seem to have brought us to one of the closing stages in the world's career, in which we can no longer *drift* with safety to our destiny. We are shut up to a perilous alternative. Immeasurable opportunities surround and overshadow us. Such, as I read it, is the central fact in the philosophy of American Home Missions." [21]

What a consummate *blunder* to live selfishly in such a generation! What food for everlasting reflection and regret in a life lived narrowly amid such infinitely wide opportunities!

Says a New York daily paper: "A gentleman died at his residence in one of our up-town fashionable streets, leaving eleven millions of dollars. He was a member of the Presbyterian church, in excellent standing, a good husband and father, and a thrifty citizen. On his deathbed he suffered with great agony of mind and gave continual expression to his remorse for what his conscience told him had been an ill-spent life. 'Oh!' he exclaimed, 'if I could only live my years over again! Oh! if I could only be spared for a few years, I would give all the wealth I have amassed in a life-time. It is a life devoted to money-getting that I regret. It is this which weighs me down, and makes me despair of the life hereafter.'" Suppose so unfaithful a steward is permitted to enter the "many mansions." When, with clarified spiritual vision, he perceives the true meaning of life, and sees that he has lost the one opportunity of an endless existence to set in motion influences, which, by leading sinners to repentance, would cause heaven to thrill with a new joy, it seems to me he would gladly give a hundred years of Paradise for a single day on earth in possession of the

[21] From letter read at the Home Missionary Anniversary in Chicago, June 9th, 1881. [Austin Phelps, "The Present Exigency in Home Missions," *Home Missionary,* 54 (December 1881), 227. See also Introduction, n. 3.]

money once entrusted to him—time enough to turn that power into the channels of Christian work.

The emergency created by the settlement of the states and territories of the West—a grand constellation of empires—is to be met by placing in the hand of every Christian agency there at work all the power that money can wield. There is scarcely a church, or society, or institution of any kind doing God service there which is not embarrassed, or sadly crippled for lack of funds. Missionaries should be multiplied, parsonages and churches built, and colleges generously endowed. The nation's salt, with which the whole land and pre-eminently the tainted civilization of the frontier, must be sweetened, is *Christian* education. The tendency, which is so marked in many of our older and larger colleges, to develop and furnish simply the intellect, is full of peril. Divorce religion and education, and we shall fall a prey either to blundering goodness or well-schooled villainy. The young colleges of the West, like Drury, Doane, Carleton, Colorado, Yankton, Fargo, and others, founded by broad-minded and far-seeing men are characterized by a strong religious influence, and send a surprising proportion of their graduates into the ministry. In view of their almost boundless possibilities for usefulness in their relations to the future of the West and of the nation, and in view of their urgent needs, it is a wonder that those who, like Boaz, are mighty men of wealth, can deny themselves the deep and lasting pleasure of liberally endowing such institutions. Said one who had just given fifty thousand dollars to a Western college: "I cannot tell you what I have enjoyed. It is like being born into the Kingdom again."

This emergency demands the acceptance of Christian stewardship, that our great benevolent societies may be adequately furnished for their work. They are kept constantly on their knees before the public, and with pleas so pitiful, so moving, the marvel to me is that, when Christian men hold their peace and their purse, the very stones do not cry out. And, notwithstanding all their efforts to secure means, they must, every one, scrimp at every point, decline providential calls to enlarge their work, and even retrench, in order to close the fiscal year without a debt.

The door of opportunity is open in all the earth; organizations have been completed, languages learned, the Scriptures translated, and now the triumph of the Kingdom awaits only the exercise of the power committed to the Church, but which she refuses to put forth. If she is to keep step with the majestic march of the divine Providence, the Church must consecrate the power which is in money.

5. Oh! that men would accept the testimony of Christ touching the blessedness of giving! He who sacrifices most, loves most; and he who loves most, is most blessed. Love and sacrifice are related to each other like seed and fruit; each produces the other. The seed of sacrifice brings forth the fragrant fruit of love, and love always has in its heart the seeds of new sacrifice. He who gives but a part is not made perfect in love. Love rejoices to give all; it does not measure its sacrifice. It was Judas, not Mary, who calculated the value of the alabaster box of ointment. He who is infinitely blessed is the Infinite Giver; and man, made in his likeness, was intended to find his highest blessedness in the completest self-giving. He who receives, but does not give, is like the Dead Sea. All the fresh floods of Jordan cannot sweeten its dead, salt depths. So all the streams of God's bounty cannot sweeten a heart that has no outlet; that is ever receiving, yet never full and overflowing.

If those whose horizon is as narrow as the bushel under which they hide their light could be induced to come out into a large place, and take a worthy view of the Kingdom of Christ and of their relations to it, if they could be persuaded to make the principle of Christian giving regnant in all their life, their *happiness* would be as much increased as their usefulness.

INDEX

THE JOHN HARVARD LIBRARY

The intent of
Waldron Phoenix Belknap, Jr.,
as expressed in an early will, was for Harvard College to use the income from a permanent trust fund he set up, for "editing and publishing rare, inaccessible, or hitherto unpublished source material of interest in connection with the history, literature, art (including minor and useful art), commerce, customs, and manners or way of life of the Colonial and Federal Periods of the United States . . . In all cases the emphasis shall be on the presentation of the basic material." A later testament broadened this statement, but Mr. Belknap's interests remained constant until his death.

In linking the name of the first benefactor of Harvard College with the purpose of this later, generous-minded believer in American culture the John Harvard Library seeks to emphasize the importance of Mr. Belknap's purpose. The John Harvard Library of the Belknap Press of Harvard University Press exists to make books and documents about the American past more readily available to scholars and the general reader.